To my little family—

Linda, Ian, and Nicole.

BOB BAXLEY

MAKING *the*
WEB WORK

DESIGNING EFFECTIVE WEB APPLICATIONS

New Riders

MAKING THE WEB WORK: DESIGNING EFFECTIVE WEB APPLICATIONS

International Standard Book Number: 0-7357-1196-8

Library of Congress Catalog Card Number: 2001094067

Printed in the United States of America

First edition: November 2002

06 05 04 03 02   7 6 5 4 3 2 1

Interpretation of the printing code: The rightmost double-digit number is the year of the book's printing; the rightmost single-digit number is the number of the book's printing. For example, the printing code 02-1 shows that the first printing of the book occurred in 2002.

TRADEMARKS

WARNING AND DISCLAIMER

PUBLISHER
David Dwyer

ASSOCIATE PUBLISHER
Stephanie Wall

EDITOR IN CHIEF
Chris Nelson

PRODUCTION MANAGER
Gina Kanouse

MANAGING EDITOR
Sarah Kearns

ACQUISITIONS EDITOR
Deborah Hittel-Shoaf

SENIOR PRODUCT MARKETING MANAGER
Tammy Detrich

PUBLICITY MANAGER
Susan Nixon

DEVELOPMENT EDITOR
Lisa Lord

PROJECT EDITOR
Jake McFarland

INDEXER
Cheryl Lemmens

PROOFREADER
Beth Trudell

COMPOSITION
Wil Cruz

MANUFACTURING COORDINATOR
Jim Conway

INTERIOR DESIGNER
Bob Baxley

COVER DESIGNER
Aren Howell

CONTENTS AT A GLANCE

TABLE OF CONTENTS

Part III   Tier 2: Behavior

ABOUT THE AUTHOR

 **Bob Baxley** is a practicing designer who lives and works in Silicon Valley. Specializing in interaction design for both Web applications and services as well as desktop products, Bob has worked in a variety of corporate and startup environments. He began his career in 1990 as the designer for ClarisWorks, and later worked on a variety of projects for Adobe Systems, Apple Computer, Epiphany, NetObjects, Ameritrade, and others. Currently, Bob runs the Design and Usability teams at myCFO, a leading wealth management firm.

In 1985, he received a B.A. in History and a B.S. in Radio/Television/Film from the University of Texas at Austin. He also received a Masters of Liberal Arts from Stanford University in 2000.

ABOUT THE TECHNICAL REVIEWERS

These reviewers contributed their considerable hands-on expertise to the entire development process for *Making the Web Work: Designing Effective Web Applications.* As the book was being written, these dedicated professionals reviewed all the material for technical content, organization, and flow. Their feedback was critical to ensuring that *Making the Web Work: Designing Effective Web Applications* fits our reader's need for the highest-quality technical information.

Scott Berkun is the training manager for user interface design and usability at Microsoft. Since 1994 he has worked as usability engineer, program manager, and lead program manager on many versions of Internet Explorer and Microsoft Windows. He writes about Web design and product usability at www.uiweb.com.

Tim Kostolansky, currently an independent consultant, has worked in the software industry for 10 years, founding two successful startup companies. He has led teams that have built custom software for Global 500 companies. Tim is a graduate of Cornell University and has completed graduate studies in computer science at Stanford University.

ACKNOWLEDGMENTS

You know those Oscar acceptance speeches that go on forever? I think I may finally understand how those folks feel.

Although it is my name that appears on the cover, don't be fooled into believing that all of it can be attributed to me alone. Endeavors such as this only reach fruition with the support, encouragement, patience, and input of others.

First and foremost, I extend the deepest thanks to my development editor, Lisa Lord, and my technical editors, Tim Kostolansky and Scott Berkun. The results of their intelligent and articulate feedback are evident on literally every page. It has been an unexpected and invaluable blessing to work alongside such a talented, supportive, and fun editorial team.

I would also like to thank my "unofficial" tech editor, Philip Haine, who was kind enough to read a number of chapters and provide his invaluable feedback and suggestions.

I would also like to acknowledge my friends and colleagues who not only read many of the chapters, but also patiently listened to me prattle on about this, that, and the other thing. A particular thanks to the "J-team": Jerrel Jimmerson, Steve Jungmann, Jacqueline Phillips, Jim Phillips, Joff Redfern, and Jerome Doran for his contributions to the model of a UI diagram.

A debt of gratitude also to Leah Williams who brought this project into New Riders, Victoria Elzey who got it off the ground, and Deb Hittel-Shoaf who shepherded it through the occasional bad storm and safely back to the terminal.

My thanks also to a handful of individuals, who helped me arrive at the point of having the necessary resources to write something like this. In particular, I owe a special thanks to Eric Olsen and Linda Paulson for their unique and long-lasting contributions. In addition, kind thanks to Liz Waymire for taking a risk and bringing me into this profession. A thanks also to my parents, Sue and Stan Baxley, for their lifelong support and encouragement of my dreams, curiosities, and pursuits.

Finally, a special thanks to my family for sharing me with this project over the past 14 months. Not only have they patiently tolerated the distraction of it all, but they have also helped keep my priorities intact during the process.

We're going to Disneyland!

TELL US WHAT YOU THINK

As the reader of this book, you are the most important critic and commentator. We value your opinion and want to know what we're doing right, what we could do better, what areas you'd like to see us publish in, and any other words of wisdom you're willing to pass our way.

As the Associate Publisher for New Riders Publishing, I welcome your comments. You can fax, email, or write me directly to let me know what you did or didn't like about this book—as well as what we can do to make our books stronger. When you write, please be sure to include this book's title, ISBN, and author, as well as your name and phone or fax number. I will carefully review your comments and share them with the author and editors who worked on the book.

Please note that I cannot help you with technical problems related to the topic of this book, and that due to the high volume of email I receive, I might not be able to reply to every message.

Fax: 317-581-4663

Email: **stephanie.wall@newriders.com**

Mail: Stephanie Wall

       Associate Publisher

       New Riders Publishing

       201 West 103rd Street

       Indianapolis, IN 46290 USA

INTRODUCTION

My career as a designer of interactive products began on the Labor Day weekend of 1990. My poor parents still aren't sure what I do, and unfortunately, they're not the only ones. Although my tenure as an interactive designer has been accompanied by an explosion in the complexity and quantity of interactive hardware and software products, the art, discipline, and craft of interactive design in general and Web design in particular remain a work in progress.

For better and for worse, the Web's openness, accessibility, and technical flexibility have enabled, if not encouraged, individual solutions to what are often collective problems. A behavioral convention or visual standard on one site might be completely different on another site. The result is a level of inconsistency detrimental to both individual users and to the Web as an interactive medium. Unfortunately, because the Web lacks a central authority to recommend, encourage, or impose consistency, the description and adoption of relevant conventions are typically preceded by years of evolution, inconsistency, and confusion.

Exacerbating the situation, the sheer newness of the Web and the speed at which it's been adopted, has failed to provide the time to develop the comprehensive methodologies, processes, or disciplines necessary for the consistent, controlled creation of truly useful and usable sites.

GOALS AND OBJECTIVES

It is these two concerns—inconsistency in implementation and inconsistency in approach—that led me to write *Making the Web Work*. The goal of this book is two-fold. On one level, it sets out to describe, analyze, and recommend solutions to common Web-based interface problems. At a higher level, it also sets out to provide a standard methodology for deconstructing and prioritizing the issues involved in the design of interactive products in general and Web applications in particular.

My hope is that *Making the Web Work* will serve as a catalog and critique of some of the visual and interactive conventions in use on the modern Web. I also hope my analysis and critique will add to your understanding and appreciation of the discipline of interactive design as well as your own ability to practice that discipline. Finally, I hope the process and methodology of my analysis will serve as a useful illustration of how to systematically deconstruct an entire application into a collection of separate but interrelated problems.

Put another way, I hope that in these pages I have given you not only a few fish and a few good fishing tips, but also a method for thinking about the practice of fishing and how to ensure that it's repeatable, sustainable, and well-managed.

WHY I WROTE *MAKING THE WEB WORK*

There are a lot of different reasons to write a book. Some authors have a particular perspective to advocate; others have a story to tell; still others, an event to report. The more altruistic say they want to give something back to their readers. I decided to write a book because I wanted to learn how to be a better designer. I wanted to develop a deeper understanding of what I had been doing for the past decade, and the best way I knew to do that was to try to explain it to somebody else.

Surely you will disagree with things you read here, and even if you don't, there will certainly be plenty of others who will. That's fine. Part of the fun and interest of working in the field of interactive design is the uncertainty and complexity of it all.

As you're reading, keep in mind that I don't have the answer to the problem you're trying to solve. I don't know the problem you're trying to solve. What I do have, however, is experience with similar problems and a way of thinking about them that you may find useful. Between these pages, you won't find any magic solutions, "Tips and Tricks," or "Top 10 Dos and Don'ts." Instead, you'll find an analysis and approach to the problems you're likely to encounter during the process of designing an interactive experience, be it an entire site or one small feature. I don't expect anything I say here to be the last word. In fact, I hope that in many cases it is but the first word, and look forward to continuing the conversation. You can reach me at bob@baxleydesign.com.

WHO YOU ARE

Like a design project, when you sit down to write a book, it's important to consider who's going to be doing the reading. For *Making the Web Work*, I envisioned three types of readers:

☐ **Practicing designers.** These are the people "on the ground" with the day-to-day responsibility of solving design problems. If you're an experienced part of this group, I suspect you already perform the type of analysis presented here; however, my catalog of problems and solutions may shortcut some of your own efforts. On the flip side, if you're a relative newcomer, my analysis and methodology may aid your understanding of the unique challenges and methods associated with interactive design.

☐ **Product marketers.** If you work in product marketing and don't have the support of a professional designer on your product, and so the responsibility for design decisions likely falls to you. And even if you do have a dedicated designer, you probably still have significant input on many design decisions because different solutions invariably have unique cost/benefit profiles. If you fall into this camp, *Making the Web Work* will give you an understanding of how to approach and prioritize the issues and decisions you're likely to encounter.

☐ **Software engineers.** Even in organizations with robust design resources, chances are good that the engineering staff outnumbers the design staff at least 10 to 1. If you're an engineer, you already know that any specification is unlikely to fully capture or anticipate every permutation and corner case the code must ultimately address. As a result, it's not uncommon for you to have to make decisions affecting the design. For you, *Making the Web Work* will provide a method for considering and prioritizing issues according to their impact on both the code and users. In addition, it will give you examples of the analysis designers typically use to solve problems and highlight some of the best practices currently in use on the Web.

WHAT YOU WILL FIND

This book starts with the assumption that you have an interest in creating Web sites that are easy to use. It presupposes the basic tenant of user-centered design: Products should serve the goals and desires of the people consuming the product, not the goals and desires of the people or organizations that created them. If you don't enter this book with at least an open mind about the value and role of design, we're going to have a difficult time.

Making the Web Work is divided into five parts. Here is an overview of what you'll encounter in each part:

Part I, Foundations, sets the stage for the rest of the book by defining common terminology, outlining the typical phases of the design process, and presenting a comprehensive model for deconstructing and prioritizing an entire application.

☐ **Chapter 1, Common Ground: Defining Web Applications and Establishing the Goals of Design**

What is a Web application, and what are its natural advantages and disadvantages?

What is the purpose and ultimate goal of a user-centric design methodology?

☐ **Chapter 2, Putting the User First: Describing Target Users and Product Goals**

What is the role of the design function?

What are some of the common process issues associated with designing Web applications?

❑ **Chapter 3, Deconstructing the Problem: Prioritizing and Categorizing Different Aspects of the Interface**

How can a complex user interface be deconstructed into discrete issues that can be prioritized and solved individually?

Part II, Tier 1: Structure analyzes the key aspects of designing the overall structure of a Web application.

❑ **Chapter 4, The Conceptual Model: Selecting a Fundamental Motif**

How can you create a fundamental model that helps users grasp the application's basic purpose and nature?

❑ **Chapter 5, The Structural Model: Understanding the Building Blocks of a Web Interface**

What are the most basic interface components of a Web application, and what are their appropriate uses?

❑ **Chapter 6, The Organizational Model: Organizing and Structuring Content and Functionality**

What are the different ways to organize content and functionality?

Which organizations and categorizations are appropriate in a given situation?

Part III, Tier 2: Behavior, addresses the behavioral aspects of a Web application's user interface. The part's chapters delve into designing navigation, manipulating the state of the application, editing information, online help, and reporting errors.

☐ **Chapter 7, Viewing and Navigation: Creating Consistent Sorting, Filtering, and Navigation Behaviors**

What are the most effect navigation devices and conventions for Web applications?

What is the best interface for sorting, filtering, and managing long lists of information?

☐ **Chapter 8, Editing and Manipulation: Using HTML Input Controls to Accurately Capture Users' Data**

What is the appropriate use of each HTML input control?

What are some of the interface options for selecting one or more items from a list?

What are the interface options for entering dates?

☐ **Chapter 9, User Assistance: Communicating with Users Through Help, Status, and Alerts**

What level of online help is appropriate for an application?

What are the interface options for reporting errors and application status?

Part IV, Tier 3: Presentation, discusses the visual and textual presentation of an application. The part's chapters address page layout, table layout, typography, color, and visual style as well as labels and other textual elements.

☐ **Chapter 10, Layout: Positioning Elements to Maximize Understanding And Readability**

What are the best options for an overall page layout?

What are the options for placement of primary, secondary, and lower-level navigation elements?

☐ **Chapter 11, Style: Defining Visual Appearance**

What are the considerations when evaluating options for an application's visual style?

What factors affect legibility of text and data. and which visual styles best communicate the behavior of buttons and links?

☐ **Chapter 12, Text and Labels: Writing for the Web and Calling Things by Their Right Names**

What is the purpose of text in a user interface?

How is writing for the Web different from writing for other mediums?

Part V, Case Studies, synthesizes the concepts introduced in the preceding parts, demonstrating how the best sites on the Web solve interface problems:

☐ **Chapter 13, Amazon.com: Browsing the Aisles of the Web's Supreme Retailer**

☐ **Chapter 14, Ofoto: Looking at the Leading Online Photo Processor**

WHAT YOU WILL NOT FIND

In the interest of setting appropriate expectations, it's good to know at the beginning what you will not be getting in the end. I have deliberately excluded a variety of topics not because I don't think they're important, but because they are well covered in other books.

Although it is a common component of books about interactive design, you will not find anything here about user research, including usability studies, ethnographic studies, contextual inquiry, market research, or focus groups. Certainly, these functions offer important input into the design process as well as validation of the design's results; however, the focus of this book is the design activity itself.

Similarly, there is nothing in *Making the Web Work* about the technical details for implementing any designs. Although successful designers must have intimate knowledge of their medium's abilities and limitations, I have chosen not to provide that knowledge here. If this were a photography book, you might say it covered composition instead of chemistry.

A more thorny exclusion involves requirements gathering and task analysis. Although both activities play a critical role in defining the problem the interface has to ultimately address, these topics are more closely related to the larger issue of product design in general than to interface design in particular.

Clearly, these topics have an important role in developing and creating Web applications. You should not assume from their absence that I don't think them important or that they shouldn't be part of the designer's vocabulary. For a detailed bibliography and recommendations for a variety of book and resources, please visit my Web site at www.baxleydesign.com.

CONVENTIONS USED IN THIS BOOK

In addition to deciding what to put in and what to leave out, writing a book forces authors to standardize terminology and other conventions. Sometimes these decisions have philosophical implications; other times they're simply ways to enforce consistency. In either case, I've settled on the following standards.

TERMINOLOGY

User interface versus user experience: The sudden and dramatic influx of graphic designers into the interactive design arena has been accompanied by a host of new terms and job titles. One of the most popular is "user experience." As I understand it, user experience encompasses every aspect of a person's interaction with an organization—everything from the company Web site, to customer support, to shipping labels, to how the receptionist answers the phone. In other words, *everything*.

Unfortunately, user experience has become entangled, confused, and synonymous with the more specific term "user interface," a term that has been used in the software industry for decades. Despite its techno-babble overtone, user interface is the correct term for describing the specific layer of an interactive product where the technology and the user come together. *Making the Web Work* is about user interface, not user experience.

Information architecture: Information architecture, as a term and a job title, was popularized by Richard Saul Wurman in his book *Information Architects*. Wurman's book profiled a number of professionals from the graphic design community, who specialized in presenting complex information in a visually digestible form. Wurman referred to them as "information architects" because he believed they were taking raw information and shaping it into a particular form to communicate a particular message.

Somewhere in the middle of the Internet explosion, the term was co-opted to refer to the design activity concerned with organizing content and functionality. Since that transformation, there has been an ongoing debate within the design community as to exactly what IA means and exactly what information architects do. I have chosen to avoid the debate by using the term "organizational model" to refer to the organization and classification aspects of the interface.

I have made this choice for two reasons. First, the title of architect is inappropriate to the creation of interactive media as well as the role of design in that medium. Second, I do not believe that information architecture is a design activity separate and distinct from other design activities. Clearly, it's a specialty at which some are more skilled than others, but it's simply a different aspect of the design. Therefore, I think of information architects as designers specializing in organization and "findability."

Conventions versus patterns: Taken from the lingo of object-oriented programming, the term "patterns" is often used to describe the set of solutions that have developed to address recurring interface problems. In a very real sense, this book serves to document some of the patterns currently in use in Web applications. Unfortunately, the use of the word "pattern" in this context, although definitely accurate, is a bit arcane. Therefore, I've chosen to use the more common word "conventions."

EXAMPLES

Books about design are a unique and challenging combination of words and pictures. Although the words are clearly the product of the author, the pictures are typically gathered from other sources.

Instead of relying on my own designs and creations, I have generally chosen to use images taken from actual Web sites that are publicly available. As a result, my examples are almost exclusively from consumer sites rather than corporate intranets, licensed software, or other proprietary sites. Although this approach results in a book that appears to be focused on consumer sites, the problems presented affect all types of Web applications, regardless of their business niche or audience.

Looking at the examples, you will notice a lack of specific URL references. The dynamic nature of Web applications generally requires programming variables and other information to be carried along in a hopelessly long, cryptic, and dynamically generated URL. Including these URLs would not only be tedious, but also useless because the programming logic and design of URLs undergo constant revision. Even without their specific addresses, however, most of the examples are shown with enough context to illustrate the point and to show you how to get to the site if needed.

ONWARD

Early on in the process, I wrote a short list of values I hoped to instill in the book. There was one for each vowel, which made them a bit easier to remember:

- ☐ Approachable
- ☐ Educational
- ☐ Inspirational
- ☐ Objective
- ☐ Useful

Of course it's you, the reader, who is the ultimate judge of whether I've pulled it off. I hope you'll let me know.

All the best…

—Bob Baxley
bob@baxleydesign.com

Foundations

PART I

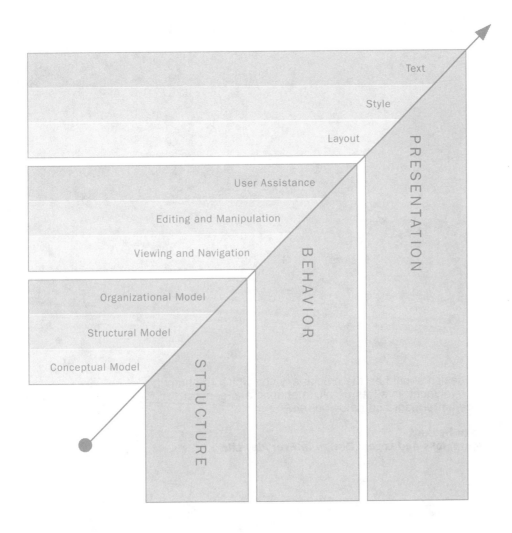

Text

Style

Layout

User Assistance

Editing and Manipulation

Viewing and Navigation

Organizational Model

Structural Model

Conceptual Model

PRESENTATION

BEHAVIOR

STRUCTURE

"…design should be the crucial anvil on which the human environment, in all its detail, is shaped and constructed for the betterment and delight of all."

John Heskett
Toothpicks and Logos: Design in Everyday Life

1

COMMON GROUND

Defining Web Applications and
Establishing the Goals of Design

When I was in the fifth grade, I submitted to a test of basic skills designed
by the state of Iowa. Staring at the blue booklet, I was filled with the anxiety of an 11-year-
old on the edge of an abyss. With the timer set to an interminable 90 minutes, Ms. Reeves
looked upon us and offered the following: "Start at the beginning."

The first step in solving any design problem, be it visual, interactive, or informational,
is to understand the medium that will express the solution. Therefore, a good beginning
for the question of how to design effective Web applications is defining and exploring the
relative advantages and limitations of Web applications as an interactive medium.

DEFINING WEB APPLICATIONS

Also known as a Web-based application, a Web app, a Web-top, and a handful of other goofy names that don't merit repeating, a *Web application* is a specific type of Web site that implicitly and explicitly stores and manipulates data unique to each of its users. Put more succinctly, a Web application is software on the Web.

Web applications differ from traditional content-based Web sites in that they interact with users in a one-to-one manner. To enable such user-specific behavior, users are typically required to identify themselves by providing a user ID and password. Once they're identified, visitors to a Web application can make permanent changes to their data by creating, editing, and deleting various types of stored information.

The one-to-one interaction possible with a Web application sets it apart from content-based sites such as CNN, The Washington Post, or Fodors. Visitors to these sites can spend all day surfing around without the site having any idea of who they are, what they are doing, or where they've been. The site simply sits there, fielding requests for one page or another and shipping them out as quickly as it can. In terms of sheer numbers, content-based sites dwarf the number of Web applications. In terms of interactivity and complexity, however, Web applications clearly dominate.

The universe of Web applications available to consumers can be placed into a handful of categories, including the following:

☐ **Online stores.** Sites that allow you to purchase goods and services
are one of the most conspicuous and popular examples of Web
applications (see Figure 1.1). Online stores are considered
Web applications because they enable users to interact with
a virtual shopping cart and a complex checkout process.
Sophisticated stores also include personalization behaviors so that
different visitors see different items, based on their past purchases.

1.1
RedEnvelope, a typical online
store, remembers shipping,
billing, and payment information
and offers reminders and an
address book.

☐ **Financial services.** Sites that provide stock trading, bill payment, and other financial services are another group of Web applications (see Figure 1.2). These applications universally require the user to log in before performing tasks such as checking account balances, paying bills, or reviewing account activity.

1.2

Customers of Charles Schwab can use Schwab.com to make stock trades, pay bills, transfer funds, request information, and interact with customer service representatives.

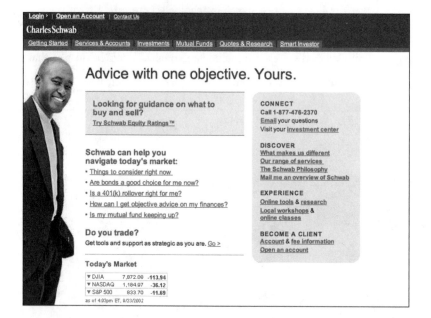

☐ **Travel services.** The Web has proved to be such a useful medium for the travel industry that almost every major airline, hotel chain, and car rental agency now has a dedicated site where customers can make reservations. In addition, a number of travel aggregation sites such as Orbitz (see Figure 1.3) provide access to a wide variety of carriers and chains in a single site. There are even specialty sites for bed-and-breakfasts, spas, adventure travel guides, and other types of travel companies. Travel sites combine content and functionality into a single application that allows users to research destinations, consult schedules, compare fares, make reservations, pay for services, store and recall travel preferences, and track flights.

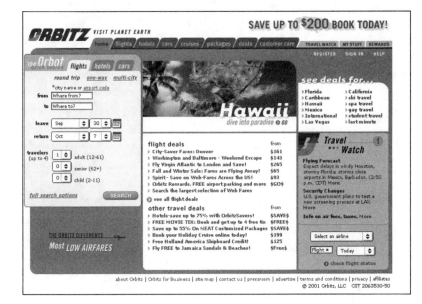

1.3
Orbitz is a Web application that allows users to plan and reserve travel.

☐ **Information portals.** Another group of Web applications includes information portals, such as myYahoo!, MSN (see Figure 1.4), Excite, Lycos, and Infoseek. Although many of these sites began as search engines, they have subsequently metamorphosed into large-scale news and information services with tools enabling users to select content and personalize the presentation.

1.4

MSN is a typical information portal offering similar content and functionality to myYahoo!, Lycos, Excite, and others.

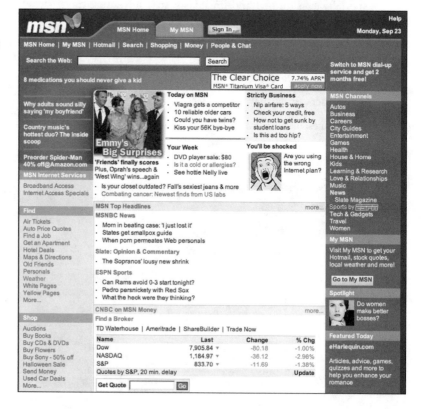

☐ **Online services.** A final broad category of Web applications encompasses tools such as online calendars, email, contact management, digital photo-processing and storage, remote file storage, group invitation services, personal Web site creation, and others. The online photo-processing service Snapfish is one example (see Figure 1.5). Although most of these online services duplicate functionality available in desktop applications, the Web environment enables them to provide unique and valuable benefits.

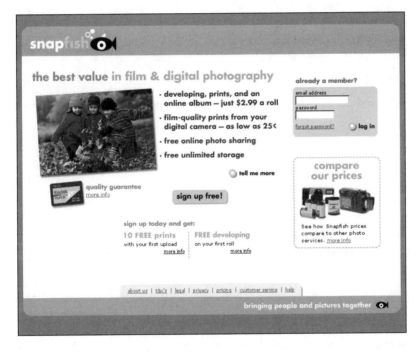

1.5
The Snapfish site offers a variety of application functionality for storing photos, sharing photos, and ordering prints.

Web applications are a relatively new phenomenon, coming onto the scene with the explosion of e-commerce, stock trading, and travel sites during the boom of the late 1990s. Although an increasing number of Web applications are taking advantage of proprietary technologies, such as ActiveX, Java, or Flash, as of this writing, the user interface for the vast majority of Web applications is built using HTML, DHTML, and JavaScript.

As an interactive medium, Web applications present a variety of unique challenges. These challenges stem from their attempt to merge two fundamentally different interaction models: the page-based hypertext model of the Web with the window-based task and actions model of data-centric applications, such as Outlook or Quicken. Although Web applications aren't likely to replace document-based productivity applications, such as Word or Photoshop, at least not any time soon, they do offer a variety of new, distinctive, and valuable capabilities.

WEB APPLICATIONS:
THE GOOD, THE BAD, AND THE UNFORTUNATE

With the dot-com excitement of the late 1990s now safely corralled in the history books, it's possible to take a more measured view of what is and isn't useful or interesting about Web applications. Using a Web browser to present an application is, after all, only one option among many. Many Web applications could also have been developed as desktop or Java applications. Web applications, however, do have some enticing advantages, including the following:

- **Access to centralized real-time data.** The most conspicuous advantage of Web application is their access to a centralized data store. Applications that offer operations such as travel reservations, real-time stock trading, and online shopping simply couldn't exist without this connectivity. In addition, as corporations increasingly move their operations to the virtual world of databases, direct access to those databases also becomes important. In addition to consumer activities, Web applications allow corporations to interact directly with each other's information systems.

- **Ease of distribution.** Web applications eliminate the physical and logistical hassles of distributing software. This improves users' experiences because they don't have to suffer through the tedium of installing and managing software; it also improves the bottom line of software developers, as they no longer have to master, press, label, or ship disks. In addition, because Web applications don't require physical distribution, their developers can afford to constantly upgrade and improve the product without having to worry about the costs of getting it to users.

- **Ubiquitous access.** Web applications are available from any computer with a Web browser and an Internet connection. That means users of Web-based email can access their messages from all over the world as well as from their local library. This is a tremendous advantage for students or other users dependent on shared computing resources.

- ☐ **Write-once coding.** Because the interface for Web applications is generally built with open-standards technology—HTML and JavaScript, to be specific—Web applications present the only practical opportunity for developers to write one version of an application that can run on any computer regardless of the operating system or browser—at least theoretically. For an industry perpetually striving to add more features and release new products, the mere idea of write-once coding is compelling enough to offset the added tradeoffs, compromises, and complexities.

- ☐ **Momentum.** As the number of Web application developers grows, there is a corresponding increase in the availability and sophistication of development tools. In addition, there is a rise in the availability and knowledge of the people needed to build them. Although this isn't an advantage of Web applications per se, it does suggest that the quantity and quality of Web applications are destined to rise.

Although the unique advantages of Web applications enable a genre of software that's otherwise impossible to create, Web applications also have their fair share of disadvantages. As you'll learn in the upcoming chapters, some of the most serious design failures affecting Web applications result from the application attempting functionality that is simply unsuitable for the Web environment. In the same way that hammers make lousy screwdrivers, Web applications aren't perfect for everything. Some of the most severe limitations include the following:

☐ **Serial interactivity.** The level of real-time interactivity available in a Web application is not enough to produce sophisticated user interactivity. By and large, every user action has to be sent to the server for processing. The results of the action then have to be transmitted back to the user in the form of a new page. The experience is about as efficient, enjoyable, and satisfying as negotiating with a car salesman who has to check with his manager on every detail.

☐ **Primitive interaction vocabulary.** Compared to the sophisticated interactions in desktop applications—drag and drop, floating palettes, and context-sensitive menus, for example—the interaction vocabulary of a Web application feels stuck in the Stone Age of radio buttons, check boxes, and command buttons. Although it can seem like you're talking to a 2-year-old with few words and poor pronunciation, Web applications can be effective communicators if you give them a bit of patience and understanding.

☐ **Bandwidth limitations.** Compounding the problem of a limited vocabulary, Web applications are also hampered by download times, server performance, and network latency. In the same way that desktop application developers once had to worry about fitting their work on 400KB disks, Web application designers have to ensure that their work can be delivered to an audience short on high-speed access and patience.

☐ **Constant connection.** The flip side of the ubiquitous access argument is the requirement that users of a Web application have to be connected to the Internet. Although free, universal, wireless access is surely just a few months away, until it arrives, Web applications will be unavailable to users away from the Web.

- **Technical complexity.** Despite the primitive nature of the user interface for Web applications, there is nothing simple about the technical infrastructure that sits behind them. Web applications depend on a multi-tier architecture that effectively isolates the application into three layers: the database layer, the application logic layer, and the presentation layer. Although isolating these components results in more manageable development environments and more maintainable code, it requires multiple types of technology working in concert to deliver a unified experience. Unfortunately, the variety of technology layers also leads to an increase in the number and complexity of errors and bugs.

- **Inconsistent presentation.** By nature, designers are control freaks; otherwise, they wouldn't be designers. As such, designers of interactive media in general, and Web applications in particular, are destined to be frustrated. Thanks to the variations in operating systems, Web browsers, monitor resolutions, and user preferences, designers of content-based sites learned long ago that precisely controlling what a user is going to see is almost impossible. Added to that challenge, designers of Web applications typically don't even know exactly what's going to be on any given page. Working in a world of such uncertainty requires the ability to finely balance multiple variables. Patience, persistence, and pragmatism are also helpful.

An intelligent solution to any design problem requires an understanding and respect for both the materials and the medium. Designers of interactive media should be no exception to this rule. In the same way that graphic designers understand the subtleties of paper, ink, and printing presses, interactive designers should understand the architecture, mechanics, and capabilities of software. For designers of Web applications, this understanding starts with an appreciation of the advantages and disadvantages of the Web as an interactive medium.

BRINGING DESIGN TO SOFTWARE

With at least some illumination shed on the question of Web applications as a medium, another room in need of sunlight is the relationship between the activities of design and software development. Unfortunately, the word *design* is about as nebulous as words like *love, faith*, and *reason*. A definition, therefore, seems in order. Unfortunately, the obligatory dictionary definition is surprisingly content-free: "v. intend, plan or propose." Thank you, Mr. Webster. Two other alternatives come closer to the point.

In his book *Toothpicks and Logos: Design in Everyday Life*, John Heskett offered the following: "…design, stripped to its essence, can be defined as the human capacity to shape and make our environment in ways without precedent in nature, to serve our needs and give meaning to our lives."[*]

---

[*]*John Heskett*, Toothpicks and Logos: Design in Everyday Life, *Oxford University Press, 2002, p. 7.*

In the specific case of design for interactive media, it's worth adding the following from Scott Berkun's post to the ACM-SIGCHI (Special Interest Group on Computer-Human Interaction) newsgroup: "Design, the skill of understanding tradeoffs and conceiving, describing, and evaluating alternatives...."[*] Slightly biased toward the sub-optimal world of software design, this definition is certainly appropriate for readers of the Web design newsgroup where it originally appeared.

In the context of Web applications, design is the activity of solving the problems that arise when you try to create a useful and desirable experience for users. Succeeding at this challenge requires not only the ability to exploit the Web's advantages and navigate its limitations, but also a clear vision of how design fits into the larger process of software development.

MARKETING AND ENGINEERING: WHAT CAN WE SELL? WHAT CAN WE BUILD?

Throughout its short but productive history, the software industry has been dominated by two competing but complementary concerns: What can we build? and What can we sell? Represented by Product Marketing and Sales on one side and Engineering on the other, most technology companies retain a bias in one direction or the other. Another way to describe this dichotomy is as a focus on the needs and desires of the marketplace versus a focus on the capabilities and limitations of the technology.

---

[*]*Scott Berkun, July 8, 1999 post to the ACM-SIGCHI (Special Interest Group on Computer-Human Interaction) newsgroup.*

Unfortunately, both approaches tend to arrive at the same end result: software containing every possible feature and capability. Software has mostly been judged by its ability to provide the maximum number of features with little regard for their usefulness or usability. Although this might sound great at first, anyone who's tried to make sense of a complex software application knows that a forest of features can be as confusing as it can be useful.

As software and Web applications attempt to extend their reach to an ever-widening group of users, the costs of complexity and instability are clearly outweighing the benefits of more functionality. Users of all levels have come to realize that a feature is not really a feature unless they can understand how to use it. Looked at from this perspective, it's clear that a critical constraint on new products and features is not the skill to write code, but the vision to design in accordance with users' needs. Granted, this phenomenon is hardly universal, but as the market for technology and software matures, so too will the products serving those markets. As products across the gamut of consumer goods—everything from automobiles to cell phones—have matured, they have become increasingly dependent on the principles of simplicity, reliability, and user satisfaction.

So if Engineering-centric organizations have the potential to push users to the edge of mental overload, what about Marketing/Sales-centric ones? Unfortunately, the question most often on the minds of Product Marketing and Sales ("What can we sell?") also fails to address users' needs.

Users and customers are often confused as one and the same, but they are two distinct groups. Customers, the focus of Marketing and Sales, are the people and organizations that give you money in exchange for goods or services. By contrast, users are the people who actually consume and interact with the goods and services. For some products, such as clothing, the customer and the user are typically the same person. For other products, however, they are not.

A 401K retirement plan is a good example of a situation in which customers and users are two different groups. The decision of selecting and contracting with a 401K provider often falls to someone in the Human Resources department. That person is a customer of the plan provider. The users of the plan, however, include every employee of the company eligible to make contributions. The desires of users—low fees, responsive customer service, and broad range of investment options—are different from those of the customer: sales relationship and ease of administration. Fortunately, the needs of the two groups aren't in actual conflict, but clearly there is little overlap.

In the world of software products and services, the manner in which software is purchased by a centralized corporate authority results in a similar relationship between customer and user needs. In those situations, the needs of the IT department—maintenance, administration, and licensing arrangements—have little in common with the desires of users: simplicity, stability, and ease of use.

Unfortunately, the conflict between customer and user needs is even more pronounced in advertising-supported mass media, such as television, newspapers, and increasingly, the Web. With advertisers as customers and visitors as users, the desires of the two groups aren't merely tangential to one another; they are downright combative. For advertising-supported Web applications, representing the needs of customers and users simultaneously requires a difficult balance between the short-term pressure to satisfy advertiser demands and the long-term danger of alienating users.

Acknowledging the differences between users and customers, it becomes clear that a single organization cannot successfully serve them both. To come straight to the point, the traditional focus on "What can we sell?" and "What can we build?" is inherently flawed because it tends to leave users alienated and frustrated. Although a focus on selling and building can succeed in a fast-moving market filled with early adopters and void of competition, its potential diminishes as product segments mature, competition increases, and users come to demand simplicity, quality, and reliability.

Accelerating the trend toward simplicity, quality, and reliability is the very nature of Web applications. Thanks to the unique advantages of Web applications—open standards, ubiquitous access, no software to install, and rapid development cycles—it is difficult to erect meaningful barriers to switching. Unlike desktop applications, where using a certain product is a commitment to a single file format, a steep learning curve, and an economically advantaged upgrade path, there is little to keep users from clicking over to the competition. Don't like Expedia? It's not hard to switch over to Orbitz.

DESIGN: WHAT DO USERS WANT?

So if a focus on building and selling fails to ensure long-term success, what will? The answer is one of balance.

A successful product is a careful balance of three competing but complementary forces:

What do users desire?

What will sustain a viable business?

What can be feasibly built?

Instead of starting with an engineering breakthrough or a business plan, this approach starts with the obvious but often ignored question of desirability. Originally proposed by Larry Keeley, president of the Chicago-based strategy firm Doblin, Figure 1.6 illustrates the intersection of desirability, viability, and feasibility.

1.6

As originally proposed by Larry Keeley, technology products with long-term sustainability balance the qualities of desirability, viability, and feasibility.

Expanding on Keeley's model, it's possible to understand how the balance of those three qualities varies with the type and maturity of the market being served. Figure 1.7 illustrates four examples: consumer software, enterprise software, technical development tools, and free online services.

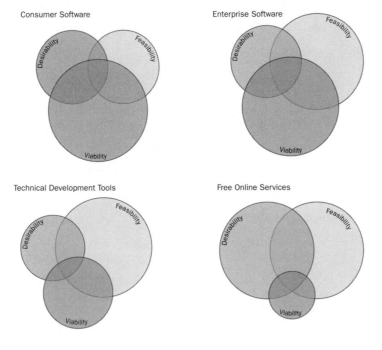

1.7
Companies producing consumer software, enterprise software, technical development tools, and free online services tend toward different balances of what's desirable, viable, and feasible.

As evidenced in the work of Keeley and others, creating products with the potential for long-term success requires that the existing power structure involving Marketing, Sales, and Engineering be opened up to include Design. Such a shift frees Product Marketing and Sales to worry about the interests and opportunities of the business, allows Engineering to remain focused on the technology's capabilities and limitations, and provides an equal partner dedicated to users' needs, limitations, and capabilities.

Bringing design to software means placing users and their needs in the forefront of the development process. It means that every decision along the way—every feature addition, every technical tradeoff, every detail of the interface—has to account for the ultimate impact on users. This does not mean, however, that user research and user opinion should sit in the driver's seat of product design and development. Rather, it means that users' needs and desires have to be carefully balanced against business concerns and technical realities.

SUMMARY

To design effective Web applications, it is necessary to have some understanding of the relative strengths and weaknesses of Web applications as an interactive medium. The most notable of these from a user's perspective include the following:

Pluses	Minuses
Real-time access	Serial interactivity
Ubiquitous access	Primitive interactive vocabulary

In addition, designing effective Web applications requires an understanding of design as an activity—shaping an environment to fit human needs—as well as its role in the overall development process. The creation of great products rests on the ability of a development organization to envision an answer that simultaneously answers three questions:

What do users want?

What will provide a sustainable business?

What can we feasibly build?

As the discussion moves on to the next chapter, the spotlight will turn to the challenge of discovering, understanding, and articulating users' needs.

"The role of the designer is to act both as visionary and troubleshooter—to provide the big picture, and to focus on every little detail as well."

Antonio Citterio
designer of the Visaroll chair

2 PUTTING THE USER FIRST

Describing Target Users and Product Goals

The designer of any interactive media confronts two significant challenges: accurately understanding users' needs and abilities, and creatively translating that understanding into an experience suitable for the medium. This process begins with the designer engaging in direct and indirect research methods, sometimes working on his or her own but preferably in concert with dedicated research professionals. Equipped with observations and facts gathered from real-world users, the designer has to extrapolate past that research—inventing a compelling product vision and ultimately translating that vision into a finished design.

A Comprehensive Product Design Process

Although a comprehensive product design process includes four phases—Understanding, Vision, Requirements, and Design (see Figure 2.1)—the focus of this chapter is the Vision phase. The remainder of the book focuses on the Design phase, leaving other authors to cover the Understanding and Requirements phases.

1 Understanding	2 Vision	3 Requirements	4 Design
User Needs	Core Design Values	Functional	Structure
Competition	Opportunity Statement	Technical	Behavior
Business Opportunity	Persona Profiles & Goals	Business	Presentation
Technical Constraints	Concept Statement	Usability	

2.1

The Vision phase of a comprehensive product design process follows the Understanding phase.

For a creative, subjective endeavor like design, however, consistently evaluating the quality and success of an alternative requires the overall team to agree on a group of relatively objective metrics. Without fixed standards, evaluating alternatives can degrade into a random contest of opinion rather than an accurate assessment of an alternative's ability to address specific user needs in a creative, comprehensive, and practical manner. Therefore, the consistent evaluation of design solutions requires two fixed positions: What is the problem to be solved, and how can the "best" solution be objectively determined? In the context of interactive design, this translates to the following:

☐ What are the specific characteristics of the individuals who will be using the product? What are their exact needs and wants?

☐ On what basis will the solutions be judged? What are the values, qualities, and metrics that will be used to compare and evaluate options?

This chapter addresses the first of those questions by detailing a variety of tools for synthesizing the needs and wants of users into a form useful to the design process. It also addresses the second question by providing a set of fixed values and qualities that can be used to judge design alternatives.

ANCHORING DESIGN: THE CORE VALUES OF CONTROL AND SATISFACTION

Desirability results from a product's overall utility and value to users. Utility and value, however, are dependent on a product's raw capabilities as well as users' capacity to take advantage of them. Although desirability is clearly affected by the overall feature set, in the more narrow context of interface design, the concern is users' ability to exploit those features. Therefore, the question here is "What are the values and principles useful for evaluating the quality of a design solution?"

Interactive designs should be judged against the metric of two specific values: control and satisfaction. *Control* is the interface's ability to provide an appropriate level of direction and power so that the user can operate the software efficiently, intelligently, and confidently. *Satisfaction* is the interface's ability to provide an enjoyable, assuring, and fulfilling experience for the user.

Although these two core design values are fundamental to interactive design as a discipline, the specific definitions and principles accorded to them result from a designer's unique philosophy, individuality, and perspective. The following sections, however, are a useful starting point.

CORE VALUE: CONTROL

Interactive design solutions should give users an appropriate level of interaction, manipulation, and communication with the software. However, for any design solution, the measure of appropriate control is based on the needs and abilities of the target users. What is appropriate to a sophisticated technical audience is unlikely to be so for a less experienced consumer audience.

The design principles that affect control include the following:

- ☐ **Consistency.** An interface that is consistent contributes to a user's control by increasing predictability and obviousness. In addition, consistency with established visual and interactive conventions reduces the time and effort needed to learn a new system by leveraging users' knowledge and experiences.

- ☐ **Simplicity.** An interface that is simple contributes to the overall sense of control by providing an experience that is clear and direct. Simplicity results from eliminating unnecessary elements, reducing the design to its most essential form. As the hallmark of all great design, simplicity requires a complete understanding of the problem and the skill to devise a thorough solution.

- □ **Orderliness.** An interface that is ordered contributes to control by removing distraction and increasing user focus. An ordered interface also creates confidence that the system has been well considered and well built.

- □ **Responsiveness.** An interface that is responsive contributes to control by improving the connection between a user's action and the system's reaction. The system should complete tasks and provide feedback in an alert and timely manner.

CORE VALUE: SATISFACTION

In addition to control, a quality interface also expresses the core value of satisfaction. A successful design solution considers the user's emotional response, offering an experience that is novel, entertaining, fulfilling, and assuring. Like the core value of control, addressing the core value of satisfaction requires the designer to find the appropriate balance between the following principles:

- □ **Efficiency.** A satisfying interface is efficient, not requiring superfluous action or unnecessary learning on the part of the user. Unlike interactions with the government in general and the IRS in particular, users should not feel that they are wasting their time.

- □ **Assurance.** A satisfying interface creates a sense of trust and assurance that the system is operating correctly and accurately. Like a skilled doctor, it should leave them with confidence in the software, even when delivering bad news.

- **Politeness**. An interface that is polite communicates in a manner that is relevant, honest, and tolerant. It does not distract the user with unimportant or irrelevant detail nor does it mislead the user. In addition, it is tolerant of users, allowing them to interact with the system in a variety of ways but preventing them from unknowingly destroying data.

- **Elegance**. An elegant interface is balanced, restrained, and harmonious. It creates an overall impression of integration, sophistication, and good taste. Elegant solutions come from people who have had long-term and repeated exposure to high-quality design in a variety of mediums.

- **Enjoyable**. A satisfying interface provides enjoyment by being novel and appropriately entertaining. Although the level of entertainment and novelty can vary widely, the principle of enjoyment should always be a goal of the design.

Remembering that these guiding principles and values are but one person's opinion, it is a useful exercise to develop your own. Writing down your own list of core design values and principles will give you a consistent metric for comparing and evaluating different design solutions. Without such metrics, design quickly spirals into a collection of unassociated decisions attributable to mood, influence, or random personal opinion.

BOUNDING THE PROBLEM: CREATING A COMPREHENSIVE PRODUCT VISION

Although the discipline of core design values sets universal metrics, it does not speak to the needs and desires of specific users working with a specific product. A different set of tools is required for that problem. These tools include a collection of documents and exercises that describe the product vision in concrete terms and replace vague and shifting concepts of users with specific descriptions of their goals and characteristics.

The purpose of the documents described here—the opportunity statement, the persona profiles, and the concept statement—is to produce a conscious, articulate, and realistic product vision. Although other documents often contribute to the product vision, these are the most germane to interface design.

The creation of truly breakthrough and sustainable product concepts requires the entire design team to seriously engage in these exercises. The written documents cannot be substituted with white-board sessions, hallway conversations, or group assumptions. The simple process of writing is the only way to reveal an articulate product vision and an accurate image of user goals. This knowledge and synthesis serve as the foundational support for everything to follow. As long as it remains in the ethereal gray matter of one's mind, the design as a whole will be shaky and fragile.

"When the outcome drives the process we will only ever go to where we've already been. If process drives outcome we may not know where we're going, but we will know we want to be there."

**—Bruce Mau
(Bruce Mau Design)
"An Incomplete Manifesto
for Growth"**

The skeptics will surely note that most software development projects do not rely on such tools and methods. The skeptics would be right. The pessimists would also be right, however, when they note that many projects fail to produce anything of true value or utility.

If the goal were to produce a simple product with a short lifespan—a mud hut, for example—the cost of careful planning and design might be questionable. If the goal were a 50-story office building, however, the costs of not planning would be disastrous. Granted, software is more malleable than glass and steel, but it doesn't take long in the industry to realize that the difference in only slight. The "code first, worry about users later" attitude rarely results in a desirable product. Unfortunately, so too do most disciplined development processes.

Tools such as the opportunity statement and the persona profiles are often the only documents that bridge the gap between the requirements documents created by Product Marketing and the technical documents produced by Engineering. Although feature lists and architecture diagrams certainly communicate important aspects of the product, they often miss the forest for the trees. *Gray's Anatomy* tells me how my body is constructed, and Darwin helps me understand the competitive environment that shaped it. Even together, however, the picture is hardly complete.

As a professional communicator, it is the designer's responsibility to interpret the descriptions produced by other functional groups, synthesizing them into a comprehensive, concise, and accurate vision that everyone on the team can understand. That vision should address four key dimensions of the product:

What is the business opportunity the product will address?

Who does the product serve?

What user goals will the product meet?

What characteristics define the product?

With a clear product vision that encompasses the business opportunity, the target user, and the product's unique qualities, the entire development process will be more focused, more productive, and more efficient. Most amazing, often the product you get in the end will bear a striking resemblance to what you set out to build at the beginning.

THE OPPORTUNITY STATEMENT: OUTLINING THE BUSINESS OPPORTUNITY

Like the story treatments used to pitch movies to producers and studios, an *opportunity statement* outlines the central themes and opportunity for the product. The statement describes why there is a product need, but stops short of describing how the need will be met.

The opportunity statement presents the product in terms of a story with a minimum of technical or business terms. Like all stories, it should include conflicts, resolutions, characters, and settings. Because the purpose of the exercise is to frame the problem without jumping to conclusions about the solution, a well-done opportunity statement is a delicate balance between the specific and the vague. Ideally, the statement takes fewer than 250 words to communicate the following:

Who is the target user?

What does the user need?

What is the technical environment (for example, Web application, desktop application, or dedicated device) of the product?

What is the business opportunity and competitive landscape?

An example of an opportunity statement is shown in the "Pika Opportunity Statement" sidebar. The statement describes a Web application codenamed Pika. The business goal of the product is to serve as an "info-mediary" for the eco-tourism industry. The statement outlines the business opportunity as well as the target users and the problems they currently experience while planning travel.

Pika Opportunity Statement

Pika is the name of a new Web application being developed for travelers and guides of eco-tourism adventures. As exotic destinations have become more accessible, a wide variety of people have started traveling to remote locales. Although eco-tourists all have a love for adventure, they desire different levels of comfort, physical activities, cultural interactions, and environmental connection.

A variety of guiding companies, services, and trips are now available to this diverse group of travelers. Most of these companies and services are small-scale operations; as a result, travelers have difficulty finding and selecting a suitable guide.

In addition, unlike travel to more developed destinations, travel to remote and exotic locations requires planning and research into appropriate clothing, gear, vaccinations, health conditions, cultural standards, political stability, physical requirements, and a host of other issues.

Although much of the content and tools for this type of trip planning are available in books, the information is constantly changing, quickly dated, and often unreliable.

The goal of Pika is to provide eco-tourists with a single Web destination that contains all the content, tools, and advice needed for the process of selecting, planning, and participating in an adventure of their own.

Although the opportunity statement might look like an easy exercise, clearly stating a problem without assuming or suggesting a solution is not a trivial task. In spite of its brevity, reading an explicit description of the product's goals and audience is likely to shatter the illusions and misconceptions of at least a few team members.

PERSONA BIOS AND GOALS: MAKING "USERS" REAL

In an ideal world, everyone involved in a development project would visit with actual users to observe their behavior and workplace environment. It would undoubtedly be an eye-opening experience for many.

Unfortunately, technology companies—particularly those in high-tech areas such as Silicon Valley, Boston, or Austin—tend to be devastatingly insular. In many cases, the very people responsible for defining, designing, and building products are those most out of touch with the needs and expectation of typical users. Peoria's a long way from Palo Alto. As a result, products are devised and created that may be interesting to the development team, but are not necessarily useful to actual users.

Personas are perhaps the most powerful tool available to penetrate such insular thinking and extend the team's collective vision outside its own area code. Although personas originally developed as a consumer marketing tool, they have been used by interactive designers since at least the early 1990s. The awareness of personas as a design tool was not widespread, however, until it was described by Alan Cooper in his book *The Inmates Are Running the Asylum*. In addition to describing personas as a design tool, Cooper also emphasized the need to classify each persona as primary, secondary, supplemental, or negative.

Personas are based on a simple concept: A fundamental requirement for developing a product that fully satisfies users' needs is to identify and articulate those needs *before* you design the product. Although this is sometimes interpreted as a simple research project—ask users what they want and then go make it—innovative, sustainable product concepts require more than a question-and-answer approach. Writing for the *Harvard Business Review*, Kim Clark and Takahiro Fujimoto put it like this:

> "It begins with customers (users), to be sure...but strong product concepts also include a healthy measure of what we call "market imagination": they encompass what customers say they want and what the concept's creators *imagine* customers will want three or more years into the future. Remembering that customers know only existing products and existing technologies, they avoid the trap of being too close to customers—and designing products that will be out-of-date before they are even manufactured."[*]

Although pure research can identify patterns of user behavior, needs, or goals, that raw information is not particularly useful during the design process. By contrast, personas are a way to synthesize and articulate information gathered from research, so that it can guide the team toward a creative, innovative product design rather than an uninspired, copycat one.

---

[*]*Kim Clark and Takahiro Fukimoto, "The Power of Product Integrity."* In Harvard Business Review, *Nov-Dec 1990, p. 113.*

Personas, or user profiles, are concise descriptions of archetypal users brought to life. Compared to demographics or other statistical descriptions, personas draw from real-life users to create a believable and specific image of a target user.

In addition to physical, psychological, and behavioral attributes, a persona also possesses goals. Compared to tasks, which are discrete, specific activities, goals reflect a persona's emotional needs. For example, improving one's self-image is a goal, but running 5 miles is a task. Although tasks support and reflect goals, they represent low-level activities rather than high-level needs. Goals are the most important aspect of a persona because they describe what tasks users will need to complete, thus determining the product's functional requirements and feature set.

A well-defined persona includes the following:

☐ **Name.** Everything has a name, whether it's your dog, your street, your best friend, or your one lonely house plant. Naming a persona makes it real and specific. It also eliminates the impersonal reference to the vague notion of a "user."

☐ **Photograph.** The maxim that a picture is worth a thousand words understates the situation. A photograph instantly communicates volumes about the persona.

☐ **Title or caption.** If your persona were being interviewed on the nightly news, what would appear under his or her name? "Vice-President of Design"? "Full-time Mom"? "Friend of dogs and confidante of children"? "9-year-old genius"? A title or caption evokes an image of the persona and his or her particular qualities.

❑ **Goals.** What are the goals this persona has for buying, using, or interacting with the product? The persona's goals are the most important aspect of the persona profile because they ultimately drive product requirements.

❑ **Other descriptive characteristics.** What are the other characteristics or interests of the persona that make it specific? Are they married? Do they have kids? Do they eat out a lot? What makes them unique?

❑ **Computing environment.** At the end of the day, this exercise is about creating software. Therefore, it's important to capture a picture of the user's computing environment. Is the persona on a on a 5-year-old PC running Windows 93 and using a 14.4 modem, or are they on a brand-new Macintosh with a personal T3 line?

❑ **Computing experience.** Is the persona a technology neophyte or an computer expert? Will he freely explore the system, or sheepishly stare at the screen, wondering if he broke something? More than a crude assignment of the "beginner, intermediate, expert" label, the goal is to describe the persona's comfort level with computers and any relevant knowledge or experience that might affect the design.

Table 2.1 contains a list of personas for the fictional Web application, Pika.

Persona #1	Bob and Ian Andelman
	Seattle, WA
Photo	
Caption	Father and son team, traveling together
Primary goal	Bond through a shared experience
Secondary goal(s)	☐ Safety
	☐ Adventure
Description	Bob is a 54-year-old financial planner. Ian is his 15-year-old son. The Hanisees want to take a guided adventure together as a father-son experience. Although they both have experience on weekend camping trips, they haven't done any extended eco-travel. They are interested in finding a trip and guiding service that will be exciting and interesting, but not necessarily dangerous.
Computing environment	Fast machine, 17-inch monitor, IE 5.0, DSL
Computing experience	☐ Daily Web usage
	☐ Experienced, savvy users
	☐ Both use online email, variety of shopping sites, and numerous content and research sites

Table 2.1

Pika Persona Bios

Table 2.1

Pika Persona Bios

Persona #2	Margie Dito Santa Barbara, CA
Photo	
Caption	Middle-aged, professional, single woman seeing the world
Primary goal	Experience other cultures
Secondary goal(s)	☐ Safety ☐ Adventure ☐ Meeting other people
Description	Margie is a 48-year-old dentist who has never been married. For the past 10 years, she has been able to afford the time and money to travel to exotic and remote destinations all around the globe. Although she enjoys her travels, she is acutely aware of the unique dangers of such locales. Because of her travel experience, Margie is also aware of the amount of planning and research required for her trips. She is looking for a service to help her identify appropriate destinations and guiding services and manage important planning details.
Computing environment	Aging machine, 15-inch monitor, Netscape 4.7, 56KB modem
Computing experience	☐ Weekly Web usage ☐ Comfortable on the Web, but not proficient with applications other than a Web browser ☐ Uses online email and content-based news sites

Persona #3	John Friday Austin, TX
Photo	
Caption	Retired attorney living his dream
Primary goal	Solitude and reflection
Secondary goal(s)	☐ Adventure ☐ See the world's 14 tallest mountains
Description	John is a 68-year-old retired attorney. Although John is married, every few years he takes an extended trip on his own. John enjoys the adventure of eco-tourism and the opportunity to quietly reflect among the world's tallest and most remote mountains. John's special interest is in seeing the world's 14 8000-meter peaks. John is looking for trips and guides to specific destinations and at specific times of year.
Computing environment	Aging machine, 15-inch monitor, AOL 6.0, 56KB modem

Computing experience	☐ Weekly Web usage
	☐ Comfortable on AOL;
	   still adjusting to the Web
	☐ Reads online news
	   and information

Table 2.1

Pika Persona Bios

Persona #4	Phil Sasaki Boston, MA
Photo	
Caption	Recent college graduate traveling the globe
Primary goal	Have a transitional experience between the end of college and the start of a career
Secondary goal(s)	☐ Adventure ☐ Physical danger and risk ☐ Excitement
Description	Phil is 22 years old and recently graduated from college. He's taking some time to see the world before he settles down to a long and profitable career as a software interface designer. Phil is an avid rock climber and extremely knowledgeable about backcountry travel. However, he has never traveled outside the U.S. and is unfamiliar with the unique requirements of exotic travel. Phil is looking for a trip and guiding service to provide him with an introductory experience as he begins his around-the-world travels.
Computing environment	Ultra-fast machine, 17-inch monitor, IE 6.0, T1 line
Computing experience	☐ Daily Web usage ☐ Highly proficient, knowledgeable, and curious ☐ Uses online email, digital photo processing, and other Web applications

Persona #5	Ana Knight Chicago, IL
Photo	
Caption	20-something woman who enjoys comfort, fun, and adventure
Primary goal	Adventure in a comfortable environment
Secondary goal(s)	☐ Safety ☐ Experience other cultures
Description	Ana is a 27-year-old investment advisor. Although she enjoys traveling, she does not necessarily enjoy extreme sports, camping, or "roughing it." Ana previously took an inn-to-inn bicycling trip through Italy and is looking for other comparable destinations and experiences. Before taking her last trip, Ana spent a lot of time talking to friends and getting personal recommendations about specific trips.
Computing environment	Fast machine, 17-inch monitor, IE 5.0, cable modem
Computing experience	☐ Daily Web usage ☐ Proficient and comfortable user of the Web ☐ Uses a wide variety of travel, community, shopping, and content Web sites

As is evident in the Pika example, the process is likely to result in more than one persona. Ideally, it results in at least five, but sometimes more and sometimes less. Regardless, the goal is create a group that is highly representative of real-world users who will be using the product.

Unfortunately, even a group of five personas contains too many variations and divergent needs to produce the level of focus and clarity that a successful design process needs. Therefore, it's important to classify the list of personas into primary, secondary, supplemental, and negative personas.

Primary Personas

The *primary personas* represent the users for whom you are ultimately designing and building the application. If they are happy, enthusiastic, and satisfied with the end product, it can deemed a success. Ideally, there will be a single primary persona, although many products require multiple primary personas. For example, in addition to Pika's public site, the product might need a private site where tour operators can list and update their offerings. In this case, there would be two primary personas: one for the traveler and one for the tour operator. Applications with more than one primary persona are often constructed of multiple sub-sites, each designed to accommodate a specific primary persona.

Identifying primary personas is a difficult decision that requires considering both business and design issues. To narrow the field to just one or two targets means answering some difficult questions:

> Who is most likely to be a profitable customer?
>
> Who is most likely to be satisfied with what the product can actually deliver?
>
> Who is most likely to use a Web application to satisfy his or her goals?

For example, the best primary persona for Pika is Ana Knight because she is comfortable with the Web, would appreciate all the research and community features a Web site could potentially offer, and will have a reason to repeatedly use the service, as she travels often. This distinguishes her from other personas—Bob and Ian Andelman, for example—who are unlikely to take more than one adventure trip. It also distinguishes her from other personas who are less interested in community or less comfortable using the Web.

Secondary Personas

In addition to the primary persona, there are typically one or more secondary personas. *Secondary personas* represent users who will be generally satisfied with the design for the primary persona, but require a few more features. Although it's important to accommodate secondary personas if possible, their needs should not overrun the primary persona's experience or satisfaction.

Of the personas described for Pika, Margie Dito is the best secondary persona. Although there are some differences that make Margie a less attractive business target, from a design perspective, a few additional features could address Margie's planning needs without affecting Ana's overall experience.

Other Types of Personas

With the primary and secondary personas identified, there are likely to be some personas still remaining. Although some of them can be dismissed as user groups not worth pursuing, others can be classified as supplemental or negative personas.

Supplemental personas—for example, John Friday and Bob and Ian Andelman—represent users who will be satisfied with a product designed for the primary and secondary personas. Supplemental personas are essentially redundant, but they should be part of the personas bio document so that it remains comprehensive.

Negative personas represent users whose needs would trash the system for the other users. For example, accommodating Phil Sasaki's interests in extreme sports and dangerous activities would diminish Ana and Margie's experience of the site.

The Benefits of Personas

Personas brings to the design process many of the same advantages as core design values. Unlike core design values, however, personas are specific to a single design project. Some of the benefits include the following:

- **Focus.** Personas focus the entire design and development teams on the needs and goals of a single, homogeneous user group. By aiming for a specific target, it is possible to avoid the compromises that occur when a product tries to satisfy a wide audience. It also helps eliminate distracting corner cases that can dilute the design.

- **Constancy.** Ever notice how everyone's mom is sometimes an expert and sometimes a novice? Personas provide a fixed, constant reference point that can be used to guide the design.

- **Connection.** By offering a synthesized, digestible view of the data collected in interviews, market research, and usability studies, personas help the design and development team connect their efforts with the real people who are ultimately going to use the product.

☐ **Objectivity.** Personas eliminate the dangerous distraction of opinion by changing design considerations from "What do I think is best?" to "What is going to be the best thing for our primary persona?"

☐ **Reality.** Personas help identify weaknesses in the business plan or marketing objectives of the application by challenging team members to invent realistic scenarios of actual users buying or interacting with their product.

Like the product treatment, creating personas is relatively simple after the technique is understood. The real challenge of personas is ensuring that they accurately represent real-world users and aren't simply sophisticated opinions.

THE CONCEPT STATEMENT: DESCRIBING THE PRODUCT'S ESSENCE

Once there is agreement on the opportunity statement and the primary and secondary personas, it is possible to start describing the product in ways that suggest a unique and innovative approach. This approach is captured in the concept statement.

The *concept statement* is a short, descriptive phrase that reflects the product's unique personality, its essence. Like great advertising tag lines, concept statements should be memorable, multivalent forms of communication. One of the best examples belongs to Disneyland: "The happiest place on Earth." In five simple words, the Disneyland concept statement communicates the unique quality of Disneyland, providing a rich and memorable concept that serves as the foundation for everything from visionary objectives to detailed decisions.

Another example comes from the "new" iMac released by Apple Computer in the spring of 2002. Unsatisfied with the early design sketches from the project, Steve Jobs found the inspiration for the final product concept as he was walking in his garden with the designer, Jonathan Ives. With the concept statement "Sunflower" guiding him, Ives ultimately produced a design of unparalleled elegance, grace, and beauty.

Although these two examples are grandiose in scale and ambition, the power of a product concept to focus and guide the design of any product cannot be overstated. Strong, well-articulated product concepts give everyone involved in the product development process a single, focused vision of what the product is about. Although this shared vision doesn't guarantee a great product, the lack of it certainly leaves the outcome to chance.

As the final element of the product vision, the concept statement should reflect the opportunity statement, the persona bios, and the persona goals. Using these elements, it is possible to create a list of potential attributes that could be part of the concept statement, as shown in the "Potential Attributes for Pika" sidebar.

Potential Attributes for Pika

Safe	Authoritative	Comfortable
Exciting	Adventurous	Reliable
Controlled	Rugged	Exotic
Remote	Strong	Integrity
Outdoors	Nature	Wilderness
Trustworthy	Moderate	Comprehensive

Starting with the list of potential attributes, the next task is to eliminate redundant or inappropriate attributes, settling on a small collection of critical themes. Because the goal of the product concept is to define a unique and compelling experience, which attributes are selected requires considering the persona's needs as well as the team's own imagination and creative insight.

Once the group of core attributes has been identified, it is also important to elaborate on the specific meaning and impact of each attribute, as shown in the "Pika Core Attributes" sidebar.

Pika Core Attributes

☐ **Safe.** Pika is a safe, private environment that fully describes and explains the potential risks and dangers of various activities or destinations.

☐ **Comprehensive.** Pika is a comprehensive service, representing the widest possible range of destinations, guiding services, and activities.

☐ **Authoritative.** Pika is *the* authoritative source for knowledgeable and articulate information on eco-tourism destinations, guiding services, and activities.

☐ **Trustworthy.** Pika is a trustworthy and reliable source of unbiased information about the guiding services and destinations.

☐ **Adventurous.** Pika exudes a spirit of adventure and excitement, celebrating the wonders of nature and the mystery of exotic cultures.

The final step in the process is to distill the core attributes into a brief, memorable concept statement. Because the final product concept should succinctly communicate the core attributes, this step requires creativity and a commitment to capture each core attribute without interjecting anything new. Arriving at the precise phrase or image takes time, effort, and experimentation. However, once found, it should excite and galvanize the entire team. The example in the "Pika Concept Statement" completes the product vision for Pika.

Pika Concept Statement

A personal assistant with the spirit of an explorer and the concern of a mother.

Like the other elements of the product vision, the concept statement is a logical but creative extension of fundamental research into users and their needs. Its goal is to synthesize and reflect the information gained through research and observation, not to replace or supersede it. Although its brevity and simplicity might lead some to believe that the product concept is little more than the sophisticated expression of opinion, its strength and integrity results from its grounding in reality.

SUMMARY

As one part of a longer, more detailed product design process, the product vision process described in this chapter sets the stage for a comprehensive user requirements and interface design phase. In particular, the goals in the persona profiles are simply the first step toward exploring and describing of the product's ultimate functionality. In addition, because the product vision process is almost exclusively user-centered, it ignores critical issues related to the product's economic viability and technical feasibility.

Still, these tools are useful but, unfortunately, often ignored methods of defining a product vision. Used in concert, they instill a sense of confidence, clarity, and certainty throughout the design and development teams. The value of the following documents, particularly compared to the minimal time and effort to produce them, cannot be underestimated:

☐ **Core design values.** Although the precise meaning can vary with an individual designer or organization's basic philosophy, the core design values of control and satisfaction provide a fixed goal and constant method of evaluating design solutions.

☐ **Opportunity statement.** The first step in defining a product vision, the opportunity statement describes in compelling terms why the product should be created.

☐ **Persona profiles and goals.** Based on research and observations of actual people, personas enable the product to aim for a single, constant, well-defined mark by describing target users as fictional archetypes.

☐ **Concept statement.** The final part of the product vision, the concept statement goes beyond the opportunity statement and the persona profiles to describe the product's essence with a powerful, engaging, and unifying phrase.

Although a product vision lacks the specific requirements and feature descriptions that are a prerequisite to the interface design, it does provide the basis for evaluating solutions and understanding the tradeoffs of various compromises.

With the next chapter, the discussion moves to the specific challenges of interface design, starting with a methodology for prioritizing and categorizing the complex set of problems associated with a comprehensive design.

"Model (n): a simplified version of something complex used, for example, to analyze and solve problems or make predictions."

The Microsoft Word Dictionary

3

DECONSTRUCTING
THE PROBLEM

Prioritizing and Categorizing Different
Aspects of an Interface

Interface design is difficult. Inventing, describing, and constructing an interactive experience that reflects one's core design values, harmonizes with users' needs and abilities, and is practical to implement is one of the most challenging, complex problems in any field of design. A skilled interface designer brings together a print designer's knowledge of visual communication, a movie director's grasp of plot, an architect's imagination for space, an anthropologist's insight into human behavior, and a software engineer's understanding of the technology.

Unfortunately, because the medium of interactive design is still in its infancy, particularly as it concerns the design of Web applications, the field lacks the structured academic training or proven methodologies associated with many other forms of design.

As a result of its youth, the field of interactive design has also become infused with a philosophy of trial and error: experimenting with different designs and observing users to see what did and didn't work. Unfortunately, although direct observation of users is a vital part of the design process, its utility is primarily as a validation tool, not as a substitute for a skilled designer's creative abilities and vision. In practice, substituting research and observation for creativity and vision is not only inefficient in terms of time and effort, it also virtually guarantees mediocrity.

Adding to the piecemeal understanding that research and direct observation provide, the field of interactive design has also been influenced by a steady stream of feedback from industry critics, pundits, and gurus. Unfortunately, such criticism is of limited use to the designer facing a difficult or unknown design problem. It would be as though a film student had only a movie critic as his instructor.

Regardless of the insight or accuracy of a critic's commentary, a collection of observations, anecdotes, and interpretations of existing designs does little to aid a designer's understanding of how the thousands of small choices work together to create a coherent whole. As a result, designers are left searching for quick fixes that will satisfy the critics or the latest user feedback without a true understanding of the medium's mechanics or how to consciously control and manipulate it.

Because interface design is a complex, multi-dimensional problem, it requires a method for deconstructing the problem so that it can be solved in a conscious, consistent, and repeatable manner. By deconstructing the overall experience into a series of smaller, interrelated problems, it is possible to design with an understanding of each discrete element of the interface as well as its influence on the whole. An intelligent deconstruction of the problem also offers a consistent basis for prioritizing problems by placing them on the continuum of foundational to supporting.

In the fields of science, various types of models are typically constructed to understand and predict the workings of complex systems. These models serve as tools for analysis by representing complex phenomena in a simplified manner. This facilitates the understanding individual components and how those components affect and are affected by the whole. Even though science is largely based on trial and error, without these models, it is often impossible to isolate the effects of individual phenomena and thus impossible to predict large-scale trends or events.

Similarly, just as modeling complex systems has obvious benefits to scientists, models can also be useful to the creators of sophisticated forms of communication, such as cinema or interactive media.

DECONSTRUCTING CINEMA: LOOKING AT MOVIES FROM THE GROUND UP

As the most complex, sophisticated, and multi-dimensional form of human communication, movies provide a good example of how a consistent model can contribute to the understanding of a particular medium. Figure 3.1 illustrates one method for deconstructing a movie into individual, interrelated layers.

The model starts with three broad tiers: the story, the production, and the presentation, and then further dissects those tiers into three layers each. From a movie-making perspective, the three tiers equate to the pre-production, production, and post-production phases.

3.1

The experience of a movie can be deconstructed into nine separate but interrelated layers. By modeling the experience in this way, it is possible to isolate individual components while understanding their influence on the whole.

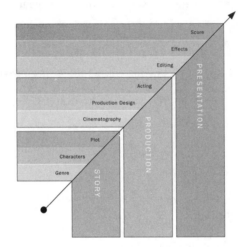

Although this model doesn't reflect the experience of watching a movie, where all the elements are experienced simultaneously, it does provide a framework for creating a movie. In particular, it gives filmmakers an understanding of the interrelationships between the components and how those components serve as foundational or supporting. For example, the Editing layer of an action movie typically supports the Genre and Plot layers by using a fast-paced, action/reaction style. The goal of the outer layer—in this case, the Editing layer—is to support, augment, and enhance the inner foundational layers.

A more specific example of the interplay between layers comes from the film *Citizen Kane*. To accent the larger-than-life quality of his main character, director Orson Welles made the creative decision to place the camera at a very low angle, literally forcing the audience to look up at Charles Foster Kane. Welles pushed the effect so far that the camera was often positioned just off the floor, requiring sets with sunken floors to accommodate the camera and crew. This meant that the sets had to have ceilings because the lower perspective allowed audiences to see the ceiling; most movies are shot from the perspective of the actors, so ceilings are almost never a visible part of a movie set. Besides the additional constraint for the set designers, the decision also created difficulty in the lighting design because lights are typically hung from above. As a result, the production's designers faced the challenge of creating sets to accommodate the unique choices made for cinematography. The relationships between these decisions are reflected in the model by placing the Production Design layer in a position that supports the Cinematography layer, and the Cinematography layer in a position that supports the Characters layer.

Even more important than its ability to provide a consistent way to deconstruct a film, however, this model gives filmmakers and screenwriters a predictive tool for understanding and creating movies. Following the model, they can recast the overwhelming challenge of creating a finished film into a series of prioritized, interrelated problems that can be solved in a systematic, controlled manner. Although it requires a different set of tiers and layers, deconstructing the user interface of an interactive product has similar benefits.

DECONSTRUCTING AN INTERFACE: DESIGNING FROM THE CONCEPTUAL TO THE CONCRETE

As shown in Figure 3.2, the user interface of any interactive product, be it hardware or software, can be modeled using three tiers and nine layers. With the layers arranged from foundational to supporting, the model not only captures the components of the interface, but also offers a useful method for understanding and designing an interactive product.

3.2
This diagram aids interface design by deconstructing an experience into a series of nine interrelated layers that can be analyzed one at a time.

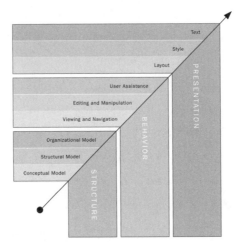

TIER 1: STRUCTURE

The *Structure* tier comprises the three lowest levels of the user interface: the conceptual model, the structural model, and the organizational model. Similar to the movie model, these three layers are not expressed in a single, concrete form that can be readily identified or touched. Rather, they represent the relationship between the interface and the world at large as well as the relationships between the pages, content, and information in the application. Although a typical user would rarely describe any of these layers in a direct manner, they form the conceptual basis of the entire experience and, as a result, are the most influential aspects of the design.

Layer 1: The Conceptual Model

The *conceptual model* is the most fundamental aspect of the interface, describing the relationship between the interface and the larger world. The purpose of the conceptual model is to place the interface within a frame of reference that draws on the user's familiarity with a physical object or experience. For example, a newspaper serves as the conceptual model of most Web portals, such as myYahoo! or MSN. Although the customization and real-time updating of these applications clearly exceeds the experience of a printed newspaper, the physical object of a newspaper nonetheless forms their conceptual basis. By relating the application to a real-world experience, users can understand the basic operation of the product and accurately predict its core functionality.

Layer 2: The Structural Model

The *structural model* is concerned with the basic components of the interface and how those components work together to support complex operations. Unlike the conceptual model, the structural model is dependent on the specific technical environment supporting the interface. For example, the structural elements of a desktop application include windows, files, dialog boxes, and floating palettes, whereas a Web application is almost entirely constructed of pages and forms. For a Web application, the structural model also describes the relationship between connected groups of pages and forms. For example, a travel site's structural model describes the multistep operation users follow to make an airline reservation. This is also referred to as the task flow.

Layer 3: Organizational Model

The *organizational model* describes how an application's content and functionality are ordered. Also known as the *information architecture*, the organizational model addresses questions such as whether the content and functionality are going to be organized hierarchically and, if so, what the exact categories and subcategories are going to be.

TIER 2: BEHAVIOR

The three middle layers of the model form the *Behavior* tier. These layers describe the interface's interactive qualities as opposed to its conceptual framework or visual presentation. Solving problems in the Behavior tier requires the designer to envision and communicate both the user's actions and the application's reaction as they unfold over time.

Layer 4: Viewing and Navigation

The *Viewing and Navigation* layer contains the behaviors that enable users to navigate between locations and change the presentation of their data. The distinguishing characteristic of these operations is that they result in a temporary change of state rather than a permanent change to stored information. Sorting, searching, and navigation are all examples.

Layer 5: Editing and Manipulation

The *Editing and Manipulation* layer describes the behaviors that allow users to make permanent changes to their stored information. In a stock portfolio application, for example, the operations for recording transactions, importing accounts, and updating values would all be contained in the Editing and Manipulation layer. These behaviors have three defining traits: they result in permanent, stored changes; they require an implicit or explicit submit action; and they typically require data validation.

Layer 6: User Assistance

As the final layer of the Behavior tier, the *User Assistance* layer contains the elements needed to inform users of the application's activity and status as well as the components dedicated to user education. In addition to online help, the User Assistance layer includes a variety of different alerts and status mechanisms.

TIER 3: PRESENTATION

The three layers of the *Presentation* tier describe the interface's visual and textual expression. In contrast to the more abstract nature of the Structure and Behavior tiers, the Presentation tier is squarely focused on the concrete and visible expression of the site.

Layer 7: Layout

The *Layout* layer contains the aspects of the visual design related to placing and ordering the interface's onscreen elements. In addition to providing an ordered visual flow, the purpose of the Layout layer is to support the Behavior tier by arranging the elements in a manner that helps communicate their behavior and usage.

Layer 8: Style

The purpose of the *Style layer* is to evoke an emotional reaction from users by establishing a unique visual tone and vocabulary. A challenge, however, is that this must be accomplished in support of established corporate brand values and adherence to Web-wide visual conventions. Although the Style layer is the most visible and conscious aspect of the interface, as the penultimate layer, it has a minimal effect on usability and is readily modified from a technical perspective.

Layer 9: Text

Separate from pure content, the *Text* layer contains the written, language-based elements of the interface. Because many of the structural and behavioral elements are represented onscreen as words, the Text layer is tightly intertwined with the lower levels of the interface. For example, the labels used in the Organizational Model layer, the names of the input and navigational controls of the Viewing and Navigation layer, and the alert messages and help text called for by the User Assistance layer are all components of the Text layer.

LIVING WITH A MODEL: WHAT THE MODEL IMPLIES ABOUT DESIGN PRIORITIES, RESOURCES, AND FEEDBACK

This model of a complete user interface is useful because it provides a common method and vocabulary for deconstructing the aspects of an interface, for prioritizing design tasks, for allocating design resources, and for interpreting user feedback. As shown in Figure 3.3, the order of the layers follows three distinct axes.

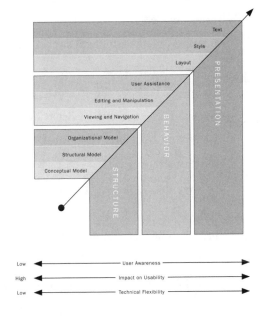

3.3
By adding the three axes to the bottom of the diagram, the implications for prioritizing and ordering design tasks are clear.

☐ **Technical Flexibility.** Because the structural layers describe the fundamental qualities and workings of the interface, they often have some representation in the architecture and functioning of the software code. This is especially true for the conceptual model.

For example, after a team starts to think of an application as "a mail system," it is very difficult not to let that concept seep into the code. As a result, modifying the structural aspects of the interface requires the most engineering effort. By contrast, it is relatively easy to modify the Presentation tier because those elements can be isolated in the code with cascading style sheets, for example.

☐ **User Awareness.** Because users can literally see the elements of the presentation layers, they are highly aware of them. By contrast, users can "see" the behavioral layers only by interacting with the interface and the structural layers. And they do this by developing an understanding of the interface. As a result, most user comments focus on the Presentation tier, with correspondingly fewer comments about the Behavior and Structure tiers.

☐ **Impact on Usability.** Paradoxically, the elements that users are least aware of are the very ones that tend to have the deepest impact on usability. And vice versa, the elements that are foremost in a user's mind are often a distraction from the more fundamental concerns of the lower layers. For example, although a striking visual design might help distract attention and resources away from a poor conceptual model, it can't fix the problem any more than a movie's music, lighting, or special effects can fix a poorly conceived story.

The message contained in these three axes is clear: **Although the foundational components, such as the conceptual, structural, and organizational models, are the elements that users comment on least often, they not only have the most impact on users' understanding and success, but also require the most engineering effort to change.** As a result, if there are time or resource constraints on the design of a new product, the priority should be on the lower layers of the interface with particular attention to the conceptual model. Similarly, if the design is for additions or enhancements to an existing product, the effort can focus more on the behavioral and presentation aspects because the structural aspects are already in place.

In addition to prioritization, the order of the layers suggests how to interpret the frequency of certain types of user comments as well as how to rate their severity and impact on engineering resources. For example, because users are most aware of the Presentation tier, comments about color, layout, and imagery should be expected. Fortunately, even if the comments are heard repeatedly, the presentation aspects of the interface do not have a major effect on usability and can be altered later with minimal impact on engineering.

Similarly, although users might be struggling to understand a product's basic purpose and operation, they will never attribute it to the conceptual model. If a designer or researcher concludes that there is a problem with the conceptual model, however, addressing the issue immediately is imperative because its detrimental effect on usability will reverberate throughout other layers of the interface, and each additional line of code increases the engineering effort required to change it.

A final way to apply the model to real-world design problems is to alter the diagram to reflect the complexity of an interface. By altering the width of each layer, the relative complexity and simplicity of each component of an interface can be easily understood. This understanding can then be used to allocate design skills, resources, and time. Figures 3.4 through 3.7 illustrate the model applied to three different Web applications and one content-based Web site.

3.4

Like other newspaper sites, the large volume of written content at washingtonpost.com requires a sophisticated organizational model, navigational system, and set of text labels.

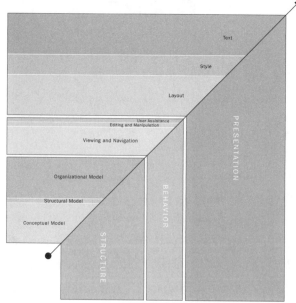

3.5

The interface for the online gift store Red Envelope reflects a limited need for editing and manipulation behaviors, and a focus on visual presentation.

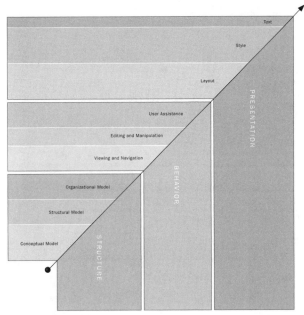

3.6

The interface for online services such as Hotmail typically requires a complex Behavior tier with a relatively limited organizational model.

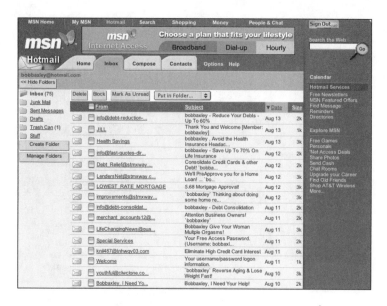

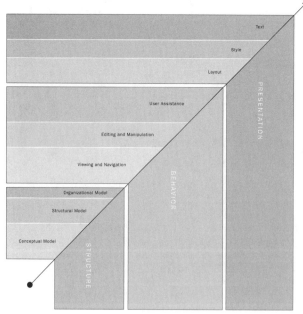

3.7
Like other travel sites, JetBlue has limited viewing and navigational functions. However, the number of steps necessary to make a reservation requires complex editing and manipulation behaviors.

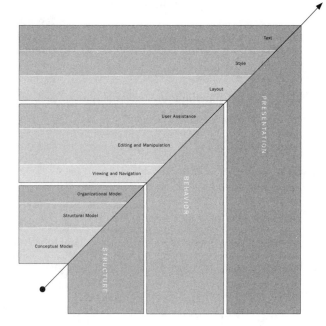

SUMMARY

Similar to the core design values and the product vision process described in the previous chapter, this model of the user interface provides a consistent and predictable method for approaching the complex, multi-dimensional problem of interface design. In particular, the model provides the following benefits:

- ☐ A common vocabulary for identifying elements of an interface
- ☐ An understanding of how individual aspects of an interface relate to one another and to the experience as a whole
- ☐ A constructive means of prioritizing design tasks so that a solid foundation is firmly established before the supporting elements are added
- ☐ An objective method for categorizing user feedback based on the impact on usability and engineering effort required to correct problems
- ☐ A rational system for allocating design resources and effort

With the end of this chapter, the book is also closed on Part I: "Foundations." Moving on to Part II, "Tier 1: Structure," the focus turns to a layer-by-layer discussion of Web applications, starting with the Conceptual Model layer.

PART II

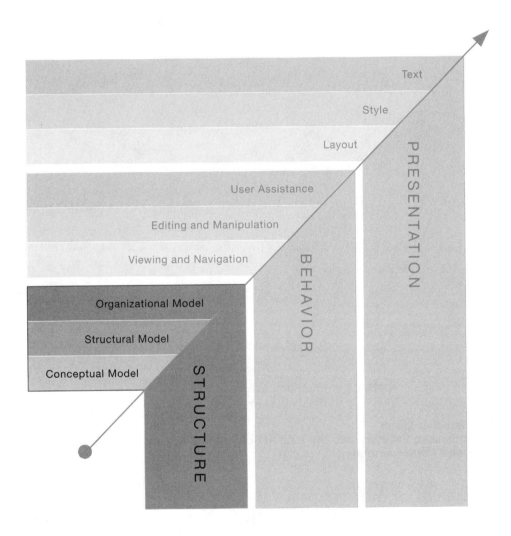

Text

Style

Layout

User Assistance

Editing and Manipulation

Viewing and Navigation

Organizational Model

Structural Model

Conceptual Model

PRESENTATION

BEHAVIOR

STRUCTURE

"Knowledge is what we get when an observer...
  provides us with a copy of reality that we can all recognize."

Christopher Lasch
"Journalism, Publicity, and the Lost Art of Political Argument"
Gannett Center Journal

4

THE CONCEPTUAL MODEL

Selecting a Fundamental Motif

As the first layer of any user interface, the conceptual model has the crucial role of placing the interface's overall function and operation into a context that the user can recognize. For example, in the same way that a movie genre sets expectations for plot, character, and setting, the conceptual model of an interactive product sets expectations about the product's capabilities and operation. In other words, the conceptual model answers the most fundamental questions on a user's mind: "What is this thing? What can it do and how do I operate it?"

To accomplish the task, the conceptual model exploits the basic cognitive mechanism humans have developed for making sense of new experiences: association. By basing an interface on a solid conceptual model, users are able to associate something new with something known, enabling them to scramble up the learning curve of novelty and quickly make accurate predictions and assumptions about a new system's behavior and capabilities.

Despite the sophistication and variety of interactive media, all conceptual models are ultimately drawn from real-world objects and experiences. For example, although information portals, online stores, and content-based Web sites are often considered experiences unique to the virtual world, they are more accurately thought of as basic extensions to objects and experiences encountered in daily life. Newspapers, catalogs, and brochures might have different characteristics and benefits than their Web counterparts, but they still form the experiential basis of sites like Yahoo!, Amazon, and Ford.

Unfortunately, without a recognizable conceptual model, users are left to wonder about a product's utility, value, and functioning. For example, the lack of a strong conceptual model that mass-market consumers can recognize makes it difficult for consumers to understand digital video recorders, such as Tivo and ReplayTV. Although there is the risk of disappointment because these devices cannot play rented movies, if the products clearly exhibited the conceptual model of a VCR, two of their most important benefits could be readily communicated: the ability to pause live TV and the availability of a sophisticated user interface for recording future programming. Without a strong conceptual model for these products, users with less technical sophistication have no way of understanding or appreciating the unique benefits of disk-based video recording.

The physical world itself is filled with conceptual models. Various types of buildings, for example, are associated with different conceptual models. Upon entering an office building, most people instantly know what it is and what they're likely to find there. They understand that people work there but don't live there, at least not by most definitions. And they also make inferences about which behaviors are appropriate and which are not. For example, in a house, they would probably have an "any port in a storm" philosophy about finding a bathroom. In an office building, however, they would dutifully search for the appropriate Boy or Girl icon, no matter how dire the situation.

Before delving into the details of conceptual models as they relate to specific Web applications, it's important to more fully understand the unique and crucial role of conceptual models in the functioning of an interface.

FIRST THINGS FIRST: THE IMPORTANCE OF A CONCEPTUAL MODEL

As the least conscious layer of the user experience, the conceptual model has the paradoxical quality of also having the most impact on usability. If an appropriate conceptual model is faithfully represented throughout the interface, after users recognize and internalize the model, they will have a fundamental understanding of what the application does and how to operate it. Without this understanding and consistent implementation, however, the user is likely to suffer through a host of usability problems, as the failure of the model reveals itself in a variety of interface components and operations.

Another critical quality of the conceptual model is its dubious distinction as the most technically rigid aspect of the interface. Unfortunately, once a product has adopted a conceptual model, that model so permeates the product that keeping it out of the technical architecture and functioning is almost impossible. As a result, redesigning the product with a different conceptual model often requires a corresponding re-architecture of the product's technical framework. Unfortunately, the engineering effort required to accomplish this is so large that such a change often amounts to a complete rewrite of the product. For this reason, the conceptual model should be considered a permanent, fixed quality of the interface. Although other aspects of the design will evolve and adapt over time, the conceptual model will remain constant. Put another way, with the right conceptual model in place, problems in any subsequent layers—whether structural, behavioral, or presentational—can be corrected later. With an inappropriate or inconsistent conceptual model, however, the interface will be fundamentally unstable with little hope for any easy repairs.

Unfortunately, despite its critical role, the conscious selection and evaluation of a conceptual model is one of the most overlooked steps of the design process. As a result, many design and development teams unwittingly commit to a conceptual model derived from an underlying aspect of the technology rather than one that truly aids users' understanding and satisfaction.

BUILDING ON THE VISION: IDENTIFYING AND SELECTING AN APPROPRIATE CONCEPTUAL MODEL

Because the conceptual model is the first layer of the interface, it is as close to a blank page as anything in the design process. However, the purpose of the conceptual model is to solve a specific problem, and the outline of that problem should be contained in the opportunity statement, persona profiles and goals, and concept statement that resulted from the product vision process. With those items in hand, it should be possible to quickly identify a variety of potential models, through either an individual or a group brainstorming session.

"The best way to get a good idea is to get a lot of ideas."

—Linus Pauling

Although a group brainstorming session is likely to produce some inappropriate or impractical suggestions, it should also produce a variety of useful ones. For example, a list of possible conceptual models for an online photo-processing and storage service might include the following:

- ☐ A physical photo-finishing store
- ☐ An operating system with file folders and printers
- ☐ An email program with an address book, messages, and attachments
- ☐ A photo album
- ☐ A shoebox full of negatives
- ☐ A darkroom
- ☐ A catalog where photos are viewed one at a time with links to similar and related photos
- ☐ A photo "toolbox" with a variety of editing operations that can be carried out on photos

Clearly, each model carries certain expectations and implications about the application's functionality, organization, and presentation. Determining which model is the best option depends on three considerations:

☐ Which model is most reflective of the concept statement developed for the product vision?

☐ Which model is most likely to be familiar and attractive to the primary and secondary personas?

☐ Which model is the most practical and appropriate to an interactive software experience?

Of the possible models listed here, the two that are most commonly implemented are the photo album and the shoebox of negatives. One advantage of a model having been implemented in another interface is that it's possible to analyze the model's success without necessarily having to apply to your situation. For example, the relative merits and weaknesses of these models is evident in the existing interface for Ofoto, as detailed in the case study in Chapter 14, "Ofoto: Looking at the Leading Online Photo Processor."

If no single model stands out as the most appropriate, other factors worth considering are whether a model is unique for the product category, and which model is most consistent with established corporate brand values. In most cases, the number of models that can be fully explored will be limited by time. In addition, limitations on the depth to which a model can be explored means that user research or other feedback is likely to be inconclusive. Therefore, the selection of a conceptual model most often relies on the experience and creative vision of the lead designer working in concert with the collective wisdom of the development and design teams.

Independent of which model is finally selected, the critical point is to spend the effort needed to consciously identify and select a conceptual model. Only through such effort is it possible to consistently select a model that supports the overall product vision and is familiar to target users.

PUTTING CONCEPTUAL MODELS TO WORK: WHAT'S IN A STORE?

One of the best methods for understanding the importance and use of conceptual models is to analyze different models as they've been applied to various situations. Fortunately, one of the most instructive models for this purpose is also one the most widely used: the online store.

Although online stores are one of the most popular types of Web applications, the efforts spent on their design and development have largely failed to produce a shopping experience as compelling as a physical store or catalog. In large part, this failing results from the conceptual model of any stores being inappropriate to the type of products they sell. Online clothing stores such as Banana Republic's are one example.

WHAT DEFINES A STORE?

[A store is] "...a machine where goods are exchanged for money."

—Paco Underhill
Why We Buy:
The Science
of Shopping

Part of the difficulty online clothing stores face is that many users come to the site with the conceptual model of a store already in mind. Unfortunately, stores are a unique physical space and experience that are impossible to represent in a virtual manner. Although the conceptual model of a store can be further dissected into specific types of stores—grocery stores, department stores, and convenience stores, for example—all stores share certain qualities, including the following:

☐ **Sensory experience.** Because they exist in the real world, physical stores offer a sensory experience impossible to reproduce on the Web. Inside a store, visitors can see, touch, smell, and hear the individual products and the store as a whole. Without direct sensory experience, comparing products such as clothing, makeup, and furniture is difficult.

☐ **Instant gratification.** A key part of the experience of shopping at a physical store is that you get the goods and you get them right now. You see something you want, you buy it, you own it. It's such a compelling experience that 12-step programs have been developed to mitigate its effect. Unfortunately, with the exception of downloadable media such as software, music, and computer games, online stores cannot reproduce the experience of instant gratification.

☐ **Social interaction.** Similar to the theme of sensory experience, shopping at a store generally requires at least some level of social interaction. Whether it's to simply pay for a soda or ask detailed questions about a digital camera, stores provide a level of direct human contact that cannot be virtually reproduced.

WHAT DEFINES A CATALOG?

Similar to stores, catalogs are another mechanism for turning money into goods. Although catalogs lack the advantages of instant gratification and sensory experience, as a shopping medium, they bring to the battlefield their own distinctive qualities:

- ☐ **Selection**. Because catalog fulfillment operations are limited by the size of their warehouses, which are cheap, instead of the size of their stores, which are expensive, they can afford to carry a bewildering selection of products that would be difficult to reproduce in a single store. With the variety of specialty and niche products available today, there's no easy substitute for a 1,000-page catalog.

- ☐ **Convenience**. Convenience comes in a number of different flavors. First off, because computers don't sleep and 800-operators can get by with only occasional naps, catalog operations tend to be open any time of the day or night. In addition, catalogs allow consumers to buy products without leaving their homes or offices. Finally, catalogs are convenient because consumers can explore them anytime, anywhere without having to worry about crowds or the availability of a salesclerk.

- ☐ **Information rich.** Catalogs can communicate vast amounts of information about a single product or group of products. Although the importance of the information depends on the products being sold, if the product is technical or complex, catalogs can be one of the best methods for evaluating and selecting a product.

Like stores, there are different types of catalogs, each based on the overall conceptual model of a catalog but developed enough to be considered a conceptual model in its own right. These two models are the magazine-style catalogs typically used to sell clothing and housewares, and the reference-style catalog typically used to sell office supplies and automotive parts. Where magazine-style catalogs are appropriate for smaller product inventories and personal goods, reference-style catalogs are useful for selling widely varied goods consumed by knowledgeable, self-directed consumers.

Both models have been used by online retailers with varying degrees of success. As shown in Figure 4.1, Pottery Barn strives for the magazine-style model by relying on elaborate photography and engaging, well-written product descriptions. By comparison, Figure 4.2 shows how OfficeMax is based on the model of a reference-style catalog, with its small product photos and elaborate index.

Other online retailers, such as Williams-Sonoma and Patagonia, exploit the magazine-style model by including content such as recipes and articles about the environment.

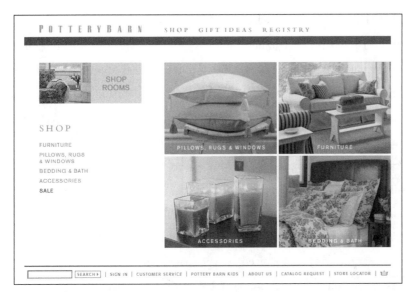

4.1

The online store for Pottery Barn follows the conceptual model of a magazine-style catalog by using elaborate photography and carefully crafted product descriptions.

4.2

OfficeMax's use of small product photos and a rich navigation index is consistent with its conceptual model of a reference catalog.

WHAT DEFINES BANANAREPUBLIC.COM?

With a more detailed understanding of the conceptual model of stores and catalogs, it's possible to more accurately assess Banana Republic's conceptual model. Based on the distinctions already made, the conceptual model for Banana Republic should be a magazine-style catalog. Unfortunately, the current design reflects the model of a reference-style catalog, so the design sets up expectations that are inappropriate to an online clothing store. As shown in Figure 4.3, these discrepancies include the following:

- **Organizational model.** Unlike a magazine-style catalog, the products are organized by type (pants, shirts, sweaters) rather than by collection (denim, cashmere, leather) or usage (business, casual, weekend). Although this is consistent with the hierarchical style commonly found on the Web, it is inconsistent with how clothing is typically presented in a catalog or a store.

- **Navigation.** Although magazine-style catalogs are typically navigated in a linear manner, one page after the next, Banana Republic's navigational design necessarily reflects the organizational model. As a result, there's no practical way for users to navigate the site in a way that would ensure they saw the entire collection. Again, this contradicts the model of a magazine-style catalog, in which consumers can clearly tell when they've see everything. In addition, the hierarchical orientation forces the user to navigate the products in a manner at odds with the browsing behavior associated with physical stores. It's simply awkward to visit this site and "just look around."

☐ **Product presentation.** Presumably for the purpose of smaller downloads, most online stores present their products with as little style, mood, and enthusiasm as possible. Even heavily merchandised stores such as Banana Republic often rely on bare-bones photography and limited copy writing. Although this is in keeping with the aesthetic standards of reference catalogs and tabloid advertising, it's not consistent with the elaborate production values of most magazine-style catalogs. By comparison, Illuminations carries the magazine-style product presentation through to its online store (see Figure 4.4).

☐ **Overhead of ordering.** An unfortunate but unavoidable aspect of online shopping is the complexity of actually completing a purchase. In comparison to the Web, physical stores and catalogs minimize the actual transaction experience in the same way that nice restaurants discreetly deliver the bill to the table. Although the quantity of interface mechanisms required to purchase an item is no worse on Banana Republic than on most other online stores, it still runs counter to the conceptual model of shopping in stores or in catalogs.

For more on ways to specify sizes and colors, see Chapter 8, "Editing and Manipulation: Using HTML Input Controls to Accurately Capture Users' Data."

Although most of these same criticisms are equally applicable to Polo, Patagonia, or J. Crew, the central point remains: The conceptual model of online clothing stores in general, and Banana Republic in particular, is inconsistent with the conceptual model of physical stores or magazine-style catalogs. As a result, the experience of shopping on those sites is unnatural for users and inappropriate for the merchandise.

4.3

Banana Republic's product details page includes many components of a reference-style catalog, even though clothing is usually sold through a magazine-style catalog.

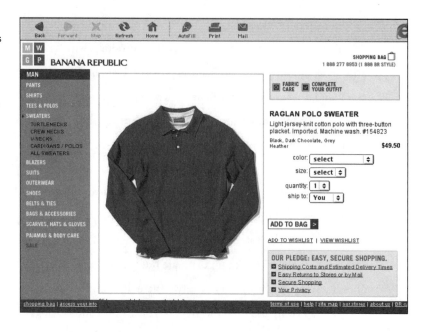

4.4

With its high visual production values and well-crafted copy, the presentation of products on the Illiuminations site is consistent with the model of a magazine-style catalog.

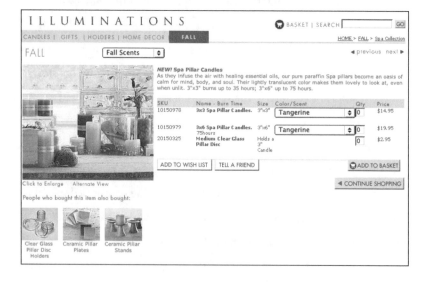

SUMMARY

Every interactive product, including every Web application, has a conceptual model at the root of its interface. It is simply impossible not to have one. Unfortunately, few design and development teams acknowledge the critical role it plays and, therefore, fail to fully explore and utilize its potential.

As the first layer of the interface, conceptual models not only have the most impact on usability, but also are the most difficult aspect of the interface to change. Therefore, a failure to identify and select an appropriate conceptual model puts the entire product at risk by placing the interface on a foundation that's shaky and costly to repair.

Fortunately, once the importance and influence of the conceptual model has been established, identifying and selecting one appropriate to the situation is relatively easy. In particular, the evaluation of conceptual models should consider the following:

☐ Does the model reflect the product's concept statement?

☐ Is the model familiar to the primary and secondary personas?

☐ Is the model practical and appropriate from a technical perspective?

Looking forward to the next chapter, the focus moves from the conceptual model to the structural model. In particular, the next chapter describes the basic building blocks of a Web interface and the structures used to connect groups of pages into unified task flows.

"Unless one is a genius, it is best to aim at being intelligible."

Anthony Hope
The Dolly Dialogues

5

THE STRUCTURAL
MODEL

Understanding the Building
Blocks of a Web Interface

Exiting the realm of the conceptual model, the second layer of the interface is the structural model. Unlike the conceptual model, which is not necessarily tied to a particular technology, the *structural model* is a direct descendant of the device or operating system underlying the application. For example, although the conceptual model of mail has been adapted to desktop applications, Web applications, dedicated devices, and custom software environments such as WebTV, a conceptual model's specific expression varies from one environment to another, depending on its unique capabilities, interactive vocabulary, and usage patterns.

In one sense, the structural model dictates the available interface components and widgets, but more importantly, it establishes the fundamental interaction paradigm. For example, in the world of desktop operating systems, the fundamental interaction paradigm revolves around files and windows. Desktop applications are essentially tools for creating, editing, and managing files, and desktop operating systems are largely tools for managing and manipulating the windows to present those files and applications. Although the desktop computing environment has developed increasingly sophisticated interface widgets, their basic orientation toward files and windows has not altered.

By contrast, the fundamental interactions of Web applications revolve around pages and links. As a rule, Web applications rely on a single window to present their interface one page at a time. Even though Web applications are typically viewed in the context of a desktop computing environment, they do not and should not exploit the file and window orientation. Rather, Web applications are designed for use in the context of a Web browser, an environment separate from the desktop environment.

As an interface designer, you have to throw off the naïve assumption that Web applications are desktop applications with a less sophisticated user interface. Web applications are a new, distinct medium and must be approached without the bias of the desktop interaction style.

Web applications are constructed from discrete pages viewed across time, one after another in a serial manner. They are not built with files and windows that can be stacked in layers, one on top of another. A usable Web application, one that's true to the medium, fully appreciates that the Web also provides a three-dimensional interface. However, the third dimension is not depth; it is time. This critical aspect of the interface, the page-based paradigm and the accompanying temporal element, is represented in the structural model. The purpose of this chapter is to explore the page-based paradigm as well as the flows and constructs appropriate to it.

PAGES: BUILDING BLOCKS OF THE WEB

Imagine for a moment the Web as a physical artifact, something you can touch and feel and look at long after the battery on your laptop has died. What are you imagining? Is it a museum? A zoo? A toolbox? What if you pictured it as a different sort of experience? Are you thinking of a movie? A stage play? A walk through the woods? Put another way, what is the conceptual model of the Web?

The answer is this: The Web is a book—a book with billions of pages, hundreds of millions of internal references, and thousands upon thousands of authors, a book that's constantly updated and revised and that in some places magically knows who you are and what you want to see. Like a book, the Web is composed of individual pages, viewed and consumed one at a time. Even the fundamental interaction of the Web, the hyperlink, is but a highly efficient way to flip pages.

So what does it mean for the design of a Web site or an application to be consistent with the conceptual model of a book? Aside from the obvious orientation toward pages, the Web's conceptual model also implies the following:

☐ **One page at a time.** Books are experienced one page a time. It is not physically possible to simultaneously view more than one page unless you're willing to do some tearing, ripping, or photocopying. Although this feature makes it difficult to easily compare multiple pages, it creates a temporal dimension to the experience, as readers consume the book page by page.

- ☐ **Clear distinction between reading and acting.** If you think of catalogs or magazines as books, there's a clear distinction between pages containing products or articles and pages with surveys or order forms. Form pages have a variety of clues and features to distinguish them from non-form pages, including different paper stock, different navigation, and even different orientation.
- ☐ **Continuation.** Books do not have navigational dead-ends. Except for the last page, you can always navigate forward. Even from the last page, you can easily navigate backward.

Of course, the Web goes well beyond the basic model of a book, incorporating features such as dynamic page resizing, hyperlink navigation, moving images, and infinite size. However, simply because an interface expands on its conceptual model does not mean it can fundamentally depart from the model. For a Web site or application to retain basic consistency with the Web's conceptual model, it must follow a handful of basic principles:

- ☐ **One page at a time.** Except on extremely rare occasions, Web applications should not require multiple windows. The normal operation of a Web application should take place in one page at a time. The only consistent exceptions are when users need to maintain their current context, such as when accessing online help.
- ☐ **Clear distinction between reading and acting.** A Web application's task flow should assume two basic modes of activity: viewing/navigating and editing/manipulating. Viewing activities should take place on pages that are clearly distinct from editing activities.

☐ **Continuation.** All Web sites and applications must be structured so that the *user is never required to use the browser's Back button.* Users should never find themselves trapped in a navigational cul de sac. From every page and in every context, there should always be at least one obvious way to keep moving forward.

The structural components and models that take up the rest of this chapter are derived from these three guiding principles. If you understand and use them appropriately, your designs will be consistent with the fundamental nature of the Web.

VIEWS: PAGES FOR VIEWING AND NAVIGATING

The term *views* describes pages used to present various types of information. In addition to the information, views typically contain navigation, searching, filtering, ordering, and other functions that do not permanently alter a user's stored information. The vast majority of the Web is made up of views.

As further proof of that "picture being worth a thousand words" maxim, the best way to understand the idea of a view is to simply look at one. Hotmail's Inbox (see Figure 5.1) serves the purpose nicely.

The purpose of the inbox is to give users a way to see an overview of their messages and select messages for viewing or other actions. To fulfill this purpose, the inbox contains a table listing messages, a mechanism for selecting messages, a series of commands that can be used on messages, and a list of the folders where messages can be stored. In other words, the inbox is all about viewing and navigating messages.

5.1

Hotmail's Inbox is a textbook example of a view page—provided, of course, that this is your textbook.

Although the page contains a variety of links and user controls, they are used to manipulate the state of the presentation, not the underlying information. Users can change the sort order of the message table, view the contents of a different folder, and even move messages from one folder to another. They cannot however, create new information or change any of the basic information being presented. In other words, the only action users can directly take on the messages is moving them from one folder to another. Even deleting a message, which seems to be a permanent action, simply moves the message from one folder to another—the Trash Can. The message isn't permanently deleted until the user actually empties the trash or the system sweeps the trash can, a few days later.

In addition to the message list, the inbox contains three command buttons: Hide Folders, Create Folder, and Manage Folders. Hide Folders does what you would expect and is obviously related to the state of the presentation. Although the other two buttons appear to create or edit user data, they both function as nothing more than navigational links. The Create Folder button links to a form where users can name a new folder, and the Manage Folders button links to a view of the current folder structure. Although the buttons' labels and visual presentation lead users to think they are creating or editing folders, the reality is that these buttons simply navigate to pages where the user can permanently affect the data. Although this is a weakness in the design, the weakness is in the way the visual design misleads the user, not in the way the functionality is structured.

Views contain five key functions that you should keep in mind. They should enable users to do the following:

- □ View information.
- □ Manipulate what information is displayed.
- □ Control how information is displayed.
- □ Select information to perform a command on it.
- □ Navigate to other parts of the application.

Views can include lists of objects, as in Hotmail's Inbox, an individual product or groups of products, search features, and a host of other functionality that does not permanently affect users' underlying information.

FORMS: PAGES FOR EDITING AND MANIPULATING

Web applications are composed of forms as well as views. Compared to views, which are used to manipulate the application's state, *forms* are used to create and manipulate the underlying data stored in the application. By definition, forms involve an interaction with the site's server and, therefore, require some type of a submit button. Although some content-only sites include forms, Web applications require a level of interaction and complexity unparalleled in typical content sites.

Sticking with Hotmail for a moment longer, as shown in Figure 5.2, the Compose page is representative of forms. It contains obvious user input controls, such as the Add/Edit Attachments button, as well as buttons that function like Submit and Cancel. In this case, they've been labeled Send, Save Draft, and Cancel, but they perform the same functions as Submit and Cancel.

5.2

Hotmail's Compose page is a typical form that enables users to permanently affect stored information.

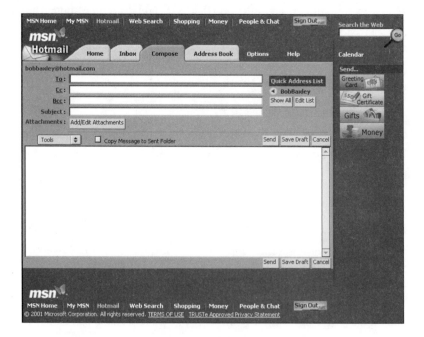

In comparison to views, forms are a readily digestible concept. We encounter countless forms in our lives: on the Web, at work, and definitely at the Department of Motor Vehicles. Although the interactive and visual design of forms is a quite complex topic, the idea of a form as a structural element of a Web application is not a huge cognitive leap for you as a designer or your users.

THE VIEW/FORM CONSTRUCT

Although the distinction between forms and views can feel cumbersome and limiting, especially compared to the dynamic interactions possible in desktop applications, the inescapable fact is that the technical realities of Web applications require this distinction. The manner in which a Web browser sends information back to an application server dictates the use of an explicit submit action. The style of interaction between the server and browser is closer to the conversational style of walkie-talkies than that of telephones. The user talks, waits for the server to answer, and then talks again. This asynchronous style is different from synchronous conversation, in which the server and the user are talking and listening at the same time. This fundamental component of any Web application's interface has to be considered in the context of the structural model.

The view/form distinction is also useful because it separates the application's functionality into the primary usage modes: viewing and editing. Again, this mirrors the asynchronous nature of Web applications and helps ensure that the design is appropriate to the Web as an interaction medium. Although the distinction between views and forms might seem obvious, what appears obvious in concept is often ignored in practice.

Unfortunately, many applications attempt to merge the functionality of views and forms into a single page, with results somewhere between quirky and bewildering. Although merging the two types of pages is possible, it's certainly difficult without introducing some ambiguity and confusion into the process. Used properly, the view/form construct supplies clear and precise commands for users to control and manipulate their data *and* their experience. Respecting the distinction between views and forms will help you avoid these potential usability issues.

If Hotmail exemplifies a clear delineation between views and forms, this example from The Motley Fool's portfolio tracker (see Figure 5.3) serves as a cautionary tale of what can happen when view and form functionality are carelessly merged into a single page.

5.3

This page from The Motley Fool's portfolio tracker combines view and form functionality into a single, confused page.

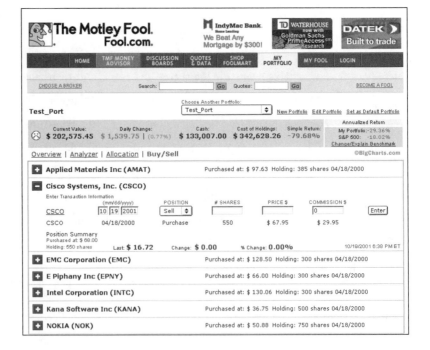

The Buy/Sell page of The Motley Fool's portfolio tracker is accessed by clicking the Buy/Sell link that follows links to Overview, Analyzer, and Allocation. A questionable organizational model to be sure, but that's another chapter.

For more on organizational models, see Chapter 6, "The Organizational Model: Organizing and Structuring Content and Functionality."

Although the user has selected a link with a clearly labeled action, when the page opens, he or she is left with little or no indication of what to do next. The design assumes that users universally understand that the + icon means "Click me and I'll show you more stuff." Again, an issue in itself, but let's move on in search of the larger point.

After users find their way to clicking the + icon, a request is sent to the server, and the page is redrawn with the area under the icon expanded to reveal controls for entering the transaction's parameters. In addition, there's information about the stock's current position and trading price and a command button labeled Enter, used to update the values in the portfolio.

The design assumes that the user will supply information for each transaction parameter and then click the Enter button to record the transaction. As long as the user proceeds accordingly, all is right with the world. If, however, the user takes a different path, the design quickly disintegrates. For example, users might inadvertently abandon their changes by simply failing to click Enter before clicking one of the navigation options. Even worse, the system cannot provide feedback that users' changes weren't saved, even though they dutifully filled out all the correct fields and options.

Two major flaws in this design relate to the view/form construct. First, the lack of obvious Submit and Cancel buttons means that no saving or editing task is clearly associated with the page. Second, including form elements alongside a full set of navigation options allows, if not encourages, users to inadvertently abandon their changes. Both problems could easily be avoided by clearly distinguishing between views and forms.

By contrast, both Quicken.com and Yahoo! (see Figure 5.4) use distinct pages for recording transactions versus viewing holdings. Placing the task of updating holdings information in its own page gives the page a clear purpose and makes it possible to eliminate almost all navigation from the form. This design helps push users toward a submit or cancel action before they exit the page.

These two examples highlight another consideration in the design of form pages: whether to include primary or persistent navigation elements, such as tab bars. Because users could abandon their changes by navigating out of the page without a submit action, removing virtually all navigation from form pages is preferable. By eliminating persistent navigation areas such as tab bars, the application clearly communicates to users that they need to complete a task before exiting the page.

Removing extraneous navigation has the added benefit of focusing users on what they're doing. Featuring a full complement of navigation options on a form distracts users from the one thing that's going to save their changes—clicking the Submit button. Forms that include a proliferation of navigation elements are akin to dialog boxes with 30 Cancel buttons.

5.4
These two forms from Quicken.com and Yahoo!'s portfolio trackers are designed exclusively for editing rather than viewing information.

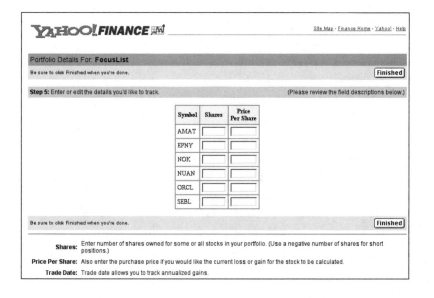

Definitions: The Meaning of Modal

Interface designers use the term *modal* to describe interactions in which the application stays in a specific state, or mode, until the user completes a task or selects a different mode. Modality is such a common style of interaction that it has become almost invisible to users. Although you might not take much notice of it, each of Photoshop's drawing tools is a different mode. Selecting different tools affects Photoshop's menu commands, palettes, and mouse behavior.

A good example of a modal interaction is the Save dialog box (see Figure 5.5). The first time a file is saved, users are required to deal with the Save dialog box before continuing their work. The system is essentially telling users "I can't do anything else until you deal with these questions."

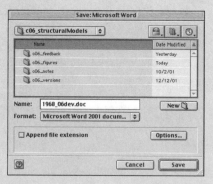

5.5

A typical modal dialog box.

Although using a model dialog box would often be ideal in Web applications, HTML does not have a mechanism for enforcing modality. The view/form construct helps create an interaction style that feels modal, but in fact is not. At the end of the day, there's nothing a Web page can do to keep a user from exiting the page by using the browser controls to navigate to a different page.

With its clear distinction between the two divergent modes of viewing and editing, the view/form construct offers users increased clarity and control by giving them a well-defined, precise moment to save changed or new data. Although it's not the whole enchilada, understanding and using the view/form construct will certainly help your design embody these qualities.

The view/form construct offers the following advantages:

- ☐ Neatly bifurcates user interactions into the well-defined modes of viewing and editing.

- ☐ Gives users explicit control over when data is submitted and saved.

- ☐ Helps prevent users from abandoning changed or new data by discouraging them from navigating out of the form without making a submit/cancel choice.

- ☐ Reduces the visual density of view pages by placing input controls on dedicated form pages.

- ☐ Offers a logical mechanism for drilling into an individual object for editing and then returning to an overview of all objects.

- ☐ Provides a predictable, logical moment for the application to check for errors and validate the user's input.

CONSTRUCTING WORKFLOWS USING VIEWS AND FORMS

With the basics of views and forms established, you can now turn to the various ways of combining them to support different workflows and tasks. In addition to the free-form hyperlink interaction that's fundamental to the Web, there are three other commonly used structural models: hubs, wizards, and guides.

In some situations, the conceptual model you select dictates a structural model. For example, the conceptual model of mail implies a structural model of a hub, and the conceptual model of a reservation system implies a wizard. However, whether you choose a structural model or have one dictated by the conceptual model, understanding its unique behaviors, characteristics, and appropriate uses is critical.

HUBS: YOU GO, YOU COME BACK

Hubs are used when there's a primary view page containing a collection of data elements and a series of one-page forms for editing the elements. Hubs are found in a variety of applications, including calendars, task managers, email, portfolio trackers, and reporting applications.

A graphic representation of a hub features a view page at the center with a variety of forms radiating out from that central page (see Figure 5.6). In essence, the central view serves as a launching pad to the individual forms required to modify and save information. The flow of a hub is a bit like flying on a commuter airline: You go, you come back. In a hub structure, users spend most of their time looking at the information displayed in the main view, navigating out and back to different forms when they need to edit or add information.

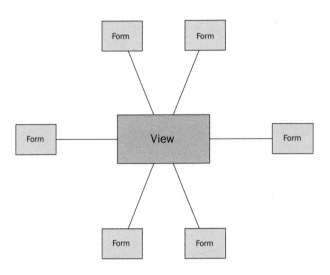

5.6
Hubs are a common structural model for applications used primarily to view information. The center of the hub is a view and the spokes are forms.

The hub structure works well for an application whose primary purpose is to present a table of data comprising a series of items edited one at a time. A fundamental assumption of the hub structure is that the possible edit operations can be grouped and performed in a manner suitable for one or more single-page forms. The primary strength of a hub is that its "out and back" flow never takes the user more than one step away from the main view, resulting in a simple, intelligible experience. Unfortunately, this strength is compromised if the design requires multipage sequences of forms.

A good example of a hub-based site was Visto. Although it no longer offers its product to consumers, Visto had an online personal information manager that included email, a calendar, an address book, a task list, and other related features. Visto's structural model relied on a series of hubs, each related to a particular realm of functionality. The calendar view was typical of Visto's implementation and use of hubs. The main calendar view page and Add Appointment form can be seen in Figure 5.7.

5.7

These two pages from Visto's
calendar are examples of a view
and form arranged as a hub.
The view calendar page is at the
center of the hub, with the Add
Appointment and other forms one
step away.

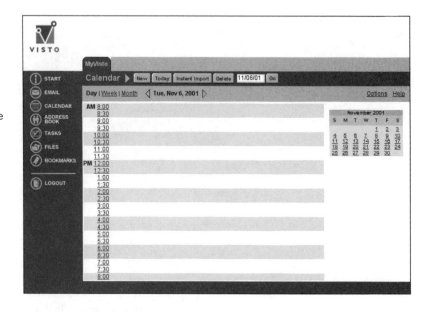

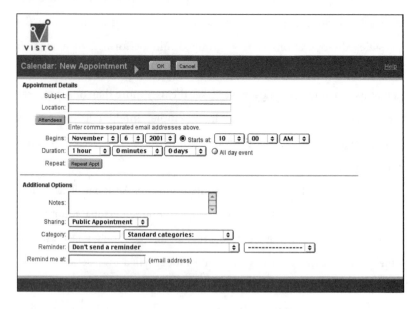

In Figure 5.8, note how the application is composed of a series of small hubs: email, calendar, address book, and tasks. In addition, certain pages are shared by all hubs, including the Delete Confirmation page and an options page not shown in this map. The natural interaction flow this structure creates is for the user to click an item in a view page, go to a form, edit an item, and return to the main view.

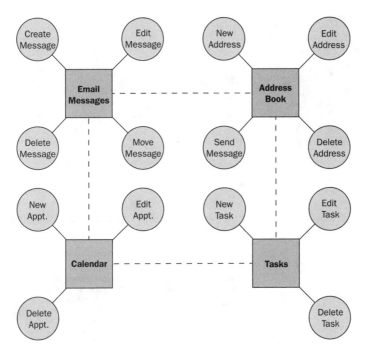

5.8
A simplified map of Visto's structural model illustrating its use of hubs.

In addition to serving as the structural model for the entire application, a hub can be used for separate areas of an application. A good example is Hotmail's user options functionality. Navigation to the different options is provided through an index page with descriptions of each group of options (see Figure 5.9). Although this implementation would be improved if the main options page served as an actual view page and displayed a summary of the user's settings, the page is still an accurate implementation of a hub structure. You go, you come back.

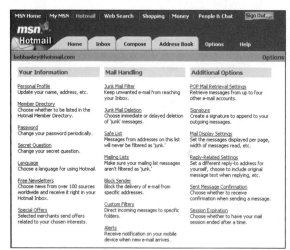

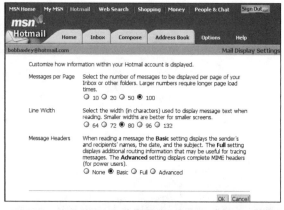

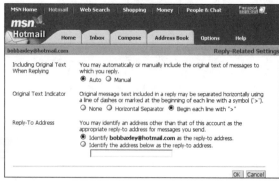

5.9

Hotmail's user options function uses a hub as its structural model. With the main index page at the center of the hub, the user navigates out to a form, changes specific options, and returns to the center.

Here are a few guidelines you should keep in mind when designing hubs:

- ☐ All options for changing the state of the presentation should be on the primary view page. For example, an online calendar might have options for changing the date as well as controls for switching between day, week, month, and year views. All controls for these options should be located directly on the main view page.

- ☐ All forms should include both Cancel and Submit buttons. If users submit a form without errors or click Cancel, they should be taken back to the view page at the center of the hub. Simply returning to the view is enough feedback to let them know their information was successfully received.

- ☐ The forms making up the spokes of the hub should not depend on one another. Users should be able to navigate to any form, make their edits, and immediately return to the main view.

WIZARDS: STEP 1, STEP 2, STEP 3

Wizards, another common structural model, are a sequence of forms linked with Previous and Next buttons. Wizards requires users to fill out forms one at a time, navigating through the process in a predetermined, fixed sequence (see Figure 5.10). After completing all the forms in the sequence, they are typically taken to a view page summarizing their choices. Wizards are common in both desktop applications and Web applications, used for everything from formatting mailing labels to installing new applications to checking out at an online store.

5.10

Wizards are an appropriate structural model for applications that require users to provide information in a specific, linear sequence.

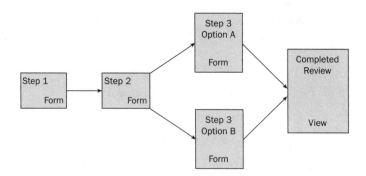

Wizards are appropriate when the possible choices and forms are dependent on one another and have to be made in a specific sequence. Wizards organize a complex set of options into small, discrete steps that can be digested and completed one at a time. Typically, the choices made in one step affect what's presented in the following steps, which enables users to make their way through intricate sets of choices without having to understand the relationships between different elements.

Wizards are also appropriate when users have to work through a complex set of interrelated tasks, particularly when the tasks must be completed in a specific sequence. By guiding users to the correct forms in the correct sequence, wizards enable even novice users to accomplish complex tasks and routines.

Like dogs, books, and hamburgers, wizards come in a variety of sizes. Toward the large end of the scale, Financial Engines is a good example (see Figure 5.11). This site helps users estimate their retirement needs by predicting their likely investment returns and comparing those returns to their projected needs. The model of a wizard is particularly appropriate for Financial Engines because it caters to users with varying levels of financial sophistication. As opposed to less structured methods of input, a wizard ensures that users complete the multiple steps needed to input the information required for the analysis.

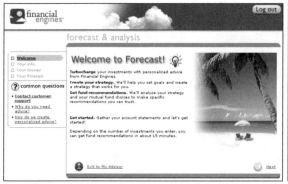

1

2

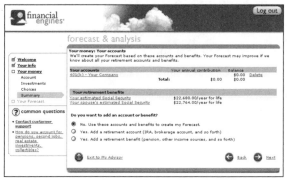

3

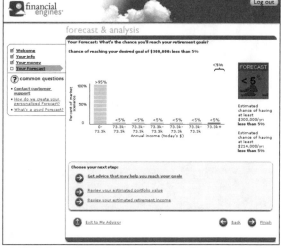

4

5.11

A representative sampling of the pages used to construct the primary input wizard at FinancialEngines.com.

Figure 5.11 illustrates how to use a left-side navigation area to communicate the user's current location in the sequence. Because sections of the wizard loop—for example, when adding retirement accounts—the wizard can't know for sure how many steps are required and, therefore, can't use a step counter. Also note that as users progress through the sequence, they can always return to earlier steps by using the left-side navigation area. However, users can progress forward only by using the Next button at the bottom right.

Instead of the structural model for an entire site, wizards are more commonly used to handle a certain feature or section of an application. Airline sites make good use of wizards for building itineraries and reserving travel (see Figure 5.12). Although there is some variation from site to site, the steps and sequence are typically as follows:

1. Enter travel parameters: departure and arrival locations, dates of travel, number of passengers, class of service, and so forth.
2. Select flights from the universe of available options.
3. Price selected flights.
4. Book selected flights.

Despite minor variation in the fields associated with each step, there is no variation in the sequence. If you want to make a flight reservation, these are the steps you're going to go through, and this is the order you're going to follow.

5.12

These figures show the three-step wizard used by almost all airline reservation sites. These steps allow users to designate an itinerary, select flights, and confirm pricing.

Like most wizards, this one finishes with an end state that allows you to review your choices and navigate back to a previous step to make changes. In this case, the end state is the step 4 described in the previous list, where you see your final itinerary and must decide whether to cough up your credit card information and complete the deal. From this final step, you can return to any previous step; however, once you return to a previous step, you have to continue the sequence from that point forward.

In the right situation, the structural model of a wizard is useful and easy to follow. Here are a few guidelines to keep in mind when you're designing a wizard:

- ☐ Wizards are appropriate for sequences of tasks in which the input entered in one step affects the options in subsequent steps. They are also appropriate for complex, multistep tasks that are likely to be unfamiliar or difficult.

- ☐ Wizards should end in a view page that summarizes users' choices and allows them to navigate to a previous step to make changes.

- ☐ When possible, each page in a wizard should include a visual indication of where the user is in the sequence. This indicator should show how many steps are in the entire sequence as well as the number of the current step.

- ☐ There should be navigational elements that make it possible for the user to return to any previous step or to exit the sequence at any point.

GUIDES: THE HUB/WIZARD HYBRID

A third commonly encountered structural model is the guide. Like butterflies, guides begin life as one beast but end life as a different one. In this case, guides begin life as wizards and end life as hubs. Not quite as romantic as the caterpillar-to-butterfly thing, but that's the way it is.

Like wizards, *guides* are composed of a collection of forms presented in a linear sequence linked by Next and Previous buttons. The key difference between guides and wizards, however, is that guides do not assume or require a particular order or dependence between the steps. As a result, after users have finished the sequence, they can return to any step and make changes without having to retrace any other steps (see Figure 5.13). In effect, the summary view page displayed at the end of the sequence functions as the center of a hub, with the steps in the guide forming the spokes.

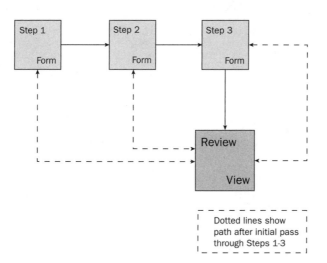

5.13
Guides are a hybrid of a hub and a wizard. Similar to wizards, they lead users through a sequence of forms. However, once the sequence is finished, they behave like hubs, providing non-sequential access to forms.

Dotted lines show path after initial pass through Steps 1-3

Guides can be used when users need to complete a set of forms, but the sequence is not important. They are particularly useful when users don't have the experience or knowledge to understand all the tasks needed to complete a operation. With guides, you have a way to make sure users supply all the necessary information to complete a complex, multistep task.

Like wizards, guides are used as the structural model for both entire applications and individual parts of applications. For example, a guide is the structural model for the entire TurboTax application as well as the checkout process at Barnes & Noble (see Figure 5.14).

A guide with these particular steps and sequence is commonly used as the checkout process for e-commerce sites. Although this flow has become standard, there's no real dependence between steps. For example, the shipping and payment steps can be presented in any order. After the user reaches the final page, the guide's behavior changes from a wizard to a hub. In the hub state, the user can navigate back to a preceding page, make changes, and return to the final confirmation step without having to repeat any other steps in the sequence.

1

2

3

4

5.14

This sequence of four pages is structured as a guide.

Most e-commerce sites use a checkout process with the following steps, closely resembling the process at Barnes & Noble:

1. Review cart
2. Shipping options
3. Payment options
4. Final review and confirmation

Although some sites insert an additional step for gift wrap options, this is the basic collection of steps on virtually every e-commerce site on the Web.

Despite its brevity, this guide illustrates a few basic principles. Other than the first and last step in the sequence, the ordering is arbitrary. The choices made in the shipping and payment forms do not have an impact on one another and could be presented in another order.

Second, at the end of the sequence, there is a metamorphosis as the structural model becomes a hub. In this state, users can return to a preceding form, make changes and return to the review page without passing through any of the other steps. In this context, the Continue button returns users to the review page because they already supplied a complete set of information.

When using guides, try to remember the following:

☐ Guides can be appropriate when a lot of input is required to complete the task.

☐ Guides should be used when data can be grouped into a series of forms, but the sequence in which the data is collected is arbitrary.

- ☐ Guides should end in a view page that summarizes users' choices and allows them to navigate back to any step in the sequence.

- ☐ Guides are appropriate for complex, multistep tasks that are likely to be unfamiliar or difficult for users.

- ☐ Guides should always include a visual indication of where the user is in the sequence and how many total steps are involved.

- ☐ On the first trip through, users should be able to return to a previous step in the sequence. After the sequence is complete, users should be able to freely move from any step to any other step.

- ☐ The destination of the buttons used to move through the sequence should link users directly to the final step after they have finished their initial pass through the sequence. As a result, the behavior of the Next and Previous buttons depends on whether the guide is behaving as a hub or wizard.

SUMMARY

Before you leave the elusive world of structural models, however, take note of a few memorable points.

Unlike their desktop cousins, Web applications reside in a page-based environment rather than a window or file-based one. To be consistent with the medium, Web applications should

- ☐ Avoid the use of secondary windows.
- ☐ Clearly distinguish between the primary modes of viewing and editing.
- ☐ Avoid, at all costs, navigational dead-ends.

Among other things, a design consistent with the Web as an interactive medium requires an understanding of the differences between, and the uses of, views and forms. Views contain content, navigational elements, and control over the information being presented. By contrast, the purpose of forms is to edit and save information. To facilitate this interaction, forms should eliminate navigation that distracts users or could cause them to accidentally abandon changes to their data.

In addition to the hypertext model that serves as the structure of all content-based Web sites, three other structural models are appropriate to the task-driven workflow of Web applications:

☐ **Hubs—You go, you come back.** Consisting of a view page and a series of independent forms, hubs are useful for applications with a collection of data elements that can be edited in simple, one-page forms. Online calendars and email clients are examples of hubs.

☐ **Wizards—Step 1, step 2, step 3.** Wizards are constructed from a group of forms in a fixed sequence; choices made in one form affect the options available in subsequent forms. Wizards are commonly used to make airline reservations and other multistep, sequenced transactions.

☐ **Guides—The hub/wizard hybrid.** Guides are similar to wizards, except there is no dependency between the forms. As a result, after users have been through the sequence, they can return to any step and make changes without affecting choices made in subsequent forms. Guides are useful for ensuring that users get through a series of steps while offering navigational flexibility.

Moving past the structural model and into the organizational model, the next chapter takes you one step farther away from the abstract and one step closer to the concrete. Less about the natural interaction style of Web technology and the flow of editing operations, the organizational model is concerned with the organization of content and functionality.

"A place for everything and
everything in its place."

Isabella Beeton
Household Management

6

THE ORGANIZATIONAL MODEL

Organizing and Structuring Content and Functionality

As the final layer of the Structure tier, the *organizational model* details how a site's functionality and content is categorized into intelligible groups. As human beings, we use organizational models as a basic cognitive tool for recognizing, experiencing, and reacting to virtually everything we encounter. For example, we categorize animals as wild or domestic, people as male or female, and nations as developed or emerging. However, we also categorize those things by a variety of other properties: large and small, exotic and conventional, cultured and swine. Selecting and defining organizational categories is an intensely personal process influenced by culture, experience, education, and bias. As children, we see everything with new eyes, but as adults, we quickly place things in predefined groups and categories, based on our personal preferences and past experiences.

As a designer and information architect, your scheme for classifying and grouping content and features has a fundamental influence on your users' perception, under-standing, and judgment of your site. The design of the organizational model not only affects your users' experience of what is on your site, but is also a key factor in setting their expectations of what could be on your site. In the same way that statistics can be used to tell a variety of stories, the organizational model of a site affects the experience and meaning of both its content and its functionality. Like a map, the organizational model defines the routes from one location to another and influences the ultimate range of destinations.

Although the functionality of some Web applications requires only minimal supporting content, other Web applications feature a tight integration between content and functionality. For example, online email clients are exclusively for sending and receiving messages, but online stores are as much about product information as they are about placing and tracking orders. In some cases, content is one of the key advantages a Web application has over its desktop counterpart. For example, online calendars combine calendaring functions with supporting content, such as sporting, entertainment, and other public events.

If an application is predominantly built around functionality, the organizational model will be minimal. However, if your application includes a substantial bit of content, the content's organization and classification will be an essential element of the site structure.

The goal of this chapter is to identify and illuminate the issues in creating effective organizational models. As always, a conscious under-standing and consideration of these issues adds another level of control and influence over the user experience. It also provides another tool for tailoring your design to the needs and expectations of your users. Because many of these issues have already been well traveled by the information and library sciences, this chapter might seem a bit like a catalog of options. In many ways, it is. As a designer, having a thorough understanding of the available materials and options is important.

DECONSTRUCTING ORGANIZATIONAL MODELS

When you encounter any grouping of people, places, or things, two fundamental aspects of the grouping are at work. First is the *classification scheme*, which determines and defines the categories for grouping individual items. Classification schemes can be based on objective, measurable properties, such as price or availability, or they can be based on subjective features, like quality or value. A well-crafted classification scheme involves not only thoughtful design and exacting definitions; it also requires consistent implementation. However, this is a good place for lofty goals, as the classification scheme is a key factor in creating an intuitive, useful, and satisfying user experience.

Second, the experience of an organized collection of information is affected by the *model of association*, which describes how the categories are related to one another. For example, if a company's classification scheme organizes employees by roles, such as contributor, director, or vice president, the model of association says that these classifications are hierarchically related to one another. The model of association works in concert with the classification scheme to fully describe how the company is organized. The organizational model, therefore, is the combination of the classification scheme and the model of association:

Classification Scheme

+ Model of Association

Organizational Model

Although classification schemes tend to be paired with models of association, these two features are independent of one another.

Understanding and appreciating how these two features of the organizational model are at once independent and interrelated gives you a powerful tool for shaping and crafting your users' experience.

In the Real World

The day begins like any other. At 10:37 a.m., a woman calls to inform you that because of your extraordinary talents as an information architect, her firm would like to hire you as one of the architects for the design and construction of a new museum. So you know you're being asked to design a space where people will go to experience art and new ideas. With visions of the Guggenheim dancing in your head, the conceptual model of the building is clear. You turn your attention to the building's structural elements: the grand entrance, galleries, hallways, a gift shop, a snack bar, and the obligatory smattering of bathrooms.

You refocus your attention and ask, "So what type of museum is this?"

"A museum about the World Wide Web. History, innovations, personalities. That sort of thing. We've contacted you to help us determine how best to organize and present the various connections, interrelationships, and developments."

Now, that's an interesting problem. You wonder what would be the appropriate organizational model for the development and evolution of the Web. Maybe by site type: e-commerce, commercial content, personal, etc.? Maybe by country to highlight the style and influence of geography? Maybe a simple chronology to stress the overall evolution? What should you use for the model of association? How do you represent a hierarchy in a museum?

You return from the distraction of possibilities to hear yourself say, "Sure, sounds interesting. I'd love to help. What's the next step?"

"Well, we know it's short notice, but we want you to put together some sketches for a meeting tomorrow. We're trying to wrap things up by the end of the week."

These are the moments that separate wisdom from youth.

CLASSIFICATION SCHEMES

The first aspect of the organizational model to consider is the classification scheme—the method or system you use for grouping the information and objects that make up your application. Classification schemes fall into one of two groups: objective and subjective.

OBJECTIVE CLASSIFICATION SCHEMES

The least complex type of classification schemes is *objective classification schemes*, which have categories with firmly fixed boundaries. In other words, the categories are so precisely defined that it's possible to objectively determine the appropriate category for any item. There are four types of objective classification schemes:

- ☐ Alphabetic
- ☐ Numeric
- ☐ Chronologic
- ☐ Geographic

A good example of an objective classification scheme is the classification of public companies into large cap and small cap. These terms describe a company's market capitalization—in other words, the total amount of money it would take to buy all outstanding shares of a company at the current stock price.

Although determining what exactly constitutes large cap or small cap is admittedly subjective, defining an exact numeric value as a precise boundary between the two categories is possible. For example, if the boundary between large and small cap is set at $5 billion, you can objectively define a company as small cap or large cap by looking at the exact value of its market capitalization. In late 2001, the market capitalization of Adobe Systems stood at about $7.6 billion, making it a large cap stock by this definition. At the same time, the market capitalization of Macromedia stood at $1.3 billion, making it a small cap stock. Even a company closer to the edge—for example, Amazon.com, at $4.2 billion—can clearly be classified as a small cap stock because that's how small cap has been defined.

The key point to remember about objective classification schemes is that even though the precise placement of the boundary between two categories may be a subjective choice, after the boundary is set, determining where to place every item in the collection is an objective decision. That means once users understand how you've defined the categories, they can easily determine where to look for an item. This creates an expectation among users that once they understand the definitions, they can accurately anticipate the placement of any item.

Be careful about confusing objective classification schemes with sorting. Just because a phone book's entries are sorted by last name does not mean it's categorized alphabetically. In fact, phone books are generally categorized by home, business, and government, with the items in each category ordered alphabetically. Fundamental to the concept of categorization is the notion of containers: Individual items are contained within a category. If all the items in the collection are presented in a list, no categorization is taking place, even though the items may be in a particular order.

Alphabetic Classification Schemes

An *alphabetic* classification scheme is a tool for clustering items into a smaller set of groups. Remember in elementary school when Ms. Crabtree asked everyone with last names starting with A–M to move to one side of the room and everyone with last names starting with N–Z to move to the other side? Ms. Crabtree was using an alphabetic classification scheme to divide the class into two groups. After she defined the border between the two categories—in this case, between M and N—it was easy to determine which group you belonged to, assuming you knew how to spell your last name and the order of the alphabet.

As adults, we continue to experience this inhumane ritual at a will-call ticket window or a conference registration counter. We arrive with our friends, only to have our conversations interrupted as we dutifully divide ourselves according to whether our last names start with A–D, E–H, and so forth. If I had known about this back in elementary school, I might have been more particular about my friends' last names.

As you've probably noticed, however, one of the downsides of alphabetic classification schemes is that they're rather impersonal, at least when you're classifying people. Because the classification is based on a property that is so specific—in this case, the item's name—the classification fails to give any real meaning to the categories. Of course, on some occasions, that might be the intent. In these examples, the classification served to divide the collection into smaller groups, not as a meaningful categorization of students or ticketholders.

Understanding this aspect of alphabetic classification schemes allows you to make an informed, conscious choice about their use. For example, the list of attorneys on many law firm sites is a flat list, sorted alphabetically. Although this listing makes it difficult for users to differentiate one attorney from another, it also sends the message that all the attorneys are equally capable. If the site is for a boutique firm with only one location and one area of practice, this meaning might be exactly what you want to convey. However, if the site is for a large firm with hundreds of attorneys in different offices and with different specialties, relying solely on an alphabetic classification scheme fails to provide any meaningful way for your visitors to differentiate between professionals. As you can see in Figure 6.1, the alphabetic listing works fine for a short list, but quickly becomes unusable as the list expands.

6.1

On the left, an alphabetic classification scheme works well for this small boutique firm with one practice area and a single office. However, a scheme built around location or practice area would offer a more useful starting point for this large law firm (on the right) with several practice areas and multiple offices.

Numeric Classification Schemes

Numeric classification schemes are used to categorize items according to a known numerical value. For example, stocks are categorized according to their market capitalization, households are categorized according to their income, people are categorized according to their age, and baseball teams are categorized according to their win/loss record.

A critical issue in designing numeric classification schemes is the placement of the boundaries between categories. You can categorize households as low-income, middle-income, and high-income, but only after you have decided on a rational boundary between each category. Is the boundary between low- and middle-income at $18,500 or $21,000? What about the boundary between middle- and high-income? Is it at $75,000, $125,000, $200,000? Where you place these boundaries obviously has a dramatic effect on the meaning of each category.

Because a numeric classification scheme can convey significant meaning about the items being classified, it is important to consider which aspect of the items best serves as the basis of the classification. For example, a financial classification of households could be based on income, net worth, or debt-to-income ratio—all reasonable categorization methods, but each with a different meaning.

Like all objective classification schemes, numeric classification schemes have both a subjective and objective component. Specifically, after the subjective decisions determining the categories and boundaries have been made, it's possible to objectively categorize any item in the collection. As a result, once users understand the classification scheme, they can accurately anticipate the classification of any item.

In the Real World

One potential danger of using objective classification schemes is that owing to their air of objectivity, users tend to sense, adopt, and trust any meaning you have consciously or unconsciously embedded in the scheme. Telephone area codes in the United States are a great example.

Although phone numbers are really nothing more than network addresses, the historical allocation of area codes has imbued what's essentially a numerical index with additional meaning. Because area codes have been assigned according to geography, we have come to naturally associate geographical meaning with a particular number. Today that association extends only to area codes, although it once also extended to the first three numbers of the seven-digit number. These three digits, known as the exchange, were allocated based on smaller geographic areas within a larger area code and could be used to identify the neighborhood associated with a phone number. For example, the 328 exchange was known as Davis-8, making it a bit easier for those of us with poor digit recall to remember phone numbers.

As the phone system has become more sophisticated, particularly with the advent of cellular phones, the need to associate area codes and exchanges with geography has disappeared. As users of the system, however, we still hold on to the earlier meaning of the organization and find ourselves occasionally baffled by the consequences. What exactly constitutes a long-distance call these days?

Here's a test: You're sitting in your office and your cube mate Jerrell is yakking away on the phone. The two of you are supposed to go to lunch, but he won't get off the phone. Just to be annoying, you call his cell phone. Although your office is in the 650 area code, his cell phone is in 415. Is it a long-distance call?

Chronologic Classification Scheme

A *chronologic* classification scheme is used to classify items according to a temporal relationship, either between two items or between a single item and time itself. Depending on the presentation, a chronologic scheme can emphasize the sequence of items, how items relate to a specific date and time, the duration of items, or any combination of the three.

You can find an example of a simple chronologic classification scheme in that high school yearbook you keep tucked away in a closet. Yearbooks are organized by a chronologic classification scheme based on expected graduation date. More specifically, students are categorized according to a relationship to time, and the categories are sorted according to sequence. This scheme is useful because "graduating class" is a defining characteristic of high school students. By contrast, preschool and kindergarten students are classified by a chronologic scheme based on age rather than expected graduation date. Although it might be fun to refer to your kid's classmates as Class of 2020, out of kindness, we simply call them "the 4-year-olds"— a more descriptive and useful distinction, to be sure.

In these cases, the application of a chronologic scheme is fairly obvious. However, complex applications of chronologic schemes, such as important events in world history, require more careful consideration. One of the common problems with chronologic schemes designed to accommodate long expanses of time is determining the appropriate intervals for categories. Selecting intervals incorrectly or inconsistently results in the distortion often found in large-scale chronological classification schemes. A good example of this problem can be seen in the History Channel's "History of the World Timeline."

The History Channel's Web site features information about historical events listed by chronology. Users can navigate to certain years, decades, or centuries by using the menus. There are pages containing a group of events for each century between 500 B.C. and A.D. 1000, for each decade between A.D. 1000 and A.D. 2000, and for each year between A.D. 1800 and A.D. 2000. Although this organization clearly establishes the sequence of events, because it does not display the items in relation to a uniform time scale, it doesn't accurately reflect how they occurred in relation to time itself. This results in a distortion of the elapsed time covered by any category. For example, the 100 years that constitute the fourth century B.C. get as much coverage as the 365 days that made up the year 2000. Knowingly or not, The History Channel is telling its viewers that the wanderings of Confucius, the beginning of the Peloponnesian Wars, and the work of Hippocrates are equivalent to Elián González's return to Cuba, a 39% decline in the NASDAQ stock index, and the Yankee's winning a third consecutive World Series title—an example of the bias toward chrono-centricity, the belief that everything important happens in our own lifetime (see Figure 6.2).

The History Channel could help mitigate this distortion by simply using different visual presentations for different time intervals—for example, one design for a century's worth of information, another for a decade, and a third for a single year. Although this would not entirely eliminate the problem, at least it would reinforce to the viewer that something different is represented on each page.

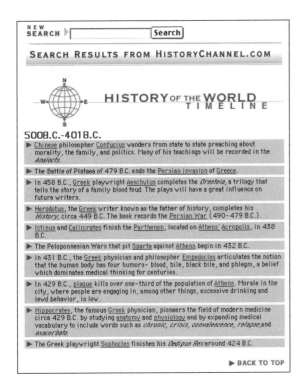

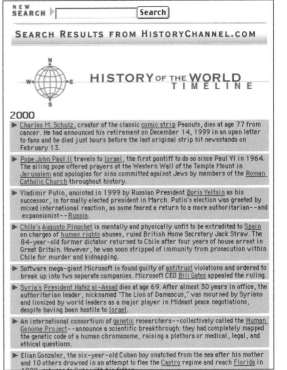

6.2

The History of the World Timeline uses a chronologic classification scheme. Although the two pages are identical in their presentation, they represent two different time periods, leaving the viewer with the impression that the Peloponnesian Wars are on par with Microsoft's antitrust problems.

In addition to considering time intervals for categories, you need to consider whether using a chronologic scheme is appropriate at all. Like the other objective classification schemes, a chronologic scheme is essentially saying that the date and/or sequence of events is the most important characteristic of the information. Because historical events influence one another, particularly in a given sphere—such as science, art, or politics— the date of an event might not be its most important feature.

For example, the History of the World Timeline is actually an amalgamation of a series of smaller, topic-specific timelines, including the history of technology, literary history, and Wall Street history. These topical timelines give users a context for the events, helping them perceive connections between events. Unfortunately, this context is lost when the items are combined into the World Timeline. Because the design fails to communicate any topical relationship between items, it emphasizes the sequence of events, even when the sequence is irrelevant. As a result, the design misses an opportunity to further the user's understanding of the information.

In addition to sequence and date, chronologic classification schemes can be used to emphasize duration. Although duration is not typically considered a chronological characteristic, it is related to the beginning and ending of events. Categorizing employees by length of service is an example of a classification scheme based on duration.

Categorizing items by duration often results in a unique and valuable view of the data. Travel destinations are one example. Although we typically think of travel time as the result of distance, my high school math teacher repeatedly made the point that it's the product of both distance and speed. From this perspective, a Northern California snowboarder can get to the snow in Lake Tahoe or Utah in about the same amount of time: four hours, depending on traffic and/or flight delays. A group of destinations classified by typical travel time would clearly look different from the same group classified by distance. Although I've never seen destinations classified by travel time, with two toddlers in tow, I can assure you that such a view would aid my travel planning.

Because chronologic classification schemes are based on the objective measurement of time, users expect them to be unbiased, predictable, and accurate. However, like other objective classification schemes, chronologic schemes also involve a subjective component. Therefore, defining categories precisely and consistently is important so that you don't distort the content or mislead users.

Geographic Classification Schemes

Geographic classification schemes use geography as the primary means for organizing and grouping items. They are appropriate in a variety of situations and can be found on sites featuring travel destinations, weather reports, shipping rates, or product availability.

Like chronologic schemes, implementing a geographic scheme can be fairly simple or quite complex. Fortunately, the slowed pace of border disputes and continental drift has left us with reasonably consistent agreement on where different cities, towns, rivers, and mountains are located. Despite this agreement, we still lack a standardized scheme for categorizing countries, regions, or continents. As a result, the subjectivity of geographic schemes tends to increase with the number of items being categorized. Although it's relatively easy to organize the major cities of the United States or Europe, creating a predictable scheme for classifying all the world's major cities is altogether different.

Geographic schemes typically appear on sites designed for a widely distributed, international audience. In these cases, the first consideration is whether the group of countries or cities is small enough to display as a simple list or large enough to require using some sort of classification.

Alphabetic lists tend to work fine if the group has fewer than 12 items. Although there isn't a definite cut-off where simple lists become unmanageable, if there are more than 20 items, you should definitely use a categorization scheme. Currently, the United Nations has 189 member states, so if your site has to deal with even a tiny subset of the world's nations, you are definitely going to need some level of categorization.

Figure 6.3 demonstrates the problem with an unwieldy list of countries and shows how Nike.com avoids the problem by using geographic classification to help the user navigate to a particular country/language version of the site.

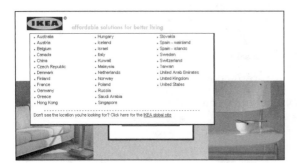

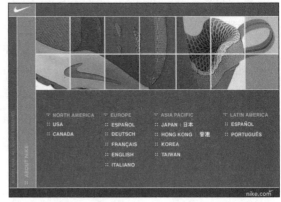

6.3

Ikea's site doesn't use a geographic classification scheme, so the user has to scan through an alphabetic list of all 33 country-specific versions. By contrast, Nike.com offers a geographic classification scheme. Unfortunately, the classification is inconsistent, with some options being grouped by country and others by language.

Sites that categorize countries typically do so by region rather than continent or hemisphere, leading to varying degrees of subjectivity and confusion. Although there is basic consistency on which countries belong in which regions, there are still cases like New Zealand. The islands have remained stationary for a few million years now, but depending on how they're being categorized, they still find themselves moving between Oceania and the Pacific Rim. One way to avoid the confusion associated with regions is to display the options on a world map. This alternative works well when the list of countries is relatively small and the site's users know where to locate a certain country. Similar to the problem of finding a word you can't spell in a dictionary, maps are useful only if you have an idea of where something is located, however. Figure 6.4 shows an example of how Volvo.com uses a world map as the navigational framework for a geographic classification scheme.

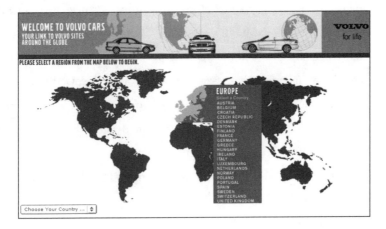

6.4
Country names are displayed as users roll over areas on the continents; users can also navigate to a country directly by selecting it in the alphabetic Choose Your Country list.

The key consideration in determining how to classify countries is the classification's intended purpose. What are you trying to say about the data? What connections are you trying to help users make? For example, if you're trying to classify countries according to sales regions, the Pacific Rim might be an appropriate classification for New Zealand. On the other hand, if you are trying to classify countries along cultural lines, it would make more sense to group New Zealand with Australia as part of Oceania. When you're using geographic classification schemes, be sure to consider what you're trying to say with the categorization.

Do you want to highlight cultural commonality, physical distance, economic interdependence, or environmental similarity? How do you want users to experience and interact with the data?

Geographic schemes are also used to classify items other than countries. For example, cities, states, mountains, rivers, and forests are all often classified by geography. Unfortunately, as the scale of the data expands, it's common to see the consistency and accuracy of the classification break down. For example, Yahoo! Weather features a single list containing Africa, Europe, Asia, Middle East, Pacific Rim, and the United States (see Figure 6.5). By combining different types of categories into a flat index, Yahoo! gives its users the message that Africa (a continent), the Pacific Rim (a region), and the United States (a country) are all equal. Even if this version of Yahoo! gets most of its visitors from the U.S., this approach is still misleading and needlessly U.S.-centric. A more appropriate approach to providing quick access to popular locations would be a "Most Popular" list, distinct from the main index.

Although you should look for ways to quickly get your users to common features and content, you should also strive to accurately represent the information. This doesn't necessarily mean you have to list the United States between the United Arab Emirates and Uruguay, but it does mean you should avoid listing California alongside Burundi and Cameroon.

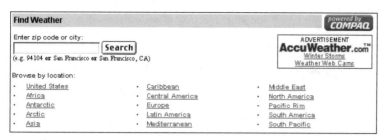

6.5

The index of locations on Yahoo! Weather contains an inconsistent collection of locations, including countries, continents, and regions.

SUBJECTIVE CLASSIFICATION SCHEMES

As you might expect, *subjective classification schemes* are the flip side of objective classification schemes. Whereas objective classification schemes benefit from well-defined boundaries between categories, subjective classification schemes suffer from the complexity of fuzzy borders. Subjective classification schemes require you to not only define the categories, but also subjectively determine the appropriate category for each item in the collection. Although a well-designed classification scheme has generally clear categories, invariably some items can reasonably fit into two different categories, and others don't neatly fit anywhere—hence the ubiquitous menu titles of Other, Miscellaneous, and Goodies. In such cases, determining classifications often devolves into an exercise in blindfolded dart throwing.

Like objective classification schemes, there are but a handful of subjective classification schemes commonly used, four of which are explored in this chapter:

- ☐ Topical
- ☐ Functional
- ☐ Audience-based
- ☐ Metaphorical

Although designing a subjective classification scheme might seem straightforward, first impressions aren't necessarily a useful guide. The scheme typically used for entertainment media, such as books, music, DVDs, and video games, is well established across a number of sites and, at first glance, appears quite solid. However, on closer inspection, cracks and inconsistencies become evident. Where, for example, do you find books on tape? What about sheet music, printed screenplays, or music videos?

When you're designing a subjective classification scheme, it's up to you to determine the definition for each category and where to place items that fall between the cracks. Even though users might understand how categories are defined, they are left guessing when it comes to the odd exceptions and corner cases. Despite these limitations, subjective classification schemes are far and away the most common method for categorizing information. Whether it's on the Web, in a library, in a store, or in your kitchen, subjective classification schemes are the dominant method of categorizing people, places, and things.

Subjective classification schemes are truly the purview of information architects. They are difficult enough to create, but even more difficult to grow and maintain—and thanks to their popularity, an unwavering source of job security. Pity the information architect at Wired.com who has only four high-level categories to work with (see Figure 6.6).

6.6
In Wired.com's subjective scheme built around four topics, where would you place a story about a congressional inquiry into the business practices of a major technology company?

As with all layers of the design, before you set out to create a subjective classification scheme, you should be armed with a thorough understanding of your audience, your content, and how your audience is likely to use your content. When it comes to designing subjective classification schemes, your job is akin to that of an American tour guide in Japan. Bilingualism helps, of course, but success also relies on your knowledge of local customs and points of interest and your ability to intersect that knowledge with the interests and goals of your American tourists. You have to simultaneously understand the intricacies of the information and the desires of users. Classification schemes derived from a good dose of both have the unique ability to guide you to items you didn't even realize were of interest: "I never thought I'd want to see a Japanese noodle factory, but now that I'm here, WOW!"

Unlike objective classification schemes, which tend to be used for relatively homogeneous content, subjective classification schemes often must accommodate a widely varied collection of items. Therefore, subjective classification schemes not only determine how content is grouped and experienced, but also influence what type of content is added in the future. Although a classification scheme begins life as a map of existing content or functionality, it quickly assumes the force of a highway or river, determining and influencing which towns will prosper, which ones will die, and where new ones will be built. The system designed to link point A with point B eventually becomes a determining factor in when and where point C gets built. A well-considered design will accommodate where you are right now *and* where you want to go in the future.

From the user's perspective, a subjective classification scheme can be particularly useful when you don't really know what you're looking for. Although objective classification schemes can be useful for organizing similar information, they require users to have a good idea of what they're looking for. Ever tried to look up a word you didn't know how to spell?

By contrast, subjective classification schemes hold the potential for greeting users with happy accidents and serendipitous discoveries. You're more likely to discover the perfect word for the first sentence of your screenplay if you rely on the subjective nature of a thesaurus rather than the objective structure of a dictionary.

As a designer, it's your responsibility to provide your guests with an enjoyable experience, happy surprises, and a desire to come back. A well-considered subjective classification schemes is one of your best opportunities to ensure that your visitors leave happy, satisfied, and wanting more.

Topical Classification Schemes

Surprisingly enough, *topical* classification schemes group information according to topic, theme, or subject. Without question, topical schemes are the most common classification scheme in use on or off the Web. The yellow pages are divided into dog groomers and wedding photographers; newspapers, into business, sports, and "lifestyle"; and menus into salads, desserts, and logo merchandise.

Many online stores—RedEnvelope, for example (see Figure 6.7)—rely on a topical classification scheme. This scheme encourages browsing and window shopping, making it possible to find what you're looking for, even when you don't know what you're looking for.

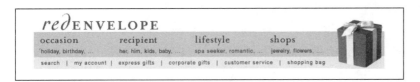

6.7

RedEnvelope relies on a topical classification scheme to direct visitors to gifts appropriate for different people and occasions—a useful scheme if you don't know exactly what you're trying to find.

What makes topical schemes particularly tricky is that not only do you have to navigate the Scylla and Charybdis of creating a useful, comprehensive set of categories, you also have to determine the appropriate category for each item. Even in the library of science, one man's paleontology can be another man's evolution. Compounding the problem is the nasty reality that virtually all information—whether it's a novel, a paragraph, or a Web page—often touches on multiple topics. As a result, you have to take on the highly subjective task of declaring what an item is actually about.

Although the Web provides a practical environment for cross-referencing, the overuse of cross-referencing renders the scheme too "squishy" to be of any real use. Even in an obviously subjective world, users expect consistency and predictability. It's simply unsettling to be cut adrift in a sea of options, cross-references, and "goodies."

Unfortunately, a topical classification is extremely specific to the content, so there are no useful "Top 10 Tips" or "Nits and Picks" for creating the perfect topical classification. However, the methodology, goals, and process of designing a topical classification scheme are consistent regardless of the situation. If you're designing a clothing site, ask yourself "Do people really think of their wardrobe in terms of jeans, chinos, leather, polo shirts, sweaters, dress shirts, and other? Is that how they shop?" If you're working on a travel site, stop to consider "What does it mean to have categories called flights, cars, hotels, cruises, and specials? Do those categories really equal travel and vacations?" The right solution will be a well-balanced synthesis of the content's unique characteristics and the unique needs, expectations, and knowledge of users.

Functional Classification Schemes

Functional classification schemes are another type of subjective classification scheme. Whereas topical schemes are typically used for organizing content and products, functional schemes usually organize commands and features. In other words, topical schemes tend to be used for organizing nouns, and functional schemes, for organizing verbs. A common example of a functional classification scheme is the organization of menu commands in a desktop application, such as Word or Quicken. Like their desktop brethren, you can use a functional classification scheme to determine how to arrange and label your application's commands and functions.

Functional classification schemes are built around specific actions. They typically use active verbs, such as *create*, *explore*, *buy*, *contact*, and *build*. The labels for functional classifications are often more engaging for users because they serve as calls to action. In other words, the scheme itself encourages users to take action and do something. For online services in particular, a functional classification scheme can make the most sense because user action is the main purpose of the site. Figure 6.8 illustrates the active nature of functional classification schemes.

6.8

These examples from Home Depot and the Container Store illustrate functional classification schemes built on user actions rather than topics.

Of course, functional classification schemes aren't without their own set of issues. Because clarity often requires you to identify both an object and an action, the labels for a functional classification scheme tend to be long. In an environment where the value of screen real estate makes Tokyo look economical, additional space requirements can be a substantial problem. For an online media store, a functional scheme might be labeled "Read Books," "Listen to Music," and "Watch Movies." By contrast, a topical scheme could support shorter labels: "Books," "Music," and "Movies," for example.

Desktop applications skirt this issue by relying on pull-down menus. For example, although the Open command would be ambiguous on its own, in the context of the File menu, it's perfectly clear. The menu title is often the object on which the menu command operates, so you open, close, save, and print *files*, but cut, copy, and paste *edits*. Unfortunately, this context is often absent in Web applications because they don't typically use pull-down menus in this way.

Audience-Based Classification Schemes

Audience-based classification schemes are typically found on sites that cater to multiple audiences or user groups. As shown in Figure 6.9, visitors to these sites are forced to select a single navigational path from two or more audience-specific options. After visitors make this choice, they are usually presented with a topical or functional classification scheme appropriate to their specific needs, knowledge, and expectations.

The key advantage of an audience-based classification is that it segments your visitors into subgroups, allowing you to create multiple classification schemes, each tailored to the needs, knowledge, and expectations of a subgroup. The downside is that some portion of the content is undoubtedly valuable to more than one part of your audience. As a result, the same content often has to be presented in more than one area of the site. Depending on your site's technological sophistication, this can quickly turn into a maintenance nightmare.

6.9
The designers of ML.com and Aetna.com used an audience-based classification scheme as a primary navigational element. Visitors are forced to select an audience segment before they're taken to the appropriate area of the site.

Metaphorical Classification Schemes

The final type of subjective classification scheme that needs mentioning, although reluctantly, is *metaphorical* classification schemes, which organize a site's functionality or content by using a metaphor from some real-world object or experience. As you can see in Figure 6.10, eWorld, Apple's defunct online service, was based on the metaphor of a town. Users accessed news by clicking on a newsstand and read their mail by clicking on a post office. Similarly, Microsoft Bob, also defunct, was built around the metaphor of a house with rooms dedicated to different types of tasks. Did I mention they were both defunct?

6.10

Remember eWorld? Not too many people do. Undoubtedly one of the best implementations of a metaphorical scheme, eWorld remains an evolutionary cul-de-sac on the road to the modern Web.

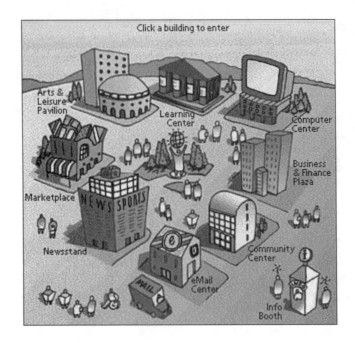

This is what I can tell you for sure about metaphorical classification schemes: Don't use them. You'll be tempted at times, but don't succumb. Because users tend to be quite literal in their interpretation of metaphors, they are quite unforgiving when the metaphor breaks. Metaphorically speaking, these schemes are the equivalent of painting yourself into a corner. For example, after decades of use, Macintosh users are still confused by having to eject a disk by dragging it to the trashcan. The metaphor simply fails to accommodate the action.

With all that said, metaphors can occasionally be useful; the shopping cart motif comes to mind. The fact that such metaphors work in small doses, however, does not mean they are necessarily appropriate at the scale of an entire classification scheme. Conceptual models are one thing; metaphors are another. Save yourself some trouble, and don't use metaphors.

EVALUATING CLASSIFICATION SCHEMES

Regardless of what type of classification scheme you use, there's a consistent set of issues you'll struggle with. The following five are at the top of the list:

☐ **Ambiguity.** All classification schemes carry with them some level of ambiguity. Whether it's in defining the categories or classifying an item, ambiguity is unavoidable. Unfortunately, it's also a source of frustration for users. If you find yourself in heated debate about the precise geography encompassed by "Pacific Rim" or in an extended thrash about the status of saltine crackers as a "snack food," don't forget to consider the knowledge and expectations of users. The question that should be foremost in your debate is "What will make the most sense to the people actually using this thing?"

☐ **Exclusivity versus inclusivity.** Thanks to ambiguity, there will also be questions of what to put in, what to leave out, and when to cross-reference. The Yahooligans get to struggle with this issue all the time. One can only imagine the late-night debates over how to categorize Messianic Judaism, Jews who believe in Christ. Do you put it with Judaism, Christianity, or both?

☐ **Homogeneity versus heterogeneity.** A large collection of content or items is unlikely to be completely consistent in detail, scale, or characteristics. In most cases, your classification scheme will have to accommodate both apples and oranges, and a whole lot more. For example, a site built to archive news events needs a categorization appropriate to text, photos, video, audio, Web sites, and other media types. The properties relevant to one media type aren't necessarily relevant to others. Who's the author of a video? What's the publication date of a Web site? A well-designed classification scheme has to find a delicate balance between what's alike and what's different.

☐ **Perspective and meaning.** All classification schemes carry a particular perspective about the information and how it should be categorized. Different people organize things differently. If you don't believe me, just try to find a file on your co-worker's computer or a mixing bowl in your neighbor's kitchen. When designing a classification scheme, you need to consider what you want to say about the information. What characteristics do you want to emphasize? What meaning do you want attached to your organization? If you were designing a site for a zoo, would you group the animals by taxonomy: big cats, bears, pachyderms? By biogeography: African animals, Asian animals, South American animals? Or by ecosystem: desert animals, forest animals, plains animals? What is it you want to say about the information you're presenting?

If the information doesn't lend itself to a single perspective or meaning, it's often possible to overlay an higher-level scheme on top of the whole thing. For example, in the zoo site, the top level of the organizational scheme could include Genetics, Habitat, and Biozone. Each could lead the viewer to a distinct classification of the animals, revealing three different perspectives in a single site. It's not something you could readily pull off with a real zoo, but it's certainly possible on the Web.

With that basic introduction to classification schemes, you'll no doubt start noticing them everywhere. Obtuse questions and obscure connections will magically appear before you. Why *do* grocery stores put cheese with meat instead of dairy? When they appear on the dinner menu, why do we refer to cows as beef and pigs as pork, but still call chickens chickens? Is bowling a sport or an activity? These are but a few of the burning questions of our day.

MODELS OF ASSOCIATION

The other half of the organizational model is the model of association. Whereas the classification scheme defines the categories composing the organizational model, the model of association describes the relationships between those categories. Three fundamental models of association are in widespread use: indexes, hierarchies, and webs (see Figure 6.11). Each model has its own set of ideal uses and unique characteristics. Depending on the specifics of your content and the needs of your users, you may find one model most useful, or you might choose to combine one or more into a hybrid model.

6.11

There are three fundamental models of association typically used to define the relationships between categories.

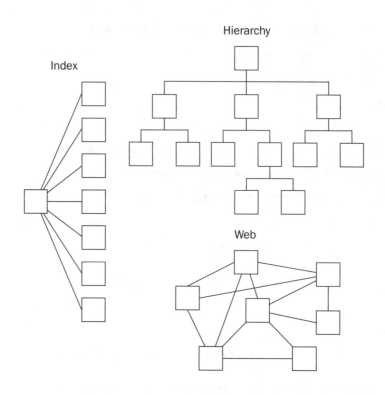

Nonfiction books are a useful example of how the three models can be combined with various classification schemes to produce a comprehensive organizational model. The first organizational model typically seen in a book is the table of contents, which is a hierarchical description of how the book is divided into parts, chapters, and sections. Like all subjective hierarchies, however, the table of contents isn't helpful if you're looking for a particular concept, person, or word. For that reason, books also include an index, which is valuable precisely because it cuts across the subjective hierarchy of the table of contents, giving readers quick access to every mention of a certain item. Depending on the book's academic level, the author might also make use of a web model through foot, side, or end notes. These pointers refer the reader to other parts of the text and to related works and are a way to insert more detail without interrupting the logical flow of the book.

This example also illustrates how the model of association defines relationships between the organizational categories as well as the range of potential navigational models. Whether the design relies on an index, a hierarchy, a web, or some combination of the three, the navigational model's flexibility and style directly result from the model of association.

Despite the unimaginable scope of information being collected, organized, and presented on the Web today, these three models remain the dominant methods for organizing and structuring information.

INDEXES

A close cousin of the laundry list, an *index* is the most simple, unbiased, and direct model of association (see Figure 6.12). The phone book, an obvious example of an index, is a list of phone numbers, grouped by whether the number is for a person, a business, or a government office. Within each category, the items are then sorted by name. The categories themselves are *peers*, the defining characteristic of an index.

6.12

Indexes are useful when users know exactly what they are looking for and the information can be organized with an objective classification scheme.

Index

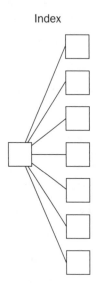

Advantages of Indexes

The key advantages of using an index as your model of association include the following:

☐ **Fast.** Indexes are appropriate when users know what they're looking for and want to get there as fast as possible. It's like running into the grocery store at midnight to buy milk. You know you want milk. You know they have milk. All you want to do is find the milk and get on with your life.

☐ **Efficient.** If the collection of items is small enough, simply listing all the items together on a single page is reasonable. By using a compact mechanism such as an index, you can reduce the amount of navigation needed to access all the items. This is the basic principle behind the portal motif seen across the Web.

☐ **Scalable.** Because indexes are typically used for homogenous groups of items, storing them in a searchable database is fairly easy. A database makes it possible to quickly search large collections, such as the card catalog for the Library of Congress or the list of DVDs available through Netflix.

☐ **Multiple perspectives.** The homogenous nature of the collections in an index also makes it easy to offer multiple perspectives on the information. For example, although you determine that the most likely way to search your company directory is by last name, some users might want to search by a different field—location, for instance. Figure 6.13 illustrates how a database could solve the problem of finding relevant attorney biographies that was mentioned earlier. With over 800 attorneys in 10 practice areas and offices in 7 cities, the designers of the Wilson Sonsini Goodrich & Rosati site use a database-index to provide multiple perspectives of the information.

6.13
Using a database enables visitors to specify one or more parameters and then quickly locate an attorney who fits their needs.

Disadvantages of Indexes

In spite of the speed, efficiency, and other benefits of an index, the model certainly isn't without its share of drawbacks. Here are some of the major ones:

- ☐ **Sans clue.** Ever try to look up someone's phone number when you didn't know his or her last name? Ever go to a hardware store and find yourself using words like "thingy" and "doohickey"? Although an index can be extremely efficient if you know what you're looking for, if you don't, they're quick to leave you without a clue.

- ☐ **Rigid.** Indexes work well only for collections of relatively homogenous items. If the items don't have a common property that clearly distinguish them from one another, there's nothing on which to base the index. For example, if you're classifying a group of books, they can easily be differentiated by name. If you're dealing with something like clothing or cars, however, there's no distinguishing property to serve as the basis of the index.

- ☐ **Uniform.** Indexes give the impression that all items in the collection are of equal value. That might be appropriate in some cases, but in many others, it's not. Before you start lumping people, places, or things into an index, make sure you want create the impression of uniformity.

There's no doubt that indexes provide a fast, efficient, and scalable mechanism for finding and navigating a group of similar items. Keep in mind, however, that they rarely offer the guidance and support users need to navigate an unknown set of items or information.

HIERARCHIES

A *hierarchical* model of association is the ideal choice if you want to express rank, inheritance, and structure (see Figure 6.14). In hierarchies, lower-level categories inherit characteristics from higher-level categories, resulting in a ranking between the levels and a clear flow from the general to the specific as you travel deeper into the hierarchy.

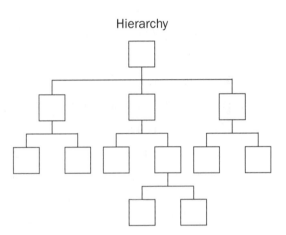

Hierarchy

6.14
Hierarchies are useful when users are freely browsing the content but still need a structural framework to understand where they are in the information space. Web applications typically combine a hierarchy and a functional classification scheme to organize functions and commands.

Not to place all the blame at the doorstep of the Victorians, but many of the complex and developed hierarchies we rely on were clearly the brainchild of people with an unusual need for order. In the modern Western world, the hierarchy expresses the fundamental structure of our businesses, our military, our government, our religions, our economy, and even our view of the natural world. For better or worse, hierarchy is such a pervasive concept that it has come to define and circumscribe how we think about information. Ubiquity, however, does not always equate with the ideal. Like everything, hierarchies have their own set of advantages, disadvantages, and usages.

Advantages of Hierarchies

Given that the hierarchical model is so pervasive, there must be something good about it. Right? Although there are undoubtedly more, here are three of the key advantages of a hierarchy:

☐ **Natural.** Resulting from a basic human need to order, rank, and organize, the hierarchy is the basis for the organization of families, authoritarian institutions, and civilization itself. Although the hierarchy is an abstract, man-made concept, it's also one of the clearest and most natural methods we have for organizing information.

☐ **Structure.** The structure of a hierarchy quickly communicates a site's overall organizational model, giving users a strong sense of location and direction. The result is a greater sense of stability and security for users as they navigate and explore. However, the importance of these benefits are declining as users become increasingly comfortable with the Web and its inherent lack of order.

Since the beginning of the Web, many designers have assumed that users rely on a hierarchical structure to develop a mental model of the site, particularly when they enter the site through some avenue other than the home page. This assumption implies, however, that users conceive of a site as a discrete unit of information and are trying to orient themselves within the site as a whole. This is similar to assuming that if you were dropped into the middle of an African jungle, you would try to figure out where you were in relation to Nairobi, Cairo, and Pretoria. In that situation, your concern is your immediate surroundings—that is, where you can go from where you currently are. If you were interested in arriving at a specific destination, you would probably start your journey from a more informative point of reference— the home page. Although the structure of a hierarchy can certainly be an advantage, exactly how much remains is open to debate.

☐ **Navigable.** Hierarchies also provide a clear model for navigation. Drilling down from the general to the specific is a powerful method for navigating and locating content, especially when you don't know what you're looking for. Hierarchies enable users to take a series of measured steps, choosing from a list of possible options at each level. This can give users the security of a multiple-choice test instead of the fill-in-the-blank experience of a searchable index. Finally, hierarchies can offer users a mental trail of breadcrumbs, enabling them to re-create the navigational path to a particular item or page.

Disadvantages of Hierarchies

As our understanding of complex systems has become more sophisticated, so has our understanding of the hierarchical model's inherent weaknesses. A hierarchical conception of systems with the complexity of nature, the global economy, or even the Web, is simply inappropriate. That isn't to say a hierarchy doesn't have its uses and advantages—only that it's important to keep in mind it's not the only game in town. Although there are others, here are two of the most important disadvantages of hierarchy:

☐ **Not scalable.** As the scope and variety of information increases, hierarchies become increasingly subjective, inconsistent, and unusable. This problem is further compounded when the users interacting with the hierarchy become more diverse. As your information set grows in ways not anticipated, the consistency, integrity, and utility in the initial design become compromised. This might not be a problem if you can narrow the collection of information, but if your information set is likely to grow and evolve, you're going to be up against a maintenance nightmare.

☐ **Single perspective.** A hierarchy necessarily represents the information in a single categorization. It says flat out: "We're going to have these things called mammals, birds, reptiles, and fish." That works great if you're interested in viewing animals grouped by genetic relationship, but what if you wanted to see all the predators in one group and all the prey in another? This view would require an entirely new hierarchy. When the information can be related in a variety of ways, forcing a single perspective on the organization can be a serious limitation.

Balances of Hierarchies

A well-designed hierarchy is one that finds the perfect balance between a variety of poles. Two of the axes that lie at the heart of a well-balanced hierarchy are depth/breadth and specific/vague.

Starting with the depth/breadth axis, at the top of everyone's list is the question "Do we go wide or do we go deep?" In other words, does the hierarchy tend toward more categories across and fewer levels down, or is it the other way around? Although there's no simple answer to this one, if there were, it would be this: Go wide (see Figure 6.15).

Example A: Three levels deep by four categories wide

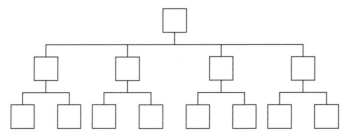

Example B: Three levels deep by three categories wide

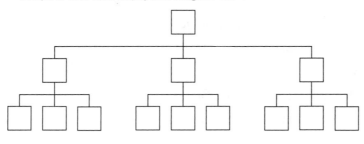

Example C: Four levels deep by two categories wide

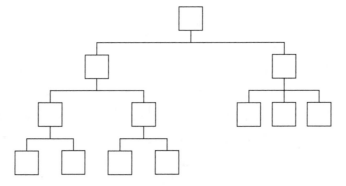

6.15
Starting with 12 items, this diagram shows a range of organizations, from wide to deep.

Because of the overhead involved in navigating down—click to go to level 1, look at the choices; click to go to level 2, look at the choices; etc., etc., etc.—it's better to maximize the number of choices at each level. Recalling the efficiency argument for the use of indexes, it's relatively easy for users to scan through a list of items and pick out the thing of interest.

Although the specific mechanisms for displaying a hierarchy will be addressed in later chapters, the point here remains one of balance. When designing an organizational model based on a hierarchy, pay careful attention to how much you feed users at each step. You need to find a balance where the bites are big enough that it doesn't take them three hours to finish the meal, but not so big that you're stuffing their faces.

In the specific/vague axis, the balance largely depends on the type of information you're presenting. If you're displaying information with universally accepted characteristics that can serve as the basis of the classification, specificity will pay off. If, however, you're classifying a bunch of "doo-hickeys" and "thing-a-ma-bobs," ambiguity will be your friend. The trick here is to set the appropriate expectation for users.

For example, if you're designing an online wine store, categories such as Cabernet, Merlot, Zinfandel, and Chardonnay would be appropriate. Because these labels are meaningful to the site's audience, they set appropriate expectations (see Figure 6.16). However, if you're designing a site with a wide variety of items that don't neatly fit into a common vocabulary, ambiguity can set a more appropriate expectation. RedEnvelope is a good example of this principle. The categories communicate something about their contents, without being so precise that they set expectations that may or may not be satisfied (refer back to Figure 6.7).

6.16

Wine.com uses categories that are specific and understood by its target users.

Because hierarchies express a parent-child relationship between categories, they require a minimum of two levels. For example, although phone books categorize listings by Personal, Business, and Government, all three categories are peers of one another. The categories don't "own" one another, so the phone book is not a hierarchy. When you're designing a hierarchy, the focus should be as much on the relationships between the categories as it is on categorizing a given piece of content.

Although there's plenty of opinion extolling the virtues of hierarchies, I, for one, remain skeptical. It's not so evident to me that a hierarchy makes the best choice for organizing information or navigating a Web site. My experience is that users spend more time clicking links than they do clicking structured navigation. From what I can tell, users care more about where they can go than where they've been or even where they are.

In the end, what's important to remember about hierarchies is that although they can be useful and easy to use, they are not without limitations. Almost inevitably, some type of hierarchy will find its way into your organizational model, but keep in mind that a hierarchy is just one possible model of association. If you carefully consider your users' needs and goals, the peculiarities of your content, and your own design goals, you will likely realize that a comprehensive solution requires combining a hierarchy with one or more of the other models.

WEBS

The *web* model of association is undoubtedly familiar, as it's fundamental to hypermedia and the World Wide Web (see 6.17). Unlike indexes and hierarchies, the structure of a web often falls somewhere between chaos and anarchy. Instead of relying on categories and classification, the web model reflects the complexity of large sets of information by linking individual bits of content based on any number of different associations.

6.17
Webs are useful when users don't necessarily know what they're looking for and the information does not lend itself to the single perspective of a rigid hierarchy.

Web

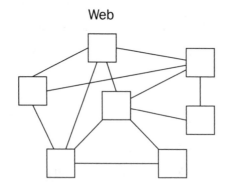

Before the dawn of the World Wide Web, content and information were linked through footnotes, bibliographies, and random notes exchanged between friends. Although it was often too time-consuming or laborious to follow links in this manner, the link certainly existed and could be exploited by the energetic reader. Lucky for us, the advent of hypermedia in general and the World Wide Web in particular finally provided a robust, standardized, usable mechanism for expressing and navigating associative linking. The result is an altogether novel method for exploring content and traversing information spaces.

Advantages of Webs

In addition to their well-established value in catching bugs, webs offer the following advantages:

- **Natural.** One of the most attractive features of the web model is that it most closely matches how the human mind works. When we encounter something, we place and define it in terms of its association with similar things we've known or encountered. Although we might rank it in terms of hierarchy, we also place it in the context of a variety of experiences that may or may not fall into a tidy order.

- **Flexible/multiple perspectives.** Webs afford an informal style of association that does not imply the primacy or superiority inherent in hierarchies or the equality and order of indexes. The web model allows designers to say to the user, "Here's something else that bears some sort of relationship to the thing you're looking at. Thought you might be interested." That statement is very different from the hierarchical model, which is more along the lines of "The thing you're looking at is the child of category X, the grandchild of category Y, and the great-grandchild of category Z. Oh yeah, and here are its 15 siblings."

☐ **Scalable.** As evidenced by the unimaginable scale of the World Wide Web itself, webs provide an extremely scalable model for associating information. Need I say more?

Disadvantages of Webs

Despite those three rather compelling advantages, you should also consider these disadvantages before turning arachnid:

☐ **Unstructured.** The most commonly heard criticism of the web model is that it fails to give users a firm sense of where they are or how they got where they are. If users decide to "go off trail," they can quickly get lost in the woods with no clear landmarks. Webs are indeed a tangled mess. They virtually preclude users from building a useful mental map of the site structure. Have you ever tried to imagine all the links and associations available on Yahoo!? Care to draw a site map? However, as I mentioned in the bit about hierarchies, this might not be much of an issue.

One caveat here: Don't use a web as the primary model of association for functional commands. In this case, users definitely need to build a mental model so that they can easily get back to certain features and functions. Do not toss them into an unstructured sea of views and forms. They'll get lost.

☐ **Hard to create.** The web model is more flexible than the hierarchy or index model, but as a result, it's also the most difficult to design and scale. Often, each item in the collection needs to be considered individually to define meaningful associations. Alternatively, developing technologies for relating items is possible, but even they require creating a useful methodology for determining appropriate links.

Although the team at Netflix hasn't determined which movies are like which other movies, it has developed a complex, sophisticated methodology for grouping certain movies with other movies. Based on the combined opinions of its user base (see Figure 6.18), Netflix's methodology, one of its most valuable and useful assets, has been codified in a software application.

The difficulty of creating a web is compounded by the fact that it's almost impossible to create a useful visualization of the design. Although hierarchies readily lend themselves to site maps and diagrams, there isn't a meaningful way to understand a web other than direct experience of it. As a result, you usually have to implement the web before you can get a clear picture of whether it works.

6.18
Netflix uses rating data to
group movies, which allows it
to use a web model to make
recommendations that cut across
any classification scheme.

Although it has challenges from both a technical and a design perspective, a web is clearly a powerful, interesting, and useful model. You as the designer get to determine which choices are available to users at any given moment, helping shape and define their experience. This brings with it a high level of responsibility for understanding your users' goals and needs, but it also offers unique flexibility. The web model enables you to relate different pieces of content without having to worry about the integrity of a global classification scheme. This model empowers you to take your visitors on unique and intelligent journeys, but it also requires you to behave as a caring guide.

CASE STUDY: THE ORGANIZATIONAL MODEL(S) OF EBAY

Up to this point, I've talked about classification schemes and models of association as though they existed in isolation from one another. Obviously, this is not the case. Like males and females, classification schemes and taxonomies can be talked about one at a time, but they don't get really interesting until you toss them together.

As the entry point to "The World's Online Marketplace," the goal of eBay's home page is to get visitors to relevant merchandise as quickly as possible. To aid in this task, the page combines a number of classification schemes and models of association (see Figure 6.19).

Searching product keywords allows cutting across subjective classifications to locate an item

Functional areas organized by combining a functional classification scheme and a hierarchical model of association

6.19

The home page of eBay, "The World's Online Marketplace."

A collection of subsites, similar to an audience-based classification

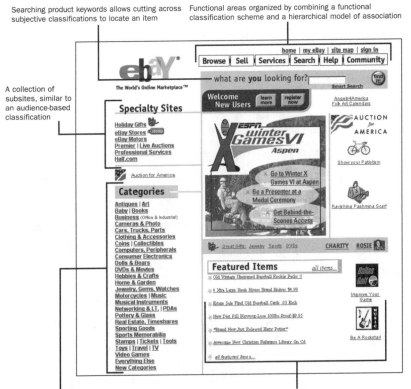

The mother-of-all product classifications, with a hierarchical subjective classification scheme; other perspectives, such as themes and regions, available under the Browse function

Combines an index with a web model of association

SUMMARY

In an effort to put a nice bow around all this, I'll leave you with a few key points. As the final layer of the Structure tier, the organizational model is the most concrete expression of how your application and/or content fits together. Although users are rarely conscious of the conceptual model or the structural model, the organizational model is certainly something they can identify and talk about. Therefore, it's also something that should be tested repeatedly with users.

When you design an organizational model, considering the classification scheme and the model of association separately is useful. Separating the categories' definition from the relationships between them enables you to see more clearly the full range of options as well as their attendant pros and cons.

In approaching the classification scheme, always keep in mind the unique nature of the items you're classifying and your users' needs and expectations. Can all these items be objectively classified by a single characteristic, or are things naturally more fuzzy than that? Are users going to know exactly what they're looking for, or are they likely to be browsing? The same considerations should be applied to determining the most appropriate model of association. Does an index work for this information and these users? Can you intelligently design a hierarchy that's appropriate to the users and the information? Will you be able to evolve and maintain the hierarchy over time? Is there some methodology you can use to automatically weave a useful web? In most cases, you'll realize that you need multiple organizational models working together to fully satisfy your users' different needs and expectations.

To increase your understanding of these issues, you should take some time to look at your favorite sites and analyze their organizational models. What does and doesn't make sense? Where are they consistent and inconsistent? Do they set the proper expectations? What does the organization say about the site's content, functionality, and experience?

In the next chapter, you'll be moving one step farther from the conceptual and one step closer to the concrete. Leaving the structure tier and entering the behavior tier, you'll look at the ways to represent the organizational model as navigation and the mechanisms for selecting objects.

Tier 2: Behavior

PART III

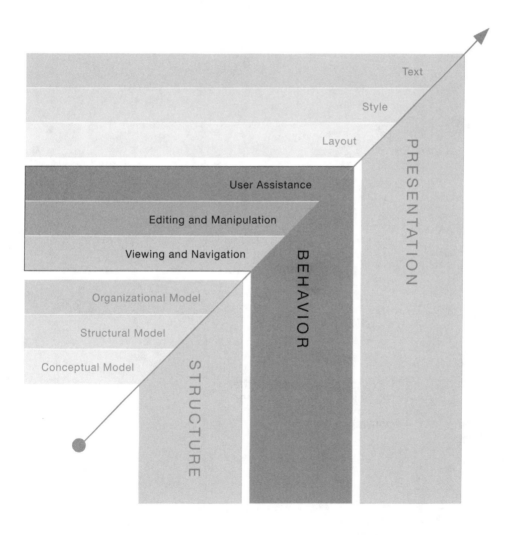

"The shortest distance between two points is a straight line."

Anonymous

7

VIEWING AND NAVIGATION

Creating Consistent Sorting, Filtering, and Navigation Behaviors

Layer 4: Viewing and Navigation marks the beginning of Tier II: Behavior and a departure from the sometimes abstract world of conceptual, structural, and organizational models. Starting with this layer and continuing through the other layers of the Behavior tier, the issues and tradeoffs affecting the design become increasingly concrete and specific.

Although the distinction between the three layers of the Behavior tier can at times be subtle, but important differences are visible upon closer inspection. Chief among them is that the behaviors of the Viewing and Navigation layer affect the state of the application, but the behaviors of the Editing and Manipulation layer affect the underlying data stored and managed by the application.

Even though users might not be as aware of the behaviors and interactions related to viewing and navigation, they spend a lot of time mucking around with them. For example, in commercial desktop applications, such as Word or Excel, a tremendous amount of activity and code is required to enable behaviors such as resizing windows, scrolling documents, moving palettes, and configuring toolbars. These actions are examples of behaviors that affect the state of the application without altering the data stored in a document. Because the behaviors of the Viewing and Navigation layer do not affect stored data, they do not require the error checking or validation typical of editing behaviors. As a group, navigational and viewing behaviors are essentially "no harm, no foul."

This chapter explores the most significant behaviors of the Viewing and Navigation layer, including navigation, selection of data objects, and list manipulation. In addition, it examines and documents the most popular interaction conventions that have developed alongside Web applications.

NAVIGATION

In support of the "all this stuff is connected" train of thought, the navigational components of the interface are a direct result of the decisions and tradeoffs embedded in the organizational model. Where the organizational model might say "We're going to have a hierarchical organization with 8 primary categories and 39 subcategories," the role of navigation is to describe the exact mechanisms allowing users to move between those categories and subcategories. The following sections examine the qualities of a well-behaved navigation scheme as well as the navigational conventions associated with different organizational models.

NAVIGATION: WHAT'S IT GOOD FOR?

Without a doubt, navigation is one of the most talked-about topics in the annals of Web design, and for good reason: It's a real hairball. Paradoxically, however, because navigation is *the* fundamental interaction component of the Web, the conversation has largely failed to consider the underlying role and purpose of navigation.

Although the most obvious purpose of navigation is to give users a way to travel from point A to point B or, more appropriately, from http://www.point-A.com to http://www.point-B.com, the navigation scheme and mechanisms of a Web application perform several other vital functions. From the user's perspective, the navigation system helps answer a variety of questions.

What Is This Thing and What Will I Find Here?

Echoing one of the central themes of the previous chapter, the organization and presentation of an application's content and functionality establishes key expectations among users. Done correctly, the combination of the organizational model and navigation scheme can instantly communicate to users what type of site they're looking at and what it can do. Notice how effective the navigation systems shown in Figure 7.1 are at communicating what the site is all about.

7.1

The use of meaningful navigation labels helps these sites quickly communicate their function and purpose.

Where Am I?

Although the Web lacks the sort of physical boundaries that define a space as we typically experience it, one purpose of navigation is to provide some level of context for the user. Combined with a well-chosen page title, the navigation system can help users place themselves within the application as a whole.

Unfortunately, the breadcrumb approach (see Figure 7.2) commonly used in hierarchical content sites, such as Books → Computers → Internet → Web Design, is often inappropriate to Web applications. Using breadcrumbs to communicate location within a hierarchy is useful only if a hierarchy is the primary method of navigation. Because users also navigate via search and non-hierarchical hyperlinks, breadcrumbs don't always provide an accurate path of how a user actually traveled from point A to point B. As a result, breadcrumbs often fail to bring much value to Web applications, in the same way that breadcrumbs would be of questionable value in Word or Photoshop. It's one thing to be able to roll back your data; it's another to be able to retrace the steps you took to arrive at a particular place.

7.2

This example shows the use of breadcrumbs as a way of communicating location within a hierarchy. In this case, the user has clicked Men's, then Outerwear, then Jackets, and then Waterproof to arrive at the current page.

A more tenable solution is to communicate the user's current location by highlighting the navigation elements. At its simplest, this can be done by highlighting the active tab with a different color. Although many sites follow this first step, the volume of secondary and tertiary navigation elements often makes it impractical to produce and display highlighted navigation controls at other levels of the hierarchy. Therefore, a clear, concise page title remains the most effective method of communicating a user's current location. Figure 7.3 illustrates how Barnes & Noble addresses this problem.

7.3
Barnes & Noble's primary navigation relies on a clear highlight to indicate the currently selected tab. Unfortunately, it doesn't follow through by also highlighting the selected secondary navigation—in this case, Baby & Preschool.

Where Can I Go?

In the same way that roads define where you can drive—can't drive to Hawaii until they build that bridge, for example—navigation determines how the user can traverse the application. Depending on the application's usage, however, this can mean different things. For example, if users typically navigate to a page and stay there for a few minutes, it might be best to simplify the page by limiting the available navigation, requiring them to return to a home page to access different areas of the application or site. By contrast, if the usage pattern is more one of quickly moving from page to page, the visual and interactive overhead of a sophisticated navigation scheme is clearly warranted. In either case, the goal is to provide meaningful and useful navigational paths for users to take out of the current page without ever driving them down a navigational dead-end.

What Are the Important Things Here?

An application's navigational mechanisms imply how its features and content are prioritized. Implementing help and logout links as small icons and sticking them in the upper-right corner tells users "You won't be needing this stuff very much, but if you do, it'll be here." By comparison, running a tab bar across the top of the page tells them "This is the stuff that's here, and the most important stuff is in the tab on the left."

Among the graphic design community, it's a well-understood principle that in Western culture the visually dominant area of the page is the upper-left corner and the least dominant is the bottom right. This is even more true in the realm of Web design because users can dynamically resize the page, which makes the upper-left corner the only consistent location on the page. When choosing a navigation mechanism or determining where to place navigation elements, make sure you keep these visual principles in mind.

Does This Company Really Care About Me?

A well-designed navigation system should help users feel welcome, comfortable, and in control. By placing the needs of the user in the forefront of the design, you can instantly demonstrate that you understand and care about your visitors. Banana Republic, for example, includes its toll-free telephone number on every page. If your site is more difficult to navigate than Disneyland at New Year's, if your customer service center is hiding behind a 6-pixel icon at the bottom of the page, or if users have to resort to the help page to find "Contact Us," you are clearly telling your users "Go away, kid. You bother me."

By carefully considering the fundamental purpose of your application's navigation system, you have a much better chance of creating a solution that serves users' needs. If you can do that, you will have traveled a goodly way down the path of building a great interface.

DECONSTRUCTING NAVIGATION

A Web application's navigation system can be deconstructed into these navigational elements:

- ☐ **High-level navigation.** Elements that move users between contexts
- ☐ **Low-level navigation.** Elements that provide additional detail and functionality within an established context
- ☐ **Utility navigation.** Elements dedicated to functions such as help and logout

In a typical online store, for example, there is high-level navigation to move between categories and subcategories, low-level navigation to see product details, and utility navigation to find the shopping cart and customer service. Figure 7.4 from Baby Gap illustrates these types of navigation.

7.4
Baby Gap's product pages include voluminous amounts of navigation.

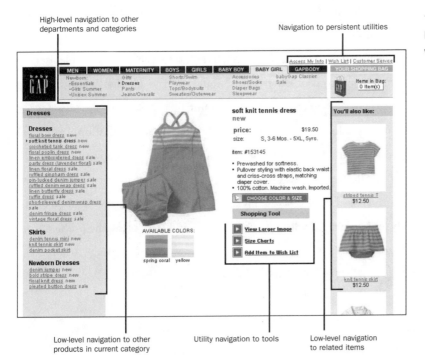

High-level navigation to other departments and categories

Navigation to persistent utilities

Low-level navigation to other products in current category

Utility navigation to tools

Low-level navigation to related items

As the example from Baby Gap shows, different conventions have been developed for each type of navigational element.

HIGH-LEVEL NAVIGATION MECHANISMS

Although low-level and utility navigational elements are typically expressed as links or icons, primary navigation tends to require a more sophisticated mechanism—tabs and trees being the two most popular.

The tab motif established its position in the pantheon of interface widgets in the era of 386 chips, 1200-baud modems, and Windows 3.0. Initially developed as a means of pushing an expanding array of options into a diminishing collection of dialog boxes, tabs are now one of the most recognizable navigation conventions on the Web.

A second common mechanism for high-level navigation is a tree. Trees effectively turn the tab motif on its side, tossing out the visual metaphor in the process. Although the tree mechanism can theoretically be expanded to fit a hierarchy of any depth, in practice trees are rarely more than two levels deep.

A primary advantage of both tabs and trees is how they enable users to quickly flip from one area of an application to another without having to return to a centralized starting point first. A second big advantage is that they allow users to progressively explore an application, instead of overwhelming them with the full set of choices. In many situations, it's more palatable to select one primary category out of seven and then one subcategory out of nine than it is to search through a list of 50 or 60 items. By letting users divide and conquer, tabs and trees break the problem into manageable steps.

Unfortunately, tabs and trees also present a few thorny difficulties and limitations:

- **Scalability.** Both tabs and trees have an inherent scalability problem. In other words, they don't. Perhaps the most famous example of this dates from the dot-com boom when Amazon.com expanded its offerings from books to music to video to everything that could be put in a box. Unfortunately, the defining interface element of the application, the tab bar, did not gracefully scale along with the product line.

  Although the vertical orientation means that trees could theoretically be expanded to an unlimited number of categories and subcategories, both trees and tabs face the practical limits of what users can reasonably view on a page and what will fit on a page. For tabs, this limit is approximately 9 categories and 11 subcategories. Because trees position subcategories between categories, their practical limits are closer to 11 categories, with 7 subcategories each. In total, that means a tab mechanism can support about 99 groupings and a tree mechanism around 77. Naturally, your mileage may vary.

- **Hidden choices.** In most implementations, both tree and tab mechanisms require users to select a category before they can see the associated subcategories. That means most subcategories are hidden from the user's view at any given time. As mentioned, however, this is also one the biggest advantages because it allows the user to navigate through the application one step at a time.

☐ **No support for lateral navigation.** In the same way that tabs and trees do not allow users to view subcategories outside the current main category, neither do they allow users to directly navigate between subcategories of different primary categories. For example, if the current location is Books: Mysteries, there is no direct way to get to Movies: Horror because the two subcategories are in different primary categories. As a result, users are required to visit an index page associated with Movies before accessing the Horror subcategory. Even if you can't eliminate this distraction, you can work to mitigate it by designing index pages that serve as useful entryways into the category.

☐ **Shifting visual relationships.** An important disadvantage unique to trees is that the visual relationship between the categories varies based on the current selection. Because subcategories appear between primary categories, the position of the primary categories in relation to one another shifts as each primary category is selected. This problem is more evident with a large number of subcategories contained in a single primary category. Figure 7.5 illustrates this problem by showing Polo's high-level navigation with two different categories selected.

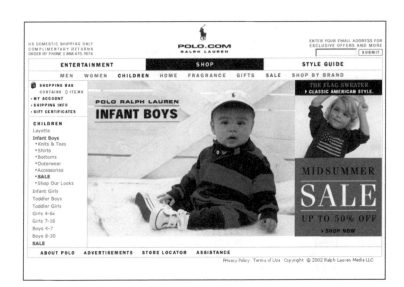

7.5

Polo uses a tree-based navigation scheme to navigate between categories and subcategories. When users click on a category, they can see the subcategories it contains.

Because high-level navigation is the most recognizable structural component of a site, the availability, position, and labeling of its elements should be consistent throughout the application. Users rely on these elements as landmarks when they navigate and explore an application, and suddenly changing their position or availability can be almost as disconcerting as finding Los Angeles in Missouri.

One way to get around most of these limitations is to implement dynamic menus, also known as pull-down, pop-up, or fly-out menus. Although dynamic menus don't do much on the scalability front, they do provide for lateral navigation and address the problem of hidden choices by not forcing the user to select a category just to see its contents.

The typical implementation of a dynamic menu shows a list of subcategories when the user clicks or rolls over the corresponding primary category. This behavior is similar to the behavior of menus in desktop applications, with the primary categories serving as menu titles and the subcategories as menu items.

Although dynamic menus can present some formidable technical and usability challenges, they remain an attractive form of high-level navigation because they enable users to directly navigate from any subcategory to any other subcategory. As a result, users have a more efficient means for both navigating and exploring the application.

Unfortunately, the lack of an established convention for the behavior of dynamic menus means that different Web applications have implemented them in different ways. Although many applications display the menu as the user rolls over the menu title (see Figure 7.6), this approach has some problems:

☐ **Ambiguous interpretation of user action.** There is no way to tell if users rolled over a category because they wanted to see its contents or because they simply moved their mouse to a different location on the screen. The result of this ambiguity is that a dynamic menu can pop up when users don't want or expect it.

☐ **Intolerant of errors.** It's not uncommon for users to accidentally move their mouse off a menu, only to have it vanish from the page. Even worse than the shock of having the menu disappear is the frustration of having to go through the whole operation again. This problem is especially frustrating for users with limited motor skills or for those stuck using an "eraser head" mouse pointer on a laptop.

☐ **Inconsistent with standard Web behaviors.** Although using rollover behavior as feedback is quite common, using a rollover to hide and show elements of the interface goes against the basic interaction model of the Web. The Web relies on the user to make explicit mouse clicks before performing an operation. This fundamental behavior should apply even when the application is simply changing the visibility of an interface element.

7.6
Crate&Barrel uses a dynamic menu to give users direct access to every subcategory. The active page is in the Dinnerware category, but the user has rolled over the Home Accessories category, revealing its contents.

A superior, although less common, implementation can be seen at the site for the American Institute of Graphic Artists (AIGA; see Figure 7.7). Instead of relying on a rollover behavior, this implementation requires the user to explicitly click on the menu title to reveal its contents. The menu disappears when the user clicks a menu item or clicks outside the menu itself. Although this design reveals a definite bias for users with 20/20 vision, from a behavior perspective, it overcomes the three problems associated with rollover behavior.

7.7
The dynamic menu is activated
when the user clicks on a menu
title. In this figure, the user is
viewing the home page and has
clicked the Main menu.

All this is not to say that dynamic menus are the best solution in every situation, regardless of the implementation. However, as Web users and Web applications both become more sophisticated, rich interaction mechanisms such as dynamic menus will become more prevalent and more useful. Whether they are ultimately appropriate for an application depends on the relative importance of the advantages and disadvantages described here.

Regardless of whether you use tabs or trees, dynamic or static menus, or some other set of mechanisms, high-level navigation is one aspect of your application that should be thoroughly tested with actual users. Sitting at a point that's fairly rigid from a technical perspective and that has a significant impact on usability, high-level navigation is something that shouldn't be left to the designer's intuition alone.

LOW-LEVEL NAVIGATION

If the purpose of high-level navigation is to allow users to establish a context, the purpose of low-level navigation is to allow them to get around inside that context. For example, in an online store, high-level navigation is used to get to a particular category, and low-level navigation is used to select information on a specific product. Similarly, in an online service, high-level navigation gets users to their calendars and low-level navigation gets them to a certain date or event.

Because low-level navigation is less about "getting around" and more about examining and transacting, it should be clearly delineated from its high-level brethren. This is typically accomplished by placing low-level navigation within the page's content area, away from high-level navigational elements.

Finally, low-level navigation should be clearly associated with the item, product, or data the user is currently viewing. By contrast, high-level navigation is associated with the application as a whole.

Although the specific options and links that compose low-level navigation vary from one context to another, low-level navigation should always follow a consistent pattern of placement and behavior.

In most applications, low-level navigation is contained in one or more dedicated navigation panels, with links to detailed information such as the following:

☐ **Item details.** Low-level navigation can be used to view more in-depth information about a product. For example, an online bike store might contain detail pages for description, technical details, photo gallery, availability, and pricing.

☐ **Related items.** Low-level navigation is appropriate for navigating to other items related to the one currently being viewed. For a book, items might be related based on the author, the subject, or the purchasing patterns of other site customers. This type of navigation is particularly useful because it cuts across the site's hierarchical organization, allowing users to blaze their own trail through the organizational model.

☐ **Navigating to specific commands.** In an online service, commands related to the current context are an appropriate use of low-level navigation. For example, Hotmail features a navigation panel with commands to add contacts, customize preferences, and check other email accounts (see Figure 7.8). By separating the commands from the high-level navigation areas, this implementation effectively communicates to users that these elements are distinct from pure navigation.

7.8

Hotmail clearly delineates low-level navigation elements from high-level elements. A dedicated navigation panel in the page's content area offers access to a variety of other locations and commands.

Like the organizational model it reflects, an application's navigation system forms the interactive backbone of any Web application, especially those connected to large volumes of content. Understanding the inherent capabilities, limitations, and conventions that affect the interface mechanisms for high-level and low-level navigation is a critical component of designing effective Web applications.

SELECTING OBJECTS AND
ISSUING COMMANDS

A common interaction problem in the Viewing and Navigation layer is the selection of data objects. In many Web applications, users are required to select a single object or a group of objects before issuing a command. For example, if users want to delete an email message, they would have to select the message, and then click the delete command. In desktop applications, this is accomplished by clicking the object and then issuing the command through a menu selection, a toolbar, or a drag-and drop-behavior. Unfortunately, the world of Web applications is void of the basic interaction mechanism of direct selection.

In place of direct selection, Web applications have to resort to different methods of indirect selection. Depending on whether the user can select more than one object at a time, the interface can use a set of command buttons working in concert with radio buttons or check boxes, or the commands can be embedded into the object's presentation. Figure 7.9 illustrates the difference between a solution using shared controls and one using dedicated controls.

Title	Type	Date	Size	Actions
Lorem ipsum dolor sit amet	Euismod tincidunt	03.31.2001	150Kb	delete
Consectetuer	Laoreet euism	03.31.2001	230Kb	delete
Euismod tincidunt ut laoreet euismod tincidunt	Tincidunt	02.28.2001	113Kb	delete
Quis nostrud exerci tation	Euismod	02.28.2001	90Kb	delete
Lorem ipsum dolor sit amet	Tincidunt ut	10.31.2000	150Kb	delete
Consectetuer	Euismod tincidunt	10.31.2000	230Kb	delete
Euismod tincidunt ut laoreet euismod tincidunt	Euismod tincidunt	09.30.2000	113Kb	delete

	Title	Type	Date	Size
●	Lorem ipsum dolor sit amet	Euismod tincidunt	03.31.2001	150Kb
○	Consectetuer	Laoreet euism	03.31.2001	230Kb
○	Euismod tincidunt ut laoreet euismod tincidunt	Tincidunt	02.28.2001	113Kb
○	Quis nostrud exerci tation	Euismod	02.28.2001	90Kb
○	Lorem ipsum dolor sit amet	Tincidunt ut	10.31.2000	150Kb
○	Consectetuer	Euismod tincidunt	10.31.2000	230Kb
○	Euismod tincidunt ut laoreet euismod tincidunt	Euismod tincidunt	09.30.2000	113Kb

[View] [Search by Type] [Delete]

7.9
With dedicated controls, shown top, the selection is inferred from the links embedded in the table. With shared controls, shown bottom, the selection is made explicit through radio buttons.

Which approach is appropriate to a situation depends on the interaction's specific requirements and the number of commands and objects involved. If users have to be able to issue a command against a group of objects in a single operation, the only solution is shared controls. However, if users can select objects one at a time, either option can work. Similarly, if there are more than five (or so) available commands, the visual noise that results from repeating every command dictates the shared controls solution.

The decision tree, shown in Figure 7.10, looks like this: Can commands be issued against a group of objects? If yes, then use the shared controls solution. Are there more than five or so commands? If yes, then use the shared controls solution. Therefore, if objects can be selected only one at a time and there are fewer than five or so commands, use the dedicated controls solution.

7.10

The decision tree for choosing indirect selection methods using shared versus dedicated controls.

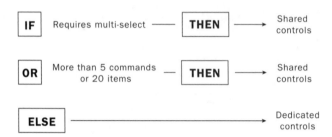

SHARED CONTROLS

A solution using indirect selection and shared controls is familiar to any user of Web-based email. A typical implementation is Visto (see Figure 7.11). In this example, the action of deleting an email requires the user to first select a message by clicking the corresponding check box and then clicking the Delete button to complete the action.

7.11

The use of shared controls in Visto's email area requires users to select one or more messages by clicking the check box(es) and then clicking the command.

MyVisto							
Email ▶ Create Msg	Check Email	Forward	Move	Delete	Folders	Alerts and Filters	
Select All	Preview	Msgs 1-12 of 12	Find:	Go	Inbox ⬍	Options Help	
Select Page	**From**	**Subject**			**Received** ▲	**Size**	
☐	Special Offers Ce...	An Exclusive Members Only Offer!			10/19/01 14:05	5.7 KB	
☐	SmartPortfolio.Co...	TheStreet.com Update: Stocks Ral...			10/19/01 13:05	27.1 KB	
☐	The Atlantic Online	Biological Weapons; Unbound Fict...			10/19/01 12:18	7.4 KB	
☐	67@china.com	Re: Your request			10/19/01 12:05	2.5 KB	
☐	KKSF, 103.7	Smooth Jazz, KKSF, 103.7 e-mail ...			10/19/01 11:35	19.8 KB	
☐	xaaqphdcwf@iobox...	in your local area			10/19/01 10:32	5.8 KB	
☐	showtimes@amazon....	Unsubscribe Weekly Movie Showtim...			10/19/01 08:30	1.5 KB	
▶☐	Conrad, Deborah	Invitation to Mitch Confer's Ope...			10/18/01 15:43	4.8 KB	
☐	executivemanageme...	IMPORTANT HOSTPRO SUPPORT AND BI...			10/12/01 13:00	4.5 KB	
☐	Chip.Swearngan@Me...	Cyberbills PR inquiry			10/11/01 15:01	1.4 KB	
☐	Lisa M. Lord	Re: Bob Baxley has sent you an A...			10/10/01 04:55	2.4 KB	
☐	Victoria.Elzey@ne...	FW: Lisa Lord			10/04/01 09:39	1.7 KB	

Although this approach to object-command interaction is common-place in Web applications, it presents a few issues to be aware of:

☐ **Geographic distance.** The shared controls solution requires users to connect two geographically distant controls, which can be a problem if the items are far apart or one of them is scrolled off the page. To alleviate this problem, always place the commands close to the table containing the data objects, preferably above and below the table. This reduces the chance of the buttons being scrolled off the page.

☐ **Limited feedback.** Because the feedback associated with changing the state of the check box or radio button is relatively subtle, altering the background color of the row containing the selected item is also useful, particularly for long lists. With cascading style sheets (CSS) and JavaScript, this feedback can occur dynamically, reinforcing the selected state.

☐ **Scalability.** Because this design relies on a series of visible buttons, the number of commands that can be presented at one time is limited by screen real estate. Although some designers have attempted to eliminate this drawback by using pull-down menus instead of buttons, such a solution hides options from users, requiring them to explore the interface to discover which operations are possible—not a good idea.

As the primary method of selecting multiple objects, the shared controls solution for object selection is one of the most common interaction conventions on the Web. If the interaction doesn't require multiple selection, however, the dedicated controls solution can be more effective.

DEDICATED CONTROLS

In the dedicated controls solution, each data object is associated with its own set of commands. As a result, instead of users explicitly selecting an object by clicking a radio button or check box, they make an implicit selection by clicking a command associated with the object.

One advantage of this solution is that it offers the flexibility to use links, buttons, or icons to issue commands (see Figure 7.12). Further, it allows the data objects' fields to function as commands. For example, in an online calendar, a date on the calendar serves to create a new event on a particular day. Similarly, an event can be used as a link to the event's details.

7.12

Metavante's online bill pay application repeats the commands in the Action column. To issue a command against a bill, the user clicks the icon in that row.

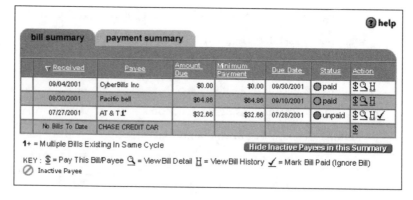

This approach can result in a cleaner, less complex experience, but selecting the appropriate fields to use as links can be tricky. Fields that function clearly as navigation can serve as links, although it's important not to overwhelm the data by using every possible field.

Although the dedicated controls approach addresses the geography and feedback issues of the shared controls solution, it is not without its own baggage:

☐ **Visual clutter.** Repeating a set of four buttons or links in row after row of a 25-row table can only look cluttered. Although this problem can't be eliminated, it can be minimized by using icons and the data itself to issue the commands.

☐ **Potential ambiguity.** Using the data to issue a command is rife with potential ambiguity. For example, on Metavante's site shown in Figure 7.12, does clicking the biller name link to the details of the bill or the details of the biller? This problem can be controlled by using dedicated links with clear names when the destination of the link might be ambiguous.

☐ **Limited scalability.** Unfortunately, the solution doesn't work well if there are more than about five commands because the additional commands lead to visual clutter and ambiguity. One way around this problem is to move the less frequently used commands to a "details" page that displays objects one at a time along with the full complement of available actions. Although this approach requires more clicks for users to get to less frequently used commands, it simplifies and streamlines access to the most common behaviors.

Which approach is best for your situation obviously depends on usage. Often it can be preferable to combine the two solutions, giving users more flexibility in working with the application. Evite is an example of how the two conventions can be combined to offer users a variety of paths (see Figure 7.13). Unfortunately, even in this implementation, the ambiguous nature of the links still presents the potential for errors.

7.13

Evite combines the dedicated
and shared controls approach
into a single hybrid solution.
Although this approach results
in additional controls and visual
weight, it supports the broadest
range of usage patterns.

Combined, the shared and dedicated controls solutions are the primary
conventions for object selection in a Web interface. Unfortunately, both
conventions have scalability challenges that represent a formidable barrier
to creating more sophisticated and feature-rich Web applications.

VIEWING LISTS OF DATA

In applications that contain a lot of user-created data—portfolio trackers, contact managers, and email, for example—a number of operations are typically available for altering the presentation of the data. Changing the sort order and changing the group of objects being viewed are two examples. This following sections examine the most common of these interaction conventions, including examples of their use and their relative advantages and disadvantages.

CHANGING COLUMN SETS

If the objects being presented are composed of many different fields, it's common to include a way for users to manipulate which fields are displayed. With stock portfolio trackers, for example, there are literally dozens of different fields for any position in a portfolio. There are fields related to the transaction (date, shares, price, and commission); fields related to the current value and gain/loss of the position; and fields related to the security (market cap, earning per share, price to earnings ratio, current trading price, 52-week range, etc., etc., etc.). With so many fields, displaying them all in a useful manner is simply impossible. Therefore, a mechanism for changing and manipulating which columns are displayed at any time is required.

The most common mechanisms for toggling between different groups of columns are menus or a series of links or icons (see Figure 7.14).

7.14

The stock research area on
Yahoo! uses links to access
different views of the data. The
Motley Fool accomplishes
the same thing with a menu.

Although the link solution displays all the potential choices, often it results in too much visual prominence for the feature. In addition, if the application allows users to create their own column sets, creating a visually pleasing design using links is even more difficult because the number of links will be unknown.

By contrast, the menu solution is more visually digestible, but it hides choices and requires more user effort. However, the solution is visually efficient and more readily accommodates an unknown number of different column sets. In general, the menu solution should be implemented as a jump menu so that the page is redrawn with the new column set immediately after the user changes the selection in the menu. In this situation, a Go or Update button adds little or no value.

In addition to the mechanism for switching from one column set to another, the design must also address which columns are going to appear together and in what order. This aspect of the design should clearly be driven by user tasks and goals.

In a stock portfolio, for example, users typically look at their portfolios from a handful of different perspectives. Therefore, the column sets should be designed with those perspectives in mind. In one context, users might be interested in the basics of companies in their portfolios; in another, they might interested in the performance of their holdings in those companies. Instead of simply cramming everything into one view and forcing the user to wade through columns and columns of data, the design should make intelligent and thoughtful decisions about which fields are relevant in which context. Although this requires the courage to leave things out, the result is a cleaner, more digestible, and more manageable experience for the user.

PAGING

Along the same theme of what to do if you have too many columns to display, there is the question of what to do if you have too many rows of data to display. If there are 564 entries in an address book to display, they can't all be displayed in a single 564-row table. Not only will the application choke on such a voluminous table, but it will also be impossible for users to manage.

The standard interaction convention for handling this problem is called *paging*, which breaks the data into smaller chunks, displaying a preset number of rows at a time. Figure 7.15 illustrates this convention in practice.

7.15

These examples from eBay and CNET demonstrate paging navigation. Note the use of Next and Previous links so that the user doesn't have to click on individual page numbers.

Despite its entry into the pantheon of Web conventions, however, there remains a handful of factors to consider when designing and implementing paging:

- ☐ **Group length.** As a general rule of thumb, it's best to initially limit the number of items in each group to around 25. The ideal solution, however, enables users to specify how many items they would prefer in each group. By providing this option as a stored user preference, high-bandwidth users aren't stuck paging through 25 items at a time.

☐ **Navigating between groups.** The ideal navigation control includes a link for each group in the set as well as Next and Previous buttons/links. Many sites have done away with Previous and Next links, but this forces the user to click on each number to navigate the list, and a one-character link is too small to be a click target. In addition, without Previous and Next buttons/links, the user must be conscious of the current page number as well as what page should come next. Although this is hardly an intellectual challenge, offering the user a Next link removes this unnecessary burden and simplifies the interaction.

☐ **Placement of navigation.** To prevent the user from having to scroll all the way to the bottom of the page simply to navigate to the next group in the collection, the navigation mechanism should always appear at both the top and the bottom of the list.

Although paging is hardly anyone's idea of a great interface, it is one of the few well-established conventions in the interactive vocabulary of Web applications. For better or worse, it will remain a part of the interface landscape until the technology of Web application matures enough to support a more sophisticated method of managing long lists.

SORTING

List sorting is another important interactive convention seen in many Web applications. Sorting interactions involve two independent but related choices: the sort key and the sort order. The *sort key* determines which field forms the basis of the sort, and the *sort order* determines whether the sort is ascending or descending. For example, if a list of addresses is to be sorted A to Z by last name, the sort key would be the last name and the sort order would be ascending.

To further the example, some situations require multiple sort keys. For instance, an address book typically uses last name as the primary key and first name as the secondary key. In other words, the list is initially sorted by last name but when two entries have the same last name, those entries are then sorted by first name.

The goal of a sorting interface is to give users control over both the sort keys and the sort order. Following in the footsteps of their desktop cousins, Web applications follow the convention of using the column title to manipulate these options. Figure 7.16 exemplifies a typical sorting interface.

7.16

Hotmail's in-box allows users to sort messages by sender, subject, date, or size. The sort key is changed by clicking a column title and indicated by a different cell background. The sort order is indicated by the arrow icon.

In this example, the column headers are displayed as links, and clicking one of the links sets the sort key to that column. The current sort key is indicated by altering the color of the cell containing the relevant column header. The sort order is similarly indicated by the arrow icon and can be reversed by clicking the column header again. Although the arrow icon can be useful to some users, it is often preferable to let the data speak for itself. If the list is sorted by a number, for example, the sort order might be perfectly obvious by simply looking at the data.

Perhaps the most difficult aspect of sorting is providing control over multiple sort keys. Although the application can often make intelligent choices for the secondary key—setting first name as the secondary key when last name is the primary key, for example—other situations require direct control for users. For example, users might want a list of addresses sorted by last name, then by city, and then by first name. Who knows? Perhaps they want to find all the Jobs in Palo Alto.

One possible solution is to derive a multikey sort by allowing users to successively click on multiple columns. In the preceding example, users would click on first name and the list would re-sort by first name. They would then click on city and the list would re-sort, with city as the primary key and first name as secondary. A third click on last name would again redraw the page, this time with last name as the primary key, city as the secondary key, and first name as the tertiary key.

A more common concern involves the relationship between sorting and paging. For example, if the list of data objects includes a paging mechanism and the user is on page 3 of 5, what happens when he or she changes the sort? The paging is reset and the user is taken to page 1.

The rational goes like this: Because the user was looking at multiple records when the sort was changed, there is no way to preserve the location when the data is re-sorted. If the list was sorted by last name and the screen was filled with Smiths, sorting the list by city will spread the Smiths across multiple pages, unless they all happen to live in the same place. As a result, the previous state of page 3 of 5 is meaningless. Therefore, the only logical option is to reset the paging mechanism and display the first page of the list.

The only exception is when the user has established a single-item selection, typically by clicking a radio button associated with an item. In this case, it is possible to determine the impact of the new sort and display the page containing the selected item.

Sorting is a basic but powerful feature of any interface involving lists of data objects. Although there are some finer points to be aware of, there is an established and useful convention in place for managing the sorting behavior of a Web application.

FILTERING

Filtering, another mechanism for providing control over the display of users' information, enables users to include or exclude items from the known set of records or data objects. Filtering is different from searching in that it doesn't allow users to specify criteria from the entire universe of options; rather, it allows them to narrow down the set of existing objects. As a result, filtering never results in a "nothing found" message. Similar to sorting and paging, filtering is integrated into the presentation of a list instead of functioning as a standalone mechanism. As shown in Figure 7.17, adding a menu to various column headers provides a simple but powerful interface for locating items. In this example, users can narrow the list by indicating a specific date range.

7.17

Note that the options in the menu are derived from the data being displayed. This prevents the "nothing found" state.

Title	Type	Date Year to date ⇕	Size	Actions
Lorem ipsum dolor sit amet	Euismod tincidunt	03.31.2001	150Kb	delete
Consectetuer	Laoreet euism	03.31.2001	230Kb	delete
Euismod tincidunt ut laoreet euismod tincidunt	Tincidunt	02.28.2001	113Kb	delete
Quis nostrud exercitation	Euismod	02.28.2001	90Kb	delete

In addition to the explicit form of filtering used in lists, many different forms of navigation also function as filters. When you visit an online store and select a category, you're filtering the complete set of available products by the category you've selected. For example, if you visit KennethCole.com, you'll see a variety of categories in the navigation. By selecting Men's Casual Shoes, you've told the application to filter the full set of products, displaying only the items that pass the filter of "men's casual shoes."

In some cases, however, a navigation path might still return a large collection of data objects. For example, navigating to the transaction history for your brokerage account might return a lists of dozens or even hundreds of transactions. In these cases, filtering is a useful interface mechanism for narrowing the list into a smaller and more manageable group.

Although paging is also a type of filtering mechanism, it allows users to filter based only on the order of items. Continuing the transaction history example, a more useful feature than simple paging would be a mechanism for filtering the list's contents by transaction type. This would allow users to quickly hone in on buy transactions, cash deposits, dividend reinvestments, and so forth. Although the same functionality could be accomplished by sorting the list by transaction type and then paging to the correct set of transactions, filtering by transaction type is a much more efficient and useful action.

In some situations filtering by multiple columns—such as transaction type and date in the transaction history example—is useful, but the additional complexity needed to support multi-field filtering is rarely worth the effort. Single-field filtering working in concert with single-key sorting typically provides enough functionality for most users and tasks.

SEARCHING

As one of the Web's most talked-about topics, search functionality is an important consideration for all types of Web sites, including Web applications. However, the challenge in creating and implementing an effective search function is largely one of requirements specifications and technical ·feasibility rather than pure interface design.

There are, however, a handful of guidelines and conventions worth keeping in mind:

- ☐ **Integrate search criteria with search results.** The controls for setting the search criteria should be replicated on the page containing the search results. This allows users to see the criteria that determined the current result set and gives them an instant way of performing a new search.

- ☐ **Provide a mechanism to begin a new search versus refining current search.** On the search results page, the controls for setting the search criteria should include an option allowing the user to either begin a new search or refine the current search.

- ☐ **Indicate the size of the found set.** The results page should contain a line of text indicating the number of items matching the current search criteria. This helps users decide whether to narrow their current search or try a different tack altogether.

☐ **Include basic and advanced search functions.** For many users, a simple text box offers enough search functionality. For example, eBay features a small search function on every page so that users can easily locate items whose titles match the criteria. This is augmented with an advanced search functionality allowing users to indicate very specific criteria, including price range, seller's name, selling region, and auction currency. By providing both forms of searching, eBay can readily accommodate all ranges of user sophistication and needs.

The importance and role of searching in the context of a Web application largely depends on the nature of the application. For applications such as address books or email, basic filtering and sorting will likely provide enough functionality. For applications connected to large volumes of content, such as online stores, searching is likely to be one of the most important and often-used features. As always, for any application, the range and sophistication of the functionality should be driven by the needs and goals of the primary persona.

SUMMARY

As the first layer of the Behavior tier, the Viewing and Navigation layer contains some of the most used and most common interface mechanisms on the Web. Because many of these behaviors, navigation in particular, also apply to content-based Web sites, there is a fairly evolved set of visual and interactive conventions that should be followed. These conventions include the following:

- **Goals of navigation.** A navigation scheme should help users understand three things: what type of application they're using, where else they can go, and what about the application is important.

- **Navigation mechanisms.** Although tabs and trees are the two most common forms of high-level navigation, they are both limited in scalability, hide choices from the user, and fail to support lateral navigation. The impact of these limitation can be mitigated but not eliminated.

- **Selection of data objects.** Two conventions are used to relate commands with data objects in a list. The convention of shared controls allows users to select multiple items at a time, but the convention of dedicated controls more tightly couples the objects and commands.

☐ **Viewing and manipulating lists.** There are four established interactive conventions useful for manipulating lists of data objects: column set selection, sorting, paging, and filtering. Working in concert, these mechanisms give users with the power and flexibility to modify the presentation of their data.

Looking forward to the next layer of the interface, Editing and Manipulation, the interaction issues become more complex and the conventions less well established.

"In saying what is obvious, never choose cunning.
 Yelling works better."

Cynthia Ozick
"We Are the Crazy Lady and Other Feisty Feminist Fables"
in *The First Ms. Reader*

8

EDITING AND MANIPULATION

**Using HTML Input Controls
to Accurately Capture Users' Data**

In contrast to the Viewing and Navigation layer, the interactions in the Editing and Manipulation layer result in persistent changes to the user's data. Owing to HTML's limited interactive vocabulary and the complex nature of these interactions, the Editing and Manipulation layer contains some of the most challenging and difficult aspects of the overall design. In addition, the technical limitations of Web applications are particularly visible in this layer. In many cases, the ideal level of sophistication and interactivity is too difficult or costly to achieve, resulting in a variety of implementation tradeoffs and compromises. Therefore, the appropriate and practical design solution requires a delicate balance between users' needs and technical feasibility.

This chapter approaches the problem from three different angles: the overall goals and purpose of forms, the proper use of HTML input controls, and how to combine input controls to facilitate complex interactions.

DESIGNING FORMS: THINKING IN TERMS OF THE WHOLE

Remember the chapter about structural models and the discussion about views and forms? When designing the structural model, the focus is on the flow of the site as a whole and how various types of pages contribute to that flow. After determining that a particular workflow requires a form, however, the challenge of the details still remains.

At the highest level, forms are essentially a mechanism for the application to ask the user questions: "When would you like to fly?," "What is your address?," and so forth. By contrast, views are essentially a mechanism for the user to do the asking: "What is the balance of my account?," "What do you have in the housewares department?," and so on.

As we all know, the rules of polite conversation are slightly different, depending on who's doing the talking and who's doing the listening. Therefore, the guidelines and conventions for form design are also slightly different from those for views.

PACE APPROPRIATELY

It's hard to hold a conversation with someone who talks too fast or asks 16 questions before giving you a chance to answer. The same is true whether you're interacting with another person or with a Web application. Therefore, determining the optimal length and density of information are two immediate concerns affecting the design of the overall form.

"We need to collect 67 fields of data. Should we create six really short forms, four medium-length forms, or one honkin' long form?"

The answer is, of course, one of balance. If the user needs to see all the options at the same time, the form will necessarily be long. Similarly, if choices in one part of the form determine the available choices in another part, the form will need to be divided into multiple pages. It's a bit like feeding babies; you want to be sure each bite is big enough to keep them interested, and you also want them to know what's coming for dessert. The balance, however, is to not stuff so much in their mouths at once that they spit it back up all over you.

When you're considering this question, a good place to start is a careful review of the functional requirements. Do you really need all those fields, or could some be eliminated? Are any fields optional? Can those fields be moved to another page or grouped together so as not to distract from the form's main elements? At a minimum, are required fields clearly differentiated from optional fields so that users can quickly identify what information they do and don't have to supply?

Complex forms can have so many input elements that the sheer volume of controls is overwhelming. Although it's acceptable to make users scroll, that doesn't give you a license to create a form of any length. Long forms are as painful and intimidating as a mortgage application and should generally be avoided. Imagine how many potential sellers get scared out of eBay simply because the form for listing auctions is so overwhelming (see Figure 8.1).

Long forms do, however, have two important advantages: efficiency and ease of error reporting. They are efficient in that they require only a single page load and they allow users to view the full set of options without additional navigation. They also enable errors to be detected, reported, and corrected in a single page. These advantages, however, bring with them the high cost of confusion, intimidation, and bewilderment, particularly for users new to the application.

8.1

The overwhelming quantity of options on eBay's selling form must intimidate any but the most determined of potential sellers.

In most cases, the better solution is to identify logical splits in the information so that the form can be presented in multiple pages. What could be presented as a single, lengthy form often turns out to be more manageable as a four-page wizard.

LIMIT NAVIGATION

As I mentioned in the context of structural models, Web applications are built from two fundamental page types: views and forms. Although a major function of views is navigation, such is not the case for forms. For all the reasons pointed out in Chapter 5, "The Structural Model: Understanding the Building Blocks of a Web Interface," the number of navigation options on form pages should be severely restricted. This applies to high-level navigation elements, such as tab bars or trees, as well as low-level navigation. If your form includes a navigational header or other ways to exit the form, at least some of your users are likely to fill out the form and then click one of the navigation paths without clicking the Submit button first. When this happens, it's impossible to know for sure if they meant to submit their changes but simply forgot to click the Submit button, or if they really meant to abandon the transaction. Even if the application is smart enough to trap every possible click out of the form and perform the submit behind the user's back, the basic problem remains: Exiting a form without using a command button creates ambiguity as to whether changes should be accepted or abandoned. Of course, you can't control the user exiting the form by way of the Back button, a bookmark, or typing in a new URL, but treating forms as modal dialog boxes with limited navigation and explicit Cancel and Submit buttons at least helps limit the problem.

INDICATE STATUS AND PROGRESS

If a form is part of a guide or a wizard, it should include clear indications of progress. If users are in step one of a seven-step process, it's only polite to let them know where they are and how many steps are left. Even when some steps are optional—choosing gift wrapping, for example—it is still important to inform users of the number of possible steps. The goal should always be to set appropriate expectations for users so that they feel some level of control over what is happening.

Figure 8.2 from the Opodo travel site is a great example of a progress indicator. Notice how the current step and all the possible steps are indicated in the progress bar.

8.2
A clear indication of where users are in the process sets appropriate expectations and keeps them in control of the experience.

SUPPORT INTELLIGENT FLOW AND KEYBOARD NAVIGATION

Well-designed forms also demonstrate balanced flow and intelligent ordering of elements. The user should be clearly drawn from the top of the form toward the bottom. Although a layout that draws the user across the page is possible, the established Web convention clearly favors vertical layouts.

In addition to enhancing their digestion of the experience, well-designed flow also enables users to quickly navigate through the form from their keyboards. This allows more sophisticated users to quickly progress through the form without having to move their hands back and forth between the keyboard and the mouse. For applications where users repeatedly interact with a form, this is particularly important. For example, the Compose Message page of an email application is a form users will interact with over and over again. Being able to use keyboard navigation to move through the form's input controls enhances the interaction's efficiency and speed. To maximize the impact, it is important to consciously design and specify the tab order rather than rely on the browser's default behavior.

PROVIDE MULTIPLE CLUES

Another key to form design is to make the use of input controls as clear as possible through the use of clues such as labels, examples, and sizing. One of the easiest things to get right—and wrong—is the label for an input control. Although the subject of labels is actually a component of Layer 9: Text, it is still worth noting here that a major factor in creating clear forms is labeling input fields appropriately.

Providing examples of the expected input when there might be confusion is important, too. For example, a text field for an email address should be labeled "Email" *and* should include a sample of the data, such as "yourname@address.com." Examples are especially important in Web applications because automatically formatting the data for the user is more difficult than in desktop applications. Without some indication of the correct format for the input, users can't be sure of precisely what's being requested. This is particularly true of dates, where so many different standards are in use.

Length is another critical clue you can provide for users. Because text fields can contain any type of text string or number, they offer few clues about the expected input and pose the biggest risk of input errors.

However, setting the length of text boxes to a dimension appropriate for the input is one clue you can easily embed in your design. For example, if you have a field for a five-digit zip code, don't use a text box 24 characters wide. By setting the text box to a size appropriate for the input length plus a few characters for editing, you give users another valuable clue to what you're asking.

Finally, indicating which fields are required and which are optional is often useful. The current convention on the Web is to add an asterisk to the field label of required fields. Unfortunately, this convention doesn't work very well when most of the fields are required because you end up with indicators at nearly every field.

Although it's possible to flip the logic and indicate the optional rather than the required fields, this runs counter to the established convention and can create confusion. Therefore, often the best solution is presenting required and optional fields in different areas of the page. Geography again proves to be an effective indicator of difference.

MAKE CHOICES VISIBLE

One of the major purposes of forms is to give users a way to view and indicate choices. To support this basic goal, it is important to make the choices as visible as possible. Although the demand for screen real estate is always present, radio buttons, check boxes, and list boxes are the best way to communicate choices. Menus offer the promise of visual efficiency, but they do so by hiding choices, increasing the amount of interaction and exploration required for the task. As a result, they should be used sparingly.

Figures 8.3 and 8.4 illustrate the tradeoffs in using menus. These figures compare the system configuration pages from the Dell Computer and Apple Computer online stores. Although the Apple design benefits from the increased visual economy of menus, the Dell site more effectively communicates the available choices, thus reducing the amount of exploration required of the user.

8.3

Apple Computer's system configuration page requires the user to explore the different menus to learn about the available options and prices.

8.4

Dell Computer's online store uses radio buttons instead of menus so that the available configuration options are instantly visible.

Well-designed forms are a delicate balance of many different factors: the length of the form, the density of the layout, the clear use of input controls, and the flow of information.

INPUT CONTROLS: PICKING THE RIGHT TOOL FOR THE JOB

Like any design medium, mastery of Web design in general and form design in particular requires a solid understanding of the available materials. In this case, that means understanding the input controls available in HTML. Although the vocabulary of radio buttons, check boxes, menus, text boxes, and list boxes might seem limited and simple, there are many subtle and not-so-subtle aspects of each control. The following sections explore each control in detail, including examples of their proper use.

CHECK BOXES

As in the printed forms from which they are derived, check boxes indicate whether an item is selected. Although they often appear in groups, check boxes do not necessarily have any relationship to one another. Correctly used, the options that check boxes present are independent choices that do not affect any other options on the form. The one exception is when a check box is nested with other input controls to indicate an explicit master-slave relationship. This style of nesting is used when an option has associated "sub-options." For example, an email application could have an option to check for spelling errors before sending a message. If the user selected the spell check option, there could be additional options to indicate which language to use, whether to ignore Internet addresses, and so forth.

Remember that check boxes, whether alone or in a group, don't require users to select anything at all. Unlike radio buttons or menus, this means check boxes typically allow for a "null" selection. However, in some situations, users can select one or more of the available options but are required to select at least one; in other words, a null selection is not valid. In these cases, check boxes can take on a hybrid radio button behavior by using JavaScript to ensure at least one check box is always selected. Figure 8.5 illustrates a common implementation of check boxes.

8.5

The use of radio buttons for the first two items under Position Data ensures that the user always has at least one of these fields selected, but allows every other field to be optionally selected.

RADIO BUTTONS

Radio buttons derived their name and behavior from the channel selectors on car stereos. In the physical world as well as the virtual one, radio buttons are used to select one, and only one, choice from an exclusive list of options.

Like check boxes, radio buttons are a fundamental element of all graphical user interfaces, including the Web. Although they have the distinct advantage of showing users all the possible options, they also have the disadvantage of scale. In other words, they don't.

Although radio buttons work great with five to seven options, if you go much past that, the required number of radio buttons simply creates too much visual clutter to be effective. In addition, if the number of options varies depending on the user's information or the application's state, radio buttons are a poor design choice because the increase or decrease in the size of the group introduces too much unpredictability into the layout. Because of those two limitations, radio buttons are most appropriate when they represent a fixed set of two to seven options.

Unlike check boxes, there is always an exclusive and dependent relationship between the radio buttons in a single group. Radio buttons are not solitary creatures and should never appear by themselves. Regardless of the size of the radio group, one and only one of the buttons is always selected. That means one of the radio buttons must always be selected by default.

Although some of the best designed applications fail to indicate a default selection within a radio group, doing so places the group in an unnatural state. For example, RedEnvelope's product-ordering pages include a two-button radio group to choose whether or not to wrap the item in its exclusive gift box (see Figure 8.6). However, the application does not indicate a default selection, so users are forced to make an explicit choice between the two radio buttons. This approach succeeds in making users more aware of the gift box option, but it does so by using radio buttons incorrectly and undoubtedly causes input errors.

8.6

No default selection is indicated for the two-item radio group—an improper use of radio buttons as input controls.

When there are only two options, using a single check box in place of two radio buttons is sometimes possible. For example, in a stock portfolio application that can include or exclude closed accounts, it is more compact to have a single check box labeled "Include Closed Accounts" rather than one radio button for include and another for exclude. However, this solution works only when the two options are obvious opposites of one another, such as include/exclude, on/off, or hide/show.

LIST BOXES

As you might guess from their name, list boxes are used to display lists of items in a fixed amount of space. List boxes can operate in a single or multi-select mode, essentially mimicking a list of radio buttons or check boxes, respectively.

Because they require less screen real estate than a comparable group of radio button or check boxes, list boxes are an effective solution when five or more options are being presented. In addition, because they take up a fixed amount of space, they are particularly effective when the number of options is unknown or variable.

The height of a list box is expressed in lines and is one of the few formatting options available. A reasonable question is "What is the optimal number of lines to display in a list box?" A slightly vague but accurate answer is "Tall enough to reveal a useful number of items but short enough to be visually manageable"—in other words, not too tall and not too short.

More precisely, you should aim for between five and seven lines, preferably five *or* seven lines. Lists with an odd number of items are generally easier to digest visually because one of the list items lies at the exact middle. As a result, it's easier to break the list into two smaller units that are quicker to scan.

The height of the list box not only affects the form's visual layout, but also gives the user an important clue about the list box contents. This is similar to how the length of a text field helps communicate the field's intended contents. A list box that displays three lines implies that the total number of items in the list is relatively short, whereas a list box with a height of seven items implies that the total list is much longer. In addition, the height conveys an impression of the list's importance, with bigger lists being perceived as more important choices than shorter lists.

In addition to the height of the list box, HTML also gives you control over the list box's behavior—specifically, whether the user can select multiple items or only a single item in the list. Put another way, does the list behave like a group of radio buttons or a group of check boxes?

The unfortunate answer is that multi-select list boxes cause a number of usability problems and are an unacceptable option for the majority of Web users. When the list box is in multi-select mode, users can make a multiple selection by holding down a modifier key (for example, the Ctrl key for Windows) while clicking additional items in the list box. However, not all users understand or are even aware of this behavior.

It is also common for a selection to include items spread out across the list. As a result, users have to scroll through the list to view the full selection, often losing track of what is and isn't selected. Depending on the selection and the scroll position, the entire selection might be displayed outside the list's visible area, giving the erroneous impression that nothing is selected.

Suffice it to say that multi-select list boxes are riddled with opportunity for error and misunderstanding. If the situation calls for a multiple selection from a long list, there are better solutions than a multi-select list box.

A final point is that list boxes, like a group of radio buttons, should always offer a meaningful default. Similarly, if a null selection is allowed, the list box should contain an option labeled "None" instead of being displayed without a selection.

MENUS

If you compressed a list box so that it displayed only one item at a time, you would end up with a menu. Despite the differences in behavior and appearance, menus provide the same function as list boxes and radio buttons: making an exclusive choice from a list of multiple options.

The primary advantage of menus is visual efficiency. In addition to their ability to present a large number of options in a small space, their "now you see it, now you don't" behavior makes them particularly appropriate when the number of options is variable.

Unfortunately, menus have one major weakness: They're hard to use. Picking an item from a menu is one of the most complicated mouse operations there is. Selecting an option from a menu requires two clicks, a complex click-and-drag movement, or a combination of keys from the keyboard. To make matters worse, the click target for an item is fairly small, and the error recovery is zilch. If you pick the wrong item, you're all the way back to square one. Finally, the menu behavior hides options from users and gives them few clues about the menus contents. As a result, menus are not only an exercise in physical dexterity, but also a challenge to understanding and recall.

Despite these caveats, however, menus still occupy an important position in the interactive landscape. The challenge is knowing when and where to use them so as to minimize their disadvantages.

In addition to the ever-present concern for how all the form's elements work together, there are two other considerations specific to menus: how many items it contains and the default selection. Because menus can be difficult to navigate, the number of options should generally be kept short. Although there's no hard-and-fast rule, a list of more than 15 items is hard to look at, and anything north of 21 is difficult to use. These limits can be expanded, however, if the contents of the menu are sorted and well understood by the target user group. For example, a menu containing the 50 U.S. states might be a reasonable solution for a site catering to users in the United States, particularly if the state choice was optional. A list of 50 hotel locations, on the other hand, would not be appropriate because users would be unfamiliar with the list's content and would have to read through each option one by one.

The second consideration when using a menu is indicating a default selection. In many cases, an application won't have the necessary information to provide an appropriate default, so the real question becomes "What is the most effective way to communicate that the user needs to make a choice?" Two methods are commonly used in such situations: Don't indicate a default so the menu is displayed without a selection, or select a dummy item labeled "Select…."

Because the fundamental behavior of a menu is to indicate a selection, not having a selection is an invalid state for the control. Therefore, the optimal solution is to select a dummy item labeled "Select…". Even better is to reference the menu's contents in the selection—for example, "Select State…."

Menus are perhaps the most overused and inappropriately used control on the Web. Of course, they're also one of the most useful. Before you place them all over your forms, however, be sure you understand and accept the usability problems they're likely to introduce.

TEXT BOXES

Text boxes are used to capture strings of text, numbers, or both. They are the most straightforward input control from a behavior perspective, but because there is no real control over what users type in them, they are also a significant source of input errors. To help alleviate this risk, giving users multiple clues about the correct input is essential. As discussed earlier, these clues include clear labels, sample text, useful defaults, and appropriate sizing.

In addition to width, HTML can also specify whether a text box should display one or more lines of text. Although most text boxes display a single line of text, in some situations—the body of an email, for example—a multiline text box is useful. Whatever the case, it still comes down to setting the text box to a size appropriate for the input.

BUTTONS

The final commonly used input control is the button. From a technical perspective, buttons come in two basic flavors: Submit and Cancel. Submit buttons send a form's contents to the server for processing, and Cancel buttons throw out a form's contents and return users to the page from whence they came. From a user's perspective, however, a button's function is known by its name.

Because there is no control over a button's appearance, most sites use images in place of standard HTML buttons. Unfortunately, some sites also use links in place of standard buttons. The two objects have different uses, however, and should not be used interchangeably. Although there are rare exceptions, in general, links should be used solely as navigational devices, not to submit or save information. Similarly, buttons should be used only to initiate commands, not as navigation. Figure 8.7 illustrates mixing up the use of links and buttons.

Although HTML provides only a small set of input controls (summarized in Table 8.1), don't let the limited vocabulary dissuade you from creating sophisticated interactions. It's true that a more dynamic set of controls would make some operations easier to design and use, but the set that *is* available can generally get the job done.

8.7
In this example from Yahoo!, the designers have inappropriately used links in place of buttons.

Table 8.1 Standard HTML Interface Controls

Name	Purpose
Check box	Select none, one, or many from a fixed list of options, preferably seven or fewer.
Radio button	Select one and only one from a fixed list of options, preferably 7 or fewer.
List box (single select)	Select one and only one from a list of any size. Also used for lists containing an unknown number of options.
Menu	Select one and only one from a list, preferably fewer than 25 items. Also used for lists containing an unknown number of options.
Text box	Input a string of any length.
Button	Perform an action or a command.
File	Upload a file.

COMMON INTERACTION PROBLEMS AND SOLUTIONS

Lest you conclude there's nothing more to forms than a series of independent, isolated input controls, this section focuses on common interaction problems requiring multiple input controls working together. These problems include the following interactions:

☐ Selecting a single item from a small, medium, or large number of options

☐ Selecting multiple items from a large set of options

☐ Selecting a date

Although it would be impossible to anticipate or explore every interaction problem, the analysis of these problems should give you an understanding of how to approach and solve complex interaction problems in general.

PICKING A SINGLE ITEM FROM A LIST

One of the most common input operations in a Web application requires the user to select a single option from a list. Depending on the situation, the user might need to select an item from a list of 2, 20, 200, or even 2,000 possible options. Regardless, the interaction requirement remains the same: an exclusive choice from an exhaustive list.

There are three basic solutions in these situations, depending on the number of options and whether the list of options is fixed or variable. The simplest solution relies on a group of radio buttons and is appropriate for a small, static number of options. The second solution, appropriate for a large set of options, uses a list box. The last solution uses a menu and is appropriate for situations somewhere in between.

Small Set of Choices

The least complex incarnation of the single-selection problem requires the user to select an item from a fixed small set of options, generally between two and seven. There are two reasonable solutions in this situation: a group of radio buttons or a menu.

Although many designers faced with this problem use menus in place of radio buttons, the advantage of visual efficiency that menus offer comes at the price of hidden options and usability concerns. Although this may be an acceptable tradeoff for seldom used features or very lengthy forms, as a general rule, options should not be hidden from users. Menus hide options; radio buttons don't. Call it a guideline, call it a rule, call it a suggestion: Whenever possible, use radio buttons instead of menus.

When the number of choices depends on the user's data or the application's state, however, this choice isn't possible. For example, a stock portfolio application typically allows users to create custom views of their portfolios, displaying the list of views as a menu in the main portfolio page. The menu is an appropriate solution in this case because it enables the page layout to remain consistent regardless of the number of views the user creates.

Online clothing stores are an instructive example of a design that uses menus when a group of radio buttons would be more appropriate. For most clothing articles, users have to indicate both a size and a color. This is typically handled as two independent selections and presented as two different menus. However, size and color are not independent selections. Rather, they are two distinct characteristics that combine to describe a single item. In addition, the number of options in either control is typically fewer than seven.

Figure 8.8 shows a typical solution that uses menus for selecting clothing size and color. Figure 8.9 shows an alternative design, with text links in place of the menus. Compared to the standard menu solution, the text link solution has these key advantages:

- **Visibility of choices.** The full set of choices is instantly visible without the user having to explore the contents of one or more menus.
- **Reduced click count.** The click count has been reduced by substituting a single link for the two menu choices and the Add to Cart button. An action that took three clicks—select size, select color, and add to cart—has been reduced to one.

□ **Simple mechanism for communicating unavailable size/ color combinations.** This solution easily handles unavailable size/color combinations. By contrast, the menu required the user to first select the size/color combination before the interface reported whether it was available.

□ **Ease of use.** As an interface control, text links are physically easier to operate than menus, so this solution is easier to use than a solution relying on menus.

As is typically the case, however, this solution also comes with some clear disadvantages. Determining whether the following disadvantages are a reasonable tradeoff compared to the advantages is no simple question:

□ **Limited scalability.** Although this solution works well in the illustrated situation, if the number of sizes or colors grew past seven, the size of the matrix would be so large that it would overwhelm the page.

□ **No clear Add to Cart action.** The most suspicious part of this design is removing the Add to Cart button. Although the text link is a reasonable way to add an item, the interaction goes against convention and could easily confuse users.

□ **Difficult error recovery.** By equating a link with the Add to Cart action, the solution does not have a simple method for users to review their selection before adding it to their Shopping Carts. This problem is compounded by the solution's inability to give users a way to recover from an incorrect selection, other than deleting the incorrect item from their Shopping Carts.

One way around these disadvantages would be to replace the text links with radio pictures, which would enable the Add to Cart button to be added, thus eliminating the two major problems. However, the visual weight of a radio picture would likely make the design even less scalable.

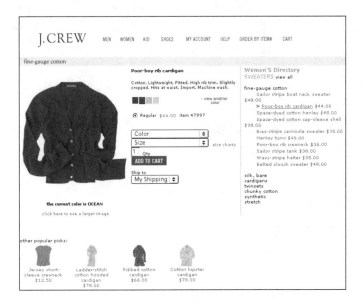

8.8

To purchase an item, the user has to navigate both the size and color menus, optionally indicate a quantity and ship-to address, and click the Add to Cart button.

8.9

In this alternative design, size and color menus have been replaced with a two-dimensional matrix of links.

In addition to their standard representation as circles, radio buttons can be represented as more meaningful icons. An iconic presentation of radio buttons is known as *radio pictures*. Although the two presentations are functionally identical (an exclusive choice from an exhaustive list of options), radio pictures are more visually efficient. A common example of a solution using radio pictures is the left, right, center, and justified text alignment icons in many desktop applications.

Other changes to the original design include eliminating the Quantity text box and placing the Ship To menu at the top of the shopping area. Because users rarely order multiple quantities of the exact same article of clothing—socks, T-shirts, and underwear being exceptions—the quantity option has been moved from the main product page to the Shopping Cart. In addition, because the Ship to option is less frequently used, it has been placed in a less visually prominent position.

Whether this solution represents a definitive, meaningful improvement over the original is a question best left to a usability study. Clearly the design represents a departure from convention—a move that should always be viewed with skepticism. In the perpetual search for improvement, however, examining the conventional solution in light of alternatives is always useful and often educational.

Medium or Unknown Number of Choices

With more choices—7 to 21, give or take—a different approach is required. The use of radio buttons is ruled out, thanks to the sheer number of options. The remaining options are a menu or a scrolling list box, although the former is suspect owing to its ever-present usability problems.

Still, menus do have their place, and Figure 8.10 is one of them. This page from The Motley Fool's portfolio tracker allows users to create a customized view of their portfolio. Instead of starting each new view from scratch, users can base a view on an existing one by selecting it from a menu.

8.10

The "Start From a View" option is an appropriate use of a menu because the control is not required and because the number of choices is variable but unlikely to be more than 20.

Three main factors justify the use of a menu in this situation:

☐ **Unknown number of items.** Depending on how many views the user has set up, the list could have 3 to 33+ different options. Because of this variability, radio buttons are inappropriate.

☐ **Small to medium range of options.** The number of options in the list, although variable, is unlikely to be more than 20. After all, how many different portfolio views is one user likely to create? With a range of 2 to 20, the number of options is reasonably manageable with a menu.

☐ **The control is optional.** Users don't have to select an existing view as a starting point. Therefore, the control doesn't warrant the visual weight and prominence of a scrolling list box.

In situations calling for the user to select a single item from a medium or an unknown number of choices, the challenge is ultimately one of balance. Although a menu or scrolling list box can be used, the optimal solution is the one that best allocates screen real estate given the situation.

Large Number of Choices

A third type of design challenge involves selecting a single item from a large list. What constitutes "large" is open to interpretation, but generally speaking, it's a number north of 21. In these cases, radio buttons and menus are ruled out by the volume of options. This leaves scrolling list boxes as the only viable alternative.

An educational point is found on almost every address entry form on the Web. The conventional design for address forms incorrectly uses a menu as the input control for U.S. states and Canadian provinces. The solution requires the user to navigate a menu of 50+ items, even though the same input could be captured with a scrolling list box (see Figure 8.11). Granted, the list box requires more screen real estate, but that cost is outweighed by the usability benefits of revealing all the options and providing an easier-to-use control.

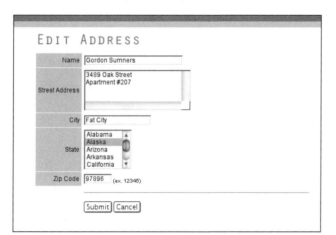

8.11

This figure illustrates the use of a scrolling list box as the input control for U.S. states and Canadian provinces.

The use of a scrolling list box has been extended in Figure 8.12 to demonstrate how the contents of an especially long set of choices can be filtered by using an additional control. In this example, the standard list of U.S. states and Canadian provinces has been divided into two smaller groups. This style of interaction works well when the list can be filtered in two to four different ways. With a larger set of filter choices, a menu can be substituted for the radio buttons.

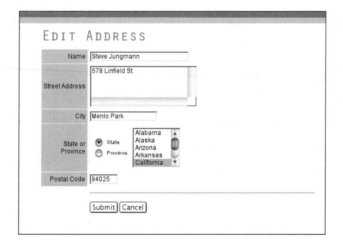

8.12

This example shows how radio buttons can be used as a filtering mechanism for a long list of choices.

When users are required to select a single item from an exhaustive list of options, there are two key considerations: the number of options and whether the number of options varies. Although radio buttons, menus, and scrolling list boxes are all acceptable solutions, the ultimate challenge is to find a balance between the need to make all the options visible, the ease of use of the input controls, and the visual weight of the different interface elements.

Picking Multiple Items from a List

A second common interaction problem is the ever-present "picking multiple items from an exhaustive list." Although multiple selection and single selection pose similar design challenges, the two are far from identical. In both cases, the elements supporting the interaction have to indicate the list of options as well as the current selection. For single–select controls, such as menus and list boxes, one interface element serves to simultaneously indicate the selection and the available options. With multiple selections, however, the interface has to communicate a selection involving any combination of options and, as a result, a different set of interaction mechanisms is required.

In situations calling for a relatively small number of choices, the issues parallel single-selection problems. Check boxes are substituted for radio buttons, and everybody moves on. As you might expect, however, that simplicity evaporates if the number of choices is variable or expands much beyond seven choices.

One potential solution for multiple selections is a scrolling list box in multiple-select mode. In this mode, users select multiple items by holding down a modifier key while simultaneously clicking items in the list. Unfortunately, multi-select list boxes have a host of usability and feedback problems, not the least of which is that many users don't even realize they exist.

An alternative solution uses two single-select list boxes working in concert with two or more command buttons. In this solution, one control contains the possible options, and the other contains the currently selected items. In addition, a group of command buttons is used to move items back and forth between the lists. Figure 8.13 from Evite shows a good example of this solution.

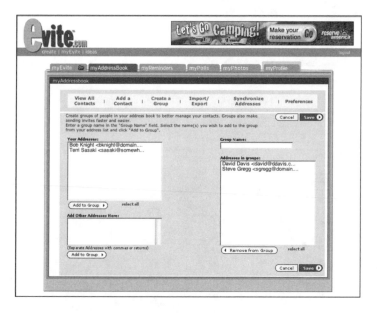

8.13
Evite's address book supports selecting multiple items through the use of a list box containing possible options and another containing the selected items. Items are moved between the lists by clicking a command button.

Harkening back to the days of Macintosh O/S 1.0, this motif is some-times called "font/DA mover" or, in the more modern vernacular, "source/target list." Although this solution requires JavaScript, it is almost always the preferred alternative, certainly warranting the extra code and effort.

A redesign of the Edit View form from Yahoo!'s portfolio tracker illustrates how source/target lists can clean up a complicated multiple-selection problem. Figure 8.14 from Yahoo! is used to customize users' views of their stock portfolio. In this implementation, the user can customize up to 16 columns, each containing one of 76 different options.

8.14

Yahoo! portfolio tracker allows users to customize the view of their portfolio. The design relies on 16 menus, each containing 76 elements.

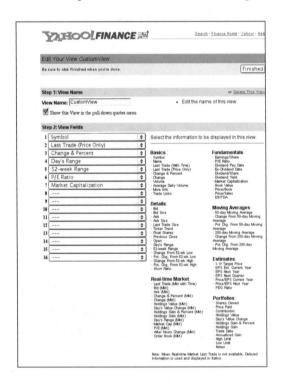

The most conspicuous problem with this design is the use of a menu containing 76 items—a poor showing in the usability race when there's only one such menu, much less 16 of them.

Aside from their function as selection mechanisms, the menus are also used to control the order of the columns. Unfortunately, although the menus are stacked vertically, the top-to-bottom ordering is translated to a left-to-right ordering when the view is being used. In addition to the oddity of this vertical to horizontal mapping, the use of menus as an ordering mechanism has another problem. Because the design doesn't provide a way to insert a column, users are required to change multiple menus if they want to place a data element between two existing elements. For example, if a user wanted to insert a new data element in column 2 but wanted to retain the order of the next 12 columns, he or she would have to reselect the elements for columns 2 through 13—a tedious task, even without 76 elements in each menu.

Finally, because there is no interactivity between the menus, this design does nothing to prevent users from displaying the same data element in more than one column.

On the positive side, the page includes a categorized list of all 76 possible data elements. By including this reference, the design mitigates some of the problems created by hiding the options.

Working backward from the implemented design, you can infer the following requirements:

- Limit the number of columns to 16.
- Do not use JavaScript or DHTML.
- Any element can appear in any column.
- Data elements can be custom sorted.

With these requirements in hand, there are a few alternatives worth exploring.

Option 1: Check Boxes

As shown in Figure 8.15, one alternative is to replace the menus with check boxes. Although this approach doesn't satisfy all the requirements, it does have some important advantages—as well as disadvantages—to consider:

Advantages

☐ Obvious presentation of available choices

☐ Simple selection interaction

☐ Prevents users from adding the same data element twice

Disadvantages

☐ No ready mechanism for limiting the selection to 16 data elements, thus requiring an error notification if more than 16 elements are selected

☐ No support for column ordering

Although the first disadvantage could be handled through an error alert, addressing the second would necessitate a reconsideration of the requirements.

Because the data elements can be grouped together in a meaningful way, the lack of support for column ordering might not be an issue. The nature of the data elements is such that determining a prescribed order that addresses most user's needs is possible. Ultimately, the questions rests on whether column ordering is essential to the primary persona and, if so, at what cost?

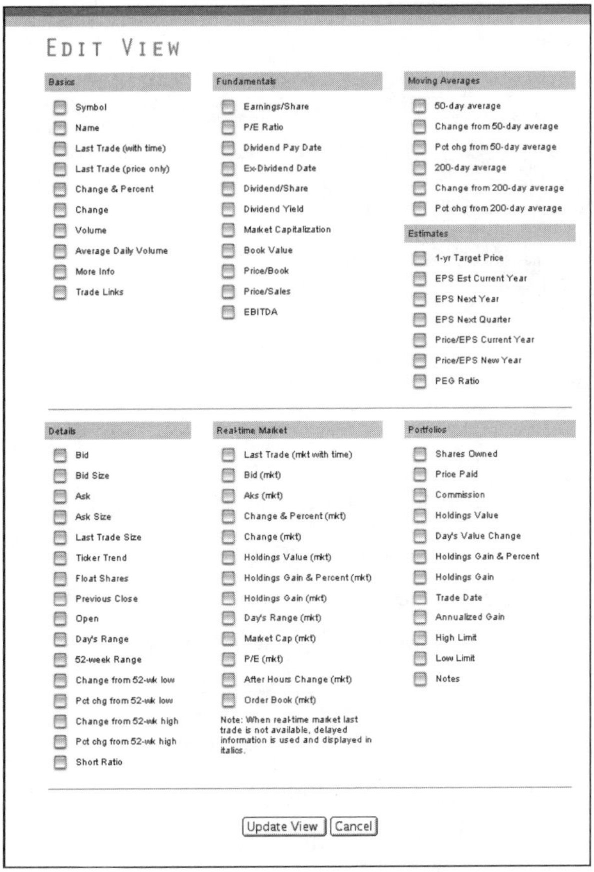

8.15

This redesign of Yahoo!'s Edit View page does not support customizing the order of the columns, but it simplifies the interaction in the original design.

Option 2: Source/Target List

A second alternative, relying on a source/target list, is shown in Figure 8.16. This option includes a source list containing the full complement of data elements and a target list containing the elements currently selected. This design also includes buttons for moving items in and out of the selection and for reordering the selected items. The combination of two list boxes and four buttons provides all the functionality of the original design but without the complexity of 16 menus.

8.16

This design simplifies the interaction by reducing the number of input controls needed. It also enables users to reorder data elements easily.

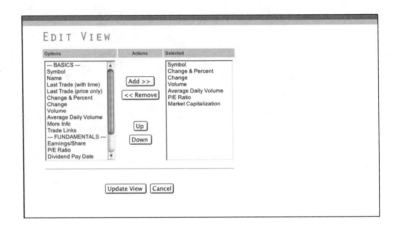

Compared to the other alternatives, this solution has the following advantages and disadvantages:

Advantages

☐ Clear communication of the current selection

☐ Easy reordering of selected items

☐ Simplified interaction using fewer input controls

☐ Visually compact and approachable

☐ Depending on the preferred use, elements can or cannot be added more than once

Disadvantages

☐ No obvious way to limit the selection to 16 items

☐ The scrolling list cannot display all options in a single glance

☐ Requires JavaScript

A variation of this design could integrate a menu as a filtering mechanism for the source list box. This would limit the number of items displayed in the list at any given time and help users locate specific items quickly.

Like the check box alternative, because this design requires JavaScript, it does not fully satisfy all the requirements. However, the improvement in the user experience is again enough to question the requirement.

As these examples show, designing an interface that allows users to select multiple items is no trivial matter. The unique environment of Web applications requires creative use of multiple input controls and a thorough understanding of the product's requirements and target users.

SELECTING DATES

The selection of dates, a problem found in many Web applications, is another complex interaction problem worth exploring. Because HTML doesn't provide any input controls specifically designed to select dates, Web applications are left to use the standard set of input controls to accomplish this rather complex task. Unfortunately, the Web's lack of interface standards is nowhere more apparent than in this particular problem. The following sections analyze the most common solutions to this problem with attention to the unique pros and cons of each.

Interface Requirements for Date Input

Not surprisingly, the purpose of a date input control is to enable users to specify a date—that is, the combination of a month, a day, and a year. In a desktop application, this is typically accomplished with a simple text box or some sort of custom UI widget. In both cases, the application has special logic allowing it to instantly recognize and report invalid dates.

With those controls as a baseline, it is reasonable to assume the following requirements for a proper date input control:

- □ **Provide context.** Where appropriate, the input control should place a date in context. A travel itinerary or future appointment should be displayed in the context of a calendar, for example, but a user's birth date or credit card expiration should not.
- □ **Prevent errors.** The input control should prevent users from selecting an invalid, a nonexistent, or an incorrect date.
- □ **Be efficient**. The input control should be quick, efficient, and simple to operate.

Although Web applications are a different medium from desktop applications, these basic requirements remain the same.

Text Boxes

As shown in Figures 8.17 and 8.18, the option at the low end of the sophistication scale relies on a single text box or a group of text boxes for date input.

8.17

Although a single text box is a simple approach, it fails to offer any context or do anything to reduce errors.

Select Date [　　　　　] example: July 12, 1965

8.18
Although a group of text boxes does not address all the short-comings of the single text box, at least it removes the question of the correct order for the three pieces of data.

Regardless of whether the design uses one text box or three, this approach fails to meet any of the requirements. Although the single text box solution offers an example of the correct date format, nothing in the interface forces the user to follow it. By contrast, the solution with multiple text boxes more clearly communicates and enforces the required format. From a technical perspective, a solution using only text boxes represents the least amount of effort, but the obvious usability shortcomings generally make it a poor choice.

Group of Menus

The most common interface for selecting dates relies on a series of menus, one each for the month, the day, and the year (see Figure 8.19). Despite the popularity of this design, however, it is not without substantial usability issues.

8.19
Despite its widespread use, this solution fails to provide context or prevent input errors.

As an improvement on the text box approach, menus help reduce some input errors by ensuring the following:

☐ Values are entered in a controlled manner.

☐ The application clearly knows which input value represents the month, day, and year.

☐ The month, day, and year values are limited to an appropriate range.

Although the design could support logic dependencies between the day and month menus—for example, limiting the options for day based on the selected month to prevent the user from selecting February 30—these dependencies have their own host of usability concerns and engineering complexities. As a result, most applications that use this motif rely on server-side validation to confirm whether the indicated date is valid. Although this approach helps limit input errors, it does not completely eliminate them.

Another concern is the failure of this solution to provide context for the date. By simply reflecting a disembodied date with no reference to a monthly or weekly calendar, the solution doesn't communicate the date's relationship to past or future time. In some cases, this relationship is not important—credit card expiration dates, for example—but in others, such as travel itineraries, it's critical for the user to quickly understand that the 15th is next Tuesday.

Two factors account for this solution's popularity: conservation of screen space and technical expediency. In some situations, these advantages clearly outweigh any of the disadvantages; in others, however, a more sophisticated solution is necessary.

Calendars

Another solution for handling date input relies on a calendar as the primary interface element. Although it's no great intellectual leap to conclude that calendars offer an easy-to-use input control, many applications don't use them because of the additional technical overhead. Of the solutions described so far, however, the calendar is the only one to satisfy the two fundamental requirements: context and error prevention.

Unfortunately, providing calendar-style input is no simple engineering task in an HTML environment. Although it is possible to create a calendar with nothing but standard HTML, changing the calendar's displayed time frame typically requires a trip to the server and page regeneration. For multiple date entries—travel reservations, for example—this behavior renders calendars disruptive and unwieldy. For a single date input, however, a fully HTML-based calendar, such as the one Evite uses (see Figure 8.20), can be a useful approach.

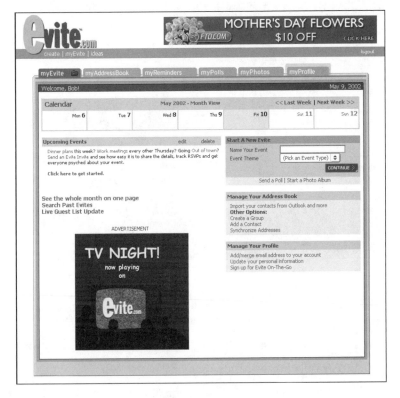

8.20

This page from Evite uses a calendar built with HTML. Clicking a date creates a new invitation for the indicated date.

Instead of placing the calendar directly in the layout, another common solution is displaying the calendar in a secondary browser window. Figure 8.21 from JetBlue exemplifies this approach. From the flight search page, the user can click the calendar icon, opening the calendar in a new window. When the user clicks a date, the calendar window closes and main page is updated to reflect the selected date.

8.21

The flight search page includes typical menus as well as a calendar option.

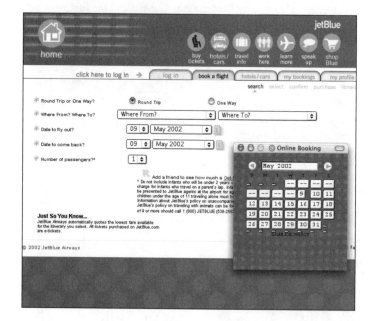

Of the options discussed so far, this is the only one that satisfies the requirements for providing context and preventing errors. Unfortunately, it also compromises this functionality by introducing a secondary window and thereby violating the basic page model of the Web.

Another solution worth consideration also relies on a calendar motif, but instead of opening the calendar in a secondary window, it is integrated directly into the form. As shown in Figure 8.22, the Broadmoor Hotel's reservation page includes two one-month calendars as well as links for changing the month being displayed. When the user selects a date, its color changes to white. In addition, after two dates have been indicated, the dates falling between the two are also highlighted, giving the user a clear, obvious way of viewing the date range of his or her stay.

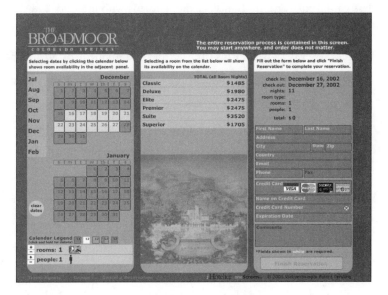

8.22
The Broadmoor's reservation form uses two monthly calendars appropriately integrated into the reservation form.

Although this implementation requires additional engineering effort and image production, it is clearly a superior design from a user's perspective. It not only satisfies the requirements for providing context and preventing errors, but it does so without introducing usability problems.

Owing to the transaction orientation of many Web applications, selecting and entering dates are common interactions. Unfortunately, the requirements for an ideal date interface dictate significant design and engineering efforts. The results of this effort, however, are more control for the user and fewer errors—two benefits worthy of substantial effort.

SUMMARY

In most applications, the number of form pages is dwarfed by the volume of view pages. A lower number, however, should not be assumed to mean less complexity or importance. Creating forms with integrity and elegance is one of the most difficult and important challenges of the interface design process. Well-designed forms are a critical component of an intelligent, enjoyable, and satisfying user experience. By contrast, poorly designed forms inevitably lead to user frustration, confusion, and disappointment.

If resources are limited and time is in short supply, forms are perhaps the single most important area in which to focus your efforts. Here are a few of the key design principles to keep in mind:

- **Pick an appropriate pace.** Do not overwhelm users with long forms that intimidate. Likewise, do not insult them with needlessly simple forms that fail to contain a task of satisfying dimension.

- **Limit navigation.** In general, the navigational paths out of a form should be limited to explicit Submit and Cancel actions. Eliminating navigational elements from a form focuses users on the task at hand and prevents them from exiting the form without definitively saving their changes.

- **Provide multiple clues.** A well-designed form takes advantage of as many different communication channels as possible. Clear labeling of fields, appropriate sizing of text boxes, examples of correct input, and obvious indications of required versus optional fields are all important clues to a form's use.

☐ **Make choices visible.** Forms should not be an advanced version of hide and seek. Relevant choices should be clearly visible at all times. Users should not be required to explore an interface to accomplish basic tasks.

A theme running throughout this chapter has been the importance of error prevention. Although a perfect world would be free of all such user or application errors, the world of Web applications is far from that ideal. In the next chapter, you'll turn from the subject of form design to the subject of help, status, and alerts.

"Accidents happen now and again."

Thomas the Tank Engine

9

USER ASSISTANCE

**Communicating with Users
Through Help, Status, and Alerts**

The third and final layer of the Behavior tier, User Assistance, enables the application to communicate with the user about problems, errors, and conditions. In short, the purpose of the User Assistance layer is to mop up the mess when users find themselves confused or when the application doesn't work as planned. Unfortunately, like an infant at an interview, the User Assistance layer is almost always about interruption.

The components of the User Assistance layer can be divided into two basic groups: help and alerts. In the context of a Web application, help provides a means for the user to ask the application a question: "Hey! How do I make you do what I want you to do?" or "What do you mean by 'obfuscate'?" Alerts, on the other hand, provide a channel for the application to communicate important news to the user: "Hey! I can't make sense of the information you just gave me," or "Are you really sure you want me to do that?"

In a perfect world, all applications would have an interface that was obvious in all interactions, accommodating of any error, and instantaneously responsive. There would simply be no need for the User Assistance layer.

However, as you have likely noticed, our world remains a few stones short of perfection. Therefore, we are left to explore how help and alerts can give users the additional information and control they need.

HELP

Of this you can be certain: Nobody reads online help. Pity the cadre of writers saddled with the unenviable task of composing manuals and help pages that are published but seldom read. But of course, there's the rub: It's not that they're *never* read; it's that they're *seldom* read. Like lifeboats on a cruise ship, online help requires effort to build, takes up precious space on the main deck, and, it is hoped, never gets used.

Clicking help is not the first action users take when they run into trouble; more likely, it's going to be the last. And because it's a bastion of last resort, meaningful and useful help is critical. You don't want the passengers to start lowering the lifeboats, only to discover they aren't seaworthy. Tempting as it might be to eliminate or skimp on help, you do so at the risk of leaving your users to drown in a storm.

Help comes in a variety of shapes and forms, some more elaborate, more appropriate, and more helpful than others. If you weren't able to establish clear requirements for help at the beginning of your project, you need to revisit your personas, look through your usability results, and honestly assess your design's simplicity and clarity. This will help you determine the appropriate balance between the substantial implementation costs and the potential user benefits of online help.

TYPES OF HELP

The type of help in Web applications comes in four varieties, each addressing certain questions:

Conceptual: "What does this thing do?"

Procedural: "How does this thing do what I want it to do?"

Definitional: "What does this thing mean by...?"

Instructional: "What does this thing want me to do now?"

Depending on the specific requirements and audience, one or more of these types of help can be appropriate. As one of the longer-lived, more stable user experience elements, a variety of conventions have been developed around help. Like the real-world reference books listed in Table 9.1, each type of help has its own advantages, disadvantages, uses, and conventions.

Table 9.1 Types of Help

Type	Related Reference Book
Conceptual help	Textbook
Procedural help	Encyclopedia
Definitional help	Dictionary
Instructional help	Footnote or legend

Conceptual Help: Help as an Online Manual

If an application is particularly complex or if users need to understand certain concepts or abstractions before they can be productive, you need to provide some level of conceptual help. Although it's hard to imagine a first-time user making sense of Illustrator or Visual BASIC without some exposure to the manual, it's equally hard to imagine users needing an education in a Web application before they can get to work. Web applications simply haven't attained the complexity of desktop applications; therefore, they don't generally require conceptual help. There are, however, exceptions.

Depending on the target user group, enterprise applications, such as customer relationship management, purchasing, or content management, can require conceptual help. Similarly, some consumer applications might also require conceptual help. For example, although photo-processing sites are generally easy for technologically sophisticated users, less-experienced users might question the site's purpose and utility. The knowledge required to upload images and order prints through a Web application is a far cry from what's required to use a one-hour photo store. For all but true technophiles, the steps, technologies, devices, and companies involved can be bewildering. In this case, help that explains each concept and step could be extremely useful.

The purpose of *conceptual help* is to explain how an application's features and commands are used to accomplish specific tasks. The explanations are structured so that the knowledge gained in one "chapter" is required to make sense of the next. As a result, users must read the material in a linear manner, from start to finish. For example, if you've read this book in the linear manner in which it was intended, you understand the statement, "Manuals are fundamentally a subjective hierarchy." If, however, you've been skipping around willy-nilly, you probably have no idea what that means. To accommodate this linear style of communication, conceptual help is best delivered following the model of printed manuals and textbooks.

Unfortunately for Web application users, the experience of reading lengthy written material on a computer is not ideal. A useful way around this problem is to deliver conceptual help by using Adobe System's Portable Document Format (PDF). The PDF technology converts a document from any application to a file that can be viewed and printed on most computing platforms with Adobe's Acrobat Reader. PDFs retain the original document's formatting and typography and can also contain hyperlinks to other locations on the Web or within the PDF. Although PDFs require the Acrobat Reader application or plug-in, both come installed on new computers and are also available as free downloads from Adobe.

As you can see in Figure 9.1, the big advantage of PDFs is that they provide a single file that can be printed and read, just like a typical software manual. Depending on the situation, it might be much easier for users to follow along with a printed document as they perform tasks on the computer instead of trying to manage the multiple windows required of a purely online help system.

On the downside, PDF files sometimes require a lengthy download. In addition, unless Adobe has slipped in some new fancy code, there is no way to open the PDF to a particular page. This means your PDFs can't provide context-sensitive help—certainly a big loss for users.

Regardless of delivery mechanism, conceptual help is appropriate only if you need to educate your users in a linear, structured manner.

9.1

The help system for
Salesforce.com includes
a PDF version of its user manual.
This 257-page manual can be
printed or viewed online.

Procedural Help: Help as Q&A

Perhaps the most widely used form of online help, *procedural help* follows the model of question-and-answer. This form of help presents information in discrete chunks designed to be consumed in any quantity or sequence fitting the user's needs. Compared to the systematic rigidity of a manual, Q&A help borders on ordered chaos.

One common expression of procedural help goes by the acronym FAQ (frequently asked questions). FAQs typically include an index page of questions, with links to a page containing the answer. Figure 9.2 is a typical example of an FAQ page.

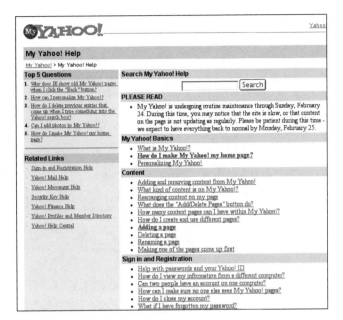

9.2
Yahoo! uses a typical FAQ-style help system. Note the Top 5 Questions area at the top left.

The problem with many FAQs is that each answer page is often a navigational cul-de-sac. This forces users to return to the main index page if they have another question or didn't get a satisfying answer. On many sites, the navigational dead-end problem is solved by opening the answer page in a small, secondary browser window. Unfortunately, this works only if the main FAQ index page appears in the main browser window—a bad choice because it requires users to flip back and forth between the two browser windows for basic navigation. A better use of the secondary window approach can be seen at Schwab.com. The Schwab site presents help information in a small helper window, but the window is opened by clicking a common help link appearing on every page in the application. Best of all, the link is context sensitive to the user's current page (see Figure 9.3).

9.3

The designers of Schwab's site chose to implement help in a secondary browser window that can be accessed from any page or from a dedicated help page.

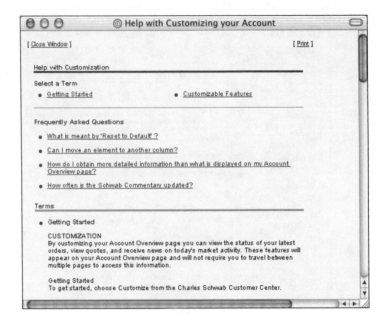

Another way out of this navigational conundrum is to present the help content in a single page composed of a two-frame layout. This is typically done with the list of questions on the left side and the corresponding answer text in the larger frame on the right. Although this style of online help can initially resemble a manual, this presentation does not force the user to read the text in a linear manner.

The items listed in the index are little more than questions masquerading as topics. Instead of "How do I add a contact?" there is "Adding contacts." More important, the explanation that corresponds to the topic does not try to place the action within a larger conceptual framework. It doesn't even attempt to explain why you might or might not want to perform such an action; it simply assumes that you want to know how to add a contact and gives the three steps needed to complete the task.

One advantage of frames is that they allow users to easily navigate to a different question or topic without having to return to a main index page, eliminating navigational dead-ends. Now I know what you're saying about frames: They're difficult to bookmark, even more difficult to print, and generally considered bad form in the design community. All those things are true. However, in procedural help, the frame caveats don't much matter. I've come to believe that frames and secondary browser windows were invented just to enable this type of help.

If you implement procedural help, your list of questions and answers will likely grow over time. In addition to having a search feature, a "Top 10 Issues" or "Most Common Problems" area on the main index page is also important. This simple mechanism helps users quickly get to the more common questions without having to wade through all the arcane problems that tend to accompany interactive products.

Because they've developed a unique style of help, e-commerce sites bear special mention here. As many e-commerce sites have matured, they've eliminated help related to the use of the Web site itself. Instead, help for e-commerce applications tends to be an online customer service center, covering return policies and order tracking, for example. Obviously, this form of help is very different from what is seen in other Web applications. The key consideration is to make sure the online customer service center actually services customers. Contact information—including phone numbers, email addresses, fax numbers, and live chat—goes a long way toward creating positive and meaningful connections with your customers. RedEnvelope has one of the best customer service areas on the Web (see Figure 9.4).

9.4

Although it's not the most prominent element on the page, the multiple contact methods and addresses communicate to customers that RedEnvelope is not trying to hide behind technology.

Big on the *how* while ignoring the *why*, procedural help is the dominant form of help on the Web. Its editorial and navigational styles are perfect for users who understand the conceptual framework of what they're doing but are having trouble with a specific task or procedure.

Definitional Help: Help as a Glossary

A third form of help is *definitional help*, the online glossary. This form of help is useful on sites that rely on specialist terms not known to the general user population. Stock trading sites, for example, make use of obscure terms to refer to the properties and statistics of different securities and trading patterns. Terms such as P/E (price to earnings ratio), EPS (earnings per share), Mkt Cap (market capitalization), moving average, and Bollinger bands all beg for definition. Unfortunately, the ever-present demand for screen real-estate makes it impractical to place definitions in the user's immediate view, so other solutions have to be found.

The most common option is to use the word in question as a link to the definition. In this solution, the definition is displayed in a secondary browser window. The ideal implementation places all the definitions in a single page so that users doesn't have to flip back and forth between the two windows. This method requires anchor tags so that the glossary page can automatically scroll to the definition. As shown in Figure 9.5, the Schwab site provides another good example of this solution in action.

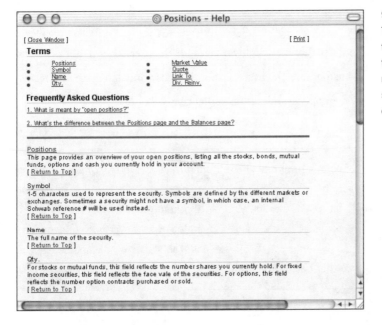

9.5
This small helper window is used to provide glossary help. Although the Return to Top links are needless clutter, the design succinctly presents the lingo of stock research.

Although Schwab's approach reduces visual clutter in the main window, it does so at the cost of opening and managing a second window, requiring a significant amount of interactive overhead just to display a definition.

Another option is to embed glossary definitions in the link's <ALT> tag so that they are displayed as Windows-style ToolTips. Although this solution requires less user interaction than opening a second window, it introduces problems of its own. First, it requires users to know what a ToolTip is in the first place. Second, it requires users to keep their mouse still long enough to discover the ToolTip. And third, it requires the definition to be short enough to fit inside a ToolTip. Because of these limitations, the <ALT> tag solution is somewhere between questionable and unacceptable.

Unfortunately, when it comes to definitional help, there aren't any ideal solutions. Whether the definitions are located somewhere on the main page, on a separate definitions page, in a secondary window, or in a ToolTip, there are disadvantages for the user. Although it's easier said than done, perhaps the best solution is to use only language and terms familiar to the application's target audience.

> What's true throughout the interface is even more so when it comes to help: Geography is everything. If there is help for an element on the page, the link to open the help must be located as closely as possible to the item in question. Users will not connect the dots between an item on the page and a help link appearing in some other part of the layout.

Instructional Help: Help as Instructions

A fourth type of help is to beat users to the punch by placing instructions directly on the page. For a simple application or simple tasks in a more complex application, the *instructional help* approach can often save users from ever having to access a dedicated help page.

As you can see in Figure 9.6, the designers of the Adobe online store went the instruction route throughout, adding a variety of help text directly inline with their form elements. In case you didn't notice them, the instructions are those bits of text appearing near the bottom of the page. And there's the catch—instructional text tends to be ignored by the impatient eye scanning for input controls and action buttons.

9.6
Although some of the instructional text contains useful information and links, it could be much shorter. Note, however, that the text fits nicely into the overall page layout.

The challenge with instructional help is to supply enough information to be useful, but not so much as to clutter the page. In addition, it requires the visual design to strike a delicate balance so that the instructions are noticeable but not distracting. The Adobe site is a nice example of such a balance.

Instructional help can be a simple, direct, and useful approach if your application needs a small push rather than a full-blown shove. Because it doesn't require a different window or even a different page, you don't have to worry about retaining the user's context nor do you have to concern yourself with bothersome navigational issues. The difficulty with instructional help, however, is to find an appropriate visual presentation and to express the instructions succinctly.

DESIGNING HELPFUL HELP

Despite its axiomatic nature, it's worth repeating: Help should be helpful. Whether you're designing a simple FAQ or a large-scale help system, you should never stray from the basic question "What is going to be helpful to the user?" The following collection of guidelines will serve you well in this quest:

☐ **Provide consistent, clear access to help.** To ensure that even the most inexperienced user can access your help system, include a single help link in the same location on every page, generally the upper-right corner. There aren't many standards on the Web, but this is one of them. Don't fight it. A user shouldn't need help finding help. Alternatively, if you're using instructional help, use a consistent placement and style for your instructions.

☐ **Retain the user's current view and context.** When users invoke help, destroying their current view and context is bad form. Rather, the polite response is to leave their current page alone and open a second browser window containing relevant help content. The last thing you want is for users to bring up help, get their questions answered, and then spend the next half hour trying to get back to where they started.

☐ **Provide help relevant to the user's immediate situation.** If your goal is to offer a meaningful level of help, your help system has to be context sensitive. In other words, when users invoke help, the application should automatically present the information that's pertinent to their current task, page, or word. Users don't go to help just to look around. They go there because they're having a specific problem and want a specific answer. It's only polite to give it to them as quickly as possible.

☐ **Offer multiple navigation methods.** Keeping in mind the merits of context sensitivity, it's also important to recognize that users often arrive at help stuck in the wrong context or task. Therefore, providing robust navigation to other elements of the help content is essential.

☐ **Balance user needs with development costs.** Help is an expensive endeavor. The trick is to find the right balance between development costs and user benefits. It's a bit like life insurance. There should be enough to be useful, but not so much that you have to sacrifice the kid's college fund to afford it.

Determining the type and degree of help to offer involves many complicated choices and tradeoffs. Before you set out to create the most elaborate help system of all time or, conversely, decide to scrap help altogether, take the time to understand your users' needs and expectations. How many of them are likely to have problems? What type of problems are they likely to be? What are the best mechanisms for addressing those problems? In the end, the need for help comes from a failure of the design to be sufficiently clear to the target audience. Therefore, the best solution remains a well-designed application that doesn't need help.

ALERTS

If you have formed the opinion that providing help is close to optional, you would be well advised not to let that attitude carry over to alerts. Help is a way for the user to ask the application for something; by contrast, alerts provide a critical communication channel for the application to talk to the user. Failure to communicate with the user is not an option. Therefore, alerts are not an option. Although you might be able to skate around offering help, there's no escaping alerts.

There are three basic categories of alerts, each informing the user of a different type of event:

Error alerts: Something is wrong.

Status alerts: Something is happening or has happened.

Confirmation alerts: Are you sure you meant to do that?

Although it can be argued that alerts result from a failure of the design
or the technology, alerts are an unavoidable by-product of the complex
communication and interaction that goes on between an application and a
user. Even if an ideal design and implementation could be conceived and
built, it is unlikely that this solution would be ideal for every user in every
situation. From a design perspective, however, alerts should be viewed as a
last resort, not a quick fix to a difficult problem.

ERROR ALERTS

Error alerts, typically associated with forms, are primarily used to notify
users that their input was incomplete, incorrect, indecipherable, or
otherwise unacceptable. Error alerts are rather dictatorial in style, in that
users have no choice but to deal with them. Usually, that means dealing
with them immediately. Error alerts come in two basic varieties: input
errors and application errors.

Input Errors

In the spirit of prevention as the best cure, the best approach to error alerts
is to prevent input errors before they happen. This requires understanding
precisely what is required from users coupled with a consistent and clear
input mechanism. As discussed in Chapter 8, "Editing and Manipulation:
Using HTML Input Controls to Accurately Capture Users' Data," well-
written instructions, a clean visual layout, easy-to-use input controls, and
appropriate examples of what input is needed are all important factors in
minimizing input errors. However, accidents do happen now and again—
hence, error alerts.

The first rule of input error alerts is that errors must be reported in the context in which they occurred. I don't have many rules, but this is one of them. It is simply unacceptable to take a user's input from a form, process the input, report the errors on a different page, and then expect the user to return to the original form, remembering and correcting the errors you reported. The only acceptable solution is to process the user's input from the form and report any errors on the form where they occurred.

The next question, then, is where on the form should the error alert be displayed? Although errors should ideally be reported next to the input controls where they occurred, the engineering efforts to make this happen can be substantial. Therefore, a common fallback is to report errors in the top portion of the page, above all the input controls. This method requires only a single area of the page to have dynamic behavior, so it's less difficult from an engineering perspective.

The best implementation of this solution also highlights the affected input areas by changing the control's label, the color of the table cell containing the control, or both. Often the color highlighting alone is enough for users to infer what the problem is and correct it without having to consult a detailed explanation. This doesn't mean you can get by without providing the text—only that the text location isn't as important as drawing the user's attention to the problem. SmartMoney's portfolio tracker shows a good example of how to report errors (see Figure 9.7).

Your Portfolio February 22, 2002 8:33 PM, EST	**Sample Port**			Print	Map	Analysis	Allocation	Log out

View | New | Buy/Sell | Edit | Splits | Dividends | Customize | Help

Number of shares cannot be zero or negative. Please enter a valid number in the indicated field.

Portfolio Name: Sample Port

Ticker	Shares	Cost	Commission	Delete
AMAT	1,060	$25.00	$29.95	☐
CSCO	0	$22.50	$29.95	☐
EPNY	830	$7.50	$89.85	☐
NOK	1,100	$22.50	$59.90	☐
ORCL	1,630	$20.00	$59.90	☐
SEBL	660	$22.00	$29.95	☐
SWPIX	241.66	$18.50	$0.00	☐
Previous Gain/Loss	$0.00			
CASH	$25,125.6			

Submit | Cancel Changes | Delete Portfolio

9.7
Note that the error is reported on the same page in which it occurred and the specific input field is highlighted. Because the input controls are placed so closely together, the location of the error text works well.

Although engineering concerns often dictate that the application's logic, including input validation, should be wholly contained on the server side of the equation, concerns about the user experience don't point to the same solution. From the user perspective, having input validation take place within the Web browser is preferable because it's immediate; users don't have to wait for the information to travel between the server and the browser only to find out they forgot to supply a phone number.

A good compromise is to provide basic input validation within the browser itself, saving the more sophisticated validation for the application's middle tier. Checking whether a required field contains a value, an email address includes an @ sign, a phone number has at least 10 digits, or an arrival time is after a departure time are examples of basic input validation that can be performed by using simple JavaScript routines. This approach can also be expanded so that error messages can be reported within the context of the input control. This is done by placing invisible images next to input controls and using error-checking routines to change those images to other images containing an error message.

Whether by accident or misunderstanding, input errors are going to happen. However, the goal should always be to minimize the possibility of their occurrence. When errors do happen, the design must be polite, succinct, and clear in identifying and describing the error. To achieve this goal, errors must be detected quickly and reported in the same context in which they occurred.

Application Errors

The other common use of error alerts is to inform users that something in the application has failed or broken. An application error can be caused when a connection times out, when an application is down for maintenance, or by a garden-variety software bug. Regardless, the application failed to complete an action, and it's only polite to let the user know what happened.

Application errors should be reported in a dedicated page with a message about the error, along with navigation controls for returning to the previous location. Depending on the type of error, a Retry button might also be appropriate.

Software is complicated, and Web applications are no exception. Even a simple application has a frightening array of things that can go wrong. Therefore, it's a good idea to create a single template for communicating application errors, modifying the message and navigation options to fit each particular error. In addition to giving users a consistent experience, it makes life easier for engineers by giving them a single mechanism for communicating the bad news.

STATUS ALERTS

Unlike error alerts and their attendant bad news, *status alerts* offer the hope of progress. They come in two flavors: progress alerts that tell the user something is happening and completion alerts that tell the user something has finished.

Progress Alerts

Any task that takes the application more than a few seconds to complete—obtaining a credit card approval, finding a travel reservation, performing a complex search, or downloading email, for example—should always be accompanied by a progress alert.

A progress alert is the application's way of saying, "I'm still working. I know it looks like I'm not doing anything, but really, I'm still going." The experiential equivalent of being put on hold, progress alerts are a painful reminder that the Web isn't quite as instantaneous as we might like.

Borrowing from everyone's favorite experience, the telephone call center, a progress alert first needs to assure users they haven't been forgotten, lost, or dropped. This is accomplished by using an alert that is continually updated to actually communicate status. Second, a progress alert needs to set accurate expectations by keeping users informed about how much time and/or processing is left, much like a call center's "Your expected wait time is 17 minutes" announcement.

Orbitz and Adobe offer good examples of progress alerts (see Figure 9.8). On the Orbitz site, the alert is shown when the user initiates a search for a flight. Although this alert does not tell users the anticipated length of the delay, at least it gives them a good reason to stick around. Unfortunately, few applications are able to report the percentage complete because they simply don't know how long the action is going to take. The alert for the Adobe online store also suffers from the "we don't know when we're going to be done" problem, although it helps mitigate the problem with a well-written text message.

9.8
Both progress alerts commit the "big lie" by using an animated GIF to simulate a progress bar, even though the animation has no relationship to actual activity.

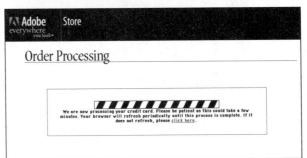

A common source of progress alerts is credit card companies' inability to supply an estimated response time to an incoming request. When an application calls Visa to approve a purchase, it has no way of knowing how long the approval will take and often displays a progress alert just in case.

However, the need for this alert could be eliminated by reordering the sequence of tasks. For example, the credit card approval could be processed after users place their orders, allowing them to go on about their day. By switching the sequence of tasks, the store could instantly confirm it received the orders, and follow up with the user if—and only if—there was a problem with the approval. Although this might be a hassle for a user whose credit card wasn't approved, it's a huge benefit to the rest of the user community because they no longer have to wait for the back-end processing to finish. If the application can carry on without the user, let it.

With a progress alert, users are basically trapped. The only options they have are to hang on until the task is done or cancel the task and hang up in frustration. It is your job to minimize their frustrations by managing expectations about how long the task is going to take and continually updating them on the progress. When you're designing progress alerts, keep this in mind: Nobody likes to wait, and nobody enjoys being on hold.

Completion Alerts

Perhaps the only alert that doesn't boil down to bad news, completion alerts inform the user that a complex task has finished or that a chunk of information has been successfully submitted and received. Completion alerts are commonly used to report when a form has been successfully submitted—for example, stock trade confirmations, new account confirmations, and purchase confirmations.

Completion alerts can be tricky owing to the difficulty in finding the ideal balance between keeping users informed and in control and not over-burdening them with details. It's a bit like working with a highly efficient executive assistant. If you ask your assistant to perform a routine task, you don't necessarily want to know when it's done. You assume it's going to get done and done in a timely manner. What you do want to know is when complex tasks, or tasks that affect other tasks, have been completed. For example, you probably want to know that a travel reservation has been made and the tickets have been sent, but you don't necessarily want to know that your email outbox has been emptied or that the to-do item you just deleted was actually deleted.

When the results of a user request aren't immediately visible in the application, completion alerts are an important way of informing users that the application has completed their requests. For example, the Fidelity stock-trading site doesn't need to tell users when they've successfully logged in to their account: It's apparent in the state of the application. However, the application does need to confirm the receipt of a trade request because there's nothing in the application to make this readily apparent.

Used in the appropriate context, completion alerts can certainly put users' minds at ease. However, their overuse or inappropriate use can just as easily drive users to distraction.

CONFIRMATION ALERTS

Confirmation alerts are the interface equivalent of asking "Huh?" Used to make sure that users actually meant to do what they just did, confirmation alerts have the redeeming characteristic of offering users an opportunity to change their minds. They are the application's way of asking the user, "I know what you said to do, but are you really sure?"

In the last salvo of the "perfect world" argument, confirmation alerts exist because of the technology's failure to allow the user to recover and undo any action.

A common confirmation alert is the "Are you sure you want to delete this?" alert. Unlike their desktop cousins, which typically move items to the "trash can" instead of immediately deleting them, most Web applications perform deletions immediately, which requires a deletion confirmation because the user cannot undo the delete and recover the item. Deleting a file folder from Hotmail or an album from Shutterfly are both examples (see Figure 9.9).

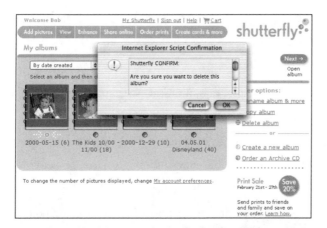

9.9
Note that Shutterfly's confirmation alert is generated by the operating system, but Hotmail uses a standard Web page. Shutterfly's approach might be faster, but Hotmail's is more consistent with the Web.

Although it's tempting to fill your application with confirmation alerts, this tendency will quickly turn your application into the little boy that cried wolf. If confirmation alerts are overused, it's not long before users develop a Pavlovian response to them, dismissing them before they can even be displayed. Even worse, because confirmation alerts in a Web application cannot be quickly dismissed, what is a simple annoyance in a desktop application is a major source of frustration on the Web.

Of course, the best solution is to engineer your application so that users can recover from any action, thereby eliminating the need for confirmation alerts. In the spirit of providing control, a fundamental goal of any interface should be to create an environment in which users can freely explore without inflicting unknown or unnecessary damage. Therefore, an undo function is far and away the most powerful assistance you can offer a user.

SUMMARY

Just as the name says, the User Assistance layer is all about offering users assistance—in other words, providing help and information when things aren't going so great. When you're designing the user assistance aspects of your application, always think in terms of being helpful, polite, and sensitive. If nothing else, make sure you don't make things worse.

Here's a summary for those of you in need of a quick fix:

☐ Whether you use conceptual, procedural, definitional, instructional, or a combination, there are well-established interface and editorial conventions for each type of help. If you concentrate on selecting an appropriate form of help, it will help guide your other decisions on delivery, design, and content.

☐ Alerts are bad news. Before you go down the alert path, stop to consider the real need and purpose of each alert. Is there some way you can redesign the workflow or the technology to eliminate the need for the alert? Is the alert there to report errors, communicate progress, or confirm an action? Again, there are well-established conventions for each type of alert, so after the alert's purpose is clearly identified, producing the appropriate interface and communication is comparatively easy.

This discussion of the User Assistance layer marks the end of the Behavior tier. As you turn the page, peering into the next constellation of concerns, you might be relieved to see the material becoming increasingly concrete and specific.

PART IV

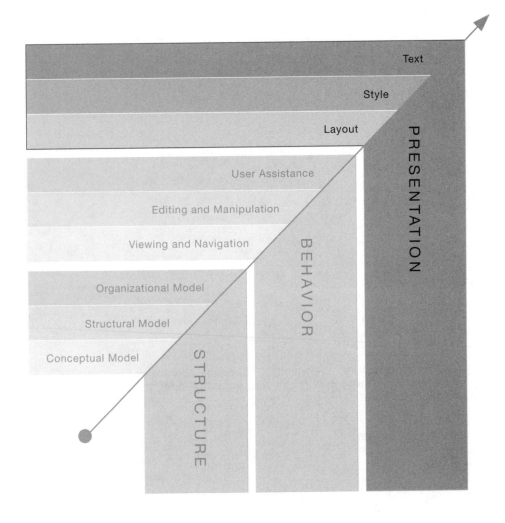

Text
Style
Layout
User Assistance
Editing and Manipulation
Viewing and Navigation
Organizational Model
Structural Model
Conceptual Model
STRUCTURE
BEHAVIOR
PRESENTATION

"Visual communication of any kind... should be seen as the embodiment of form and function: the integration of the beautiful and the useful."

Paul Rand
Thoughts On Design

10   LAYOUT

**Positioning Elements to Maximize
Understanding And Readability**

As the first layer of the Presentation tier, the Layout layer encompasses the specific placement and spatial arrangement of onscreen elements. Put another way, the Layout layer serves as a sort of visual skeleton on which to support the skin of color, imagery, typography, and style.

Compared to the Style layer, the goal of the Layout layer is less about creating a mood or evoking an emotion and more about supporting the Behavior and Structure tiers by lending an air of order, focus, and prioritization to the interface.

Designing an effective layout requires an understanding and application of three core design values:

☐ Simplicity

☐ Consistency

☐ Order

The purpose of the following sections is to examine those values and the visual principles associated with them.

DESIGN VALUE: SIMPLICITY

As the first place where the rubber of the ideal finally hits the road of screen space, the Layout layer is often where the presence of complexity is first felt. In the light of black-and-white line drawings and wireframe layouts, it finally becomes apparent that a single page really can't support 5 levels of navigation, 42 different input fields, and 4 banner ads. Something has to go.

Resulting from the careful consideration and the evaluation of every detail, true simplicity requires the designer to make difficult choices—accenting a small set of elements while minimizing or eliminating others.

To aid in the pursuit of simplicity, the three design principles of clarity, reduction, and leverage are worth mastering. Although these principles should be applied to every layer of the interface, they are especially relevant in the layout.

CLARITY: SIMPLE, DIRECT EXPRESSION

Clarity, the principle of clear expression, contributes to simplicity by freeing users from the mental overhead of figuring out what is or isn't possible on a page. With respect to the application's layout, clarity requires that the visual solution effectively communicate critical information to users in the manner and locations they expect it. All these questions should be addressed at the user's first glance:

☐   "What is the purpose of this page?"

☐   "Where can I or should I click?"

☐   "Where can I go from here?"

This requires a combination of focus, prioritization, and, as always, the ability to remove unnecessary and distracting elements. By reducing the number of items users have to comprehend and process, you increase their ability to recognize and understand the page's purpose.

In an effort to provide multiple navigational paths and maximize an application's "flexibility," some designs fill the page with duplicate and rarely used options. They do this with the false belief that users who don't need the options will simply ignore them. Unfortunately, this is rarely true. At first glance, it is impossible for users to quickly distinguish important from optional elements. As a result, they typically examine every element on the page, meaning that every additional element is one more thing to process and understand—and one more opportunity for confusion.

For example, Google's interface (see Figure 10.1) is relatively clear because there are so few elements on the page. Even this layout could be improved, however, by removing or clarifying the I'm Feeling Lucky button. The layout could also be improved by adding white space between the two command buttons and between the buttons and the text box. However, even with these and other minor problems, the layout succeeds in effectively communicating the page's functionality.

10.1

Google's function is clearly expressed by this simple, minimalist layout that visually prioritizes the text box and command buttons.

By contrast, the interface for Ask Jeeves in Figure 10.2 is filled with distraction and visual competition. Although the presentation is more sophisticated and interesting from an aesthetic perspective, it lacks a clear visual hierarchy, making it hard to comprehend the page's essential functionality and purpose.

10.2

This layout distracts from the page's functionality by including tabs, links, text, and icons that compete with the core interface elements: the text box and the Ask button.

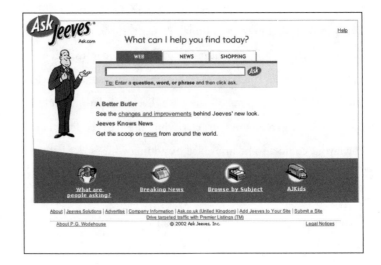

The principle of clarity rests on the solution's ability to focus the user's attention on the page's content and functionality. Creating this focus demands that users' needs—their work, their task, and their information—be placed at the top of the visual priority, above the din of marketing messages and advertisements. For advertising-based services and applications, this means balancing the needs of your users against the demands of your advertisers in the same way that magazines, television networks, and radio stations balance the conflicting demands of their viewers and advertisers.

In the world of licensed or subscription-based Web applications, however, users are a captive audience. They've already bought the software, signed up for an account, logged into the service. You don't need to keep fighting for their attention; you've already got it. If you want to keep it, help them focus on what they're doing, which ensures a productive and satisfying experience.

REDUCTION: ARRIVING AT ESSENTIAL ELEMENTS AND FORMS

Like the principal of clarity, *reduction*—paring down a design to its essential elements and forms—requires the elimination of nonessential elements. However, unlike clarity, the goal of reduction is less about clearly expressing fundamental purpose than it is about achieving visual efficiency. Where clarity is the ability to make sure someone understands what you're saying, reduction is the ability to say it in as few words as possible.

Throughout the interface, the value of simplicity requires every element and interaction to be reduced to its essential form. In terms of the layout, reduction means determining the minimum elements required for the page and the most efficient means of expressing those elements.

As the designer, it's natural to believe that every element is critical to the overall product. However, a bit of ruthless trial and error can often identify elements to cut without weakening the overall design. By examining each element to determine how it supports the communication, the page, or the application as a whole, you can identify potentially extraneous elements. If you find an element that can possibly be cut, test the design without it. As often as not, the design will be improved.

LEVERAGE: USING A SINGLE ELEMENT FOR MULTIPLE ROLES

The Viewing and Navigation layer is discussed in Chapter 7, "Viewing and Navigation: Creating Consistent Sorting, Filtering, and Navigation Behaviors."

Leverage is the technique of using a single element to play multiple roles. Examples of how leverage can be applied include:

☐ **Stock quote and search forms.** The number of elements needed for simple search or stock quote forms can be reduced by using the form's Submit button to identify and label its function. For example, instead of a Quotes title, a text box, and a Submit button labeled Go, you can represent the same function by eliminating the title and renaming the command button as Quotes.

☐ **Using dynamic data as links.** As discussed in the chapter on the Viewing and Navigation layer, applications that present users' data can use the data itself as links. For example, Web-based email applications typically use a message's subject as a link to the message, eliminating the need for a Read command and leveraging the message's subject by having it serve as both content and functionality.

☐ **"Click here" links.** A decidedly anti-leverage design is the dreaded Click Here link. As Web design has become increasingly sophisticated, however, most designers have realized that embedding the link in the text is a more efficient use of hyperlinking. Where you once saw "Registered users <u>click here</u>" you now see simply "<u>Registered users</u>."

Figure 10.3 from myCFO's portfolio tracker illustrates several examples of the principle of leverage. The stock quote form in the top-right corner of the page has been reduced to an input field and a single button. The current location is communicated by highlighting the Investments tab and the Portfolio Tracker secondary navigation. Finally, dynamic data functions as both content and functionality because the stock symbols in the first column also act as links to stock research.

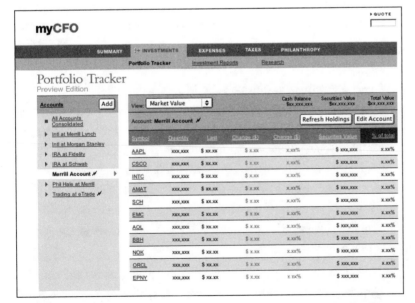

10.3

This page from myCFO's portfolio tracker shows how to use leverage to reduce the number of elements on the page and therefore simplify the design.

Although leverage can be a useful way to reduce the number of elements on a page, it can easily create confusion if done to the extreme. Leveraging a single element to play multiple roles can require a level of subtlety that's incompatible with the values of obviousness and predictability. With experience, good judgment, and appropriate user-testing, however, you can find the balance between being efficient and being invisible.

Layout Behavior: Fixed Versus Dynamic

A fundamental constraint governing the design of physical objects is form factor. For print designers, it often translates to page size. For Web designers, it's a bit more complex. Unlike the physical world of print design, one of the first questions in creating a layout for a Web page is whether it should be a fixed width or should dynamically resize to fit the browser window. Considering all the other factors affecting visual design, creating a fixed-width layout is a big enough challenge; dynamics layouts, however, are definitely taking things up a notch.

Fixed-width layouts maintain a specific page width, regardless of the browser window's dimensions. Although fixed-width layouts go against the grain of allowing the user to resize the content, they are useful in some situations. For example, because images cannot be dynamically resized with the browser window, fixed-width layouts are better for image-intensive applications, such as online stores, online art museums, and photo-processing services. Because the images have fixed dimensions, a dynamic layout can affect only the spacing between images.

Fixed-width layouts are commonly sized to accommodate a monitor resolution of 800×600. After subtracting space for the browser window, a width of around 755 pixels remains for the page. The unfortunate result is that users with monitors set below the fixed

---

dimension cannot see the entire page, and users with monitors set above the fixed dimension are going to see extra blank space. To minimize the frustration of users with large monitors, the layout's alignment should support the orientation of the primary navigation. For tab-based navigation, this means the layout should be vertically centered on the page; for tree-based navigation, it should be left-aligned.

In keeping with the ethics of the Web, *dynamic layouts* give users control over content presentation by resizing to match the browser window. These layouts are appropriate, if not mandatory, for applications that use text-based content or tabular data. However, they present a unique design problem. Because effective dynamic layouts don't simply adjust every element on the page as the window is resized, identifying which elements should dynamically resize and which should stay fixed is a challenge unfamiliar to most graphic designers.

For example, in a layout that features tabular data, it is important to determine which columns are likely to contain data of varying length so that those columns can be made dynamic. This enables the user to adjust the layout to fit the specifics of the data, without causing the entire layout to shift based on the window width. For example, a dynamic layout for the inbox of an online email application might vary only the column containing the message subject, leaving the sender, date, and size columns fixed.

Whether an application should rely on a fixed-width or dynamic layout involves considering a number of factors. Does the application primarily present images or text? Is the computing environment of target users relatively heterogeneous or homogeneous? What is the optimum balance of control between the designer and the user? Once the decision between fixed-width or dynamic has been made, however, there are well-established conventions for the specific behavior of the layout.

DESIGN VALUE: CONSISTENCY

Fundamental to all forms of verbal communication is the core design value of consistency. Any software interface, on the Web or elsewhere, is essentially an alternative, virtual world that users have to understand and master. The only way to ensure that they can succeed in that goal is to establish obvious, well-understood, and consistently applied rules for the functioning of the interface. Those rules encompass not only the visual details of layout, color, and typography, but also the behavioral and structural details discussed in previous chapters.

Along with simplicity, the importance of consistency cannot be overstated. Consistency is fundamental to the concepts of usability and user satisfaction. In its absence, users will be faced with confusion, frustration, and disappointment. Although it's critical at every layer of the interface, a lack of consistency in the layout is particularly evident.

As a core design value, consistency has to be considered at several levels. For example, each page in an application should be consistent with the Web as a whole, with the application as a unique interface, and with other page-specific elements. Although each level of consistency dictates certain boundaries for the design, it also leaves a bit of wiggle room. Therefore, finding a solution that embodies both consistency and individuality requires an understanding of the established conventions and the skill to modify those conventions without completely violating them.

CONSISTENCY WITH THE WEB: CONVENTIONS

Because the environment of Web design is free from the dictates of a single visual style or an authoritarian keeper of guidelines, Web-wide conventions, such as they are, are the result of natural evolution. This evolution occurs as designers encounter solutions to common visual and interactive problems and adopt the best solutions for their own use. Although there are a handful of dominant Web applications whose influence owes more to their sheer mass of users than the quality of their design solutions—eBay and Yahoo!, for example—the conventions in use generally result from Darwinian survival of the fittest.

Although the strict adherence to convention can be a stifling experience for any creative professional, convention can also serve as a highly productive co-worker and educator. Because conventions save you from having to reinvent the wheel, they reduce the designer's workload. More important, they also allow users to apply their experiences from other sites, reducing the amount of learning and orientation required for them to become productive.

A good example of a convention is the ubiquitous "shopping cart" found at online stores. What started out as one person's solution to the problem proved to be so useful that it has become one of the most well-established conventions on the Web—so much so that it's often reduced to little more than a 12-pixel icon.

Another convention dictates that every page contain certain elements. For example, in addition to their actual content, view pages should include the following:

- Company logo or identifier
- Page title
- High-level navigation
- Low-level navigation
- Utility navigation
- Footer

The placement and arrangement of these elements can vary greatly, but the elements should always be present.

What makes the use of Web conventions tricky and interesting is their constant evolution. Who's to say what will survive and become a long-lived, usable convention versus some short-term fashion trend? There's no perfect measure to distinguish one from another, but you can save yourself and your users considerable time and effort by seeking out a suitable solution to your current problem on other sites before turning to your own efforts at invention.

CONSISTENCY IN PLACEMENT AND VISUAL FLOW: TEMPLATES AND GRIDS

Consistency can also be increased by establishing a robust, flexible set of page templates and using them throughout the application. Fortunately, this is an almost inescapable aspect of designing Web applications because their dynamic, data-driven nature requires them to be template driven. Because the visual appearance of most pages results from a combination of the page's content and a predefined template, it is possible to enforce consistency by consciously designing the templates as a unit and by keeping the overall number of templates to a minimum.

For example, the following set of templates might be enough to handle almost every page of an online store:

- ☐ Product details
- ☐ Category overview
- ☐ Input forms
- ☐ Input error alerts

In addition to the template-based pages, the application would likely require a handful of one-off pages, such as the home page and the logon page. The goal, however, is to approach the entire set of pages as a single unit that shares the same visual characteristics of color, typography, and layout.

A critical part of achieving a consistent layout is the strict adherence to a single grid system. Grids, a long-standing technique in the graphic design profession, uniformly divide a page into smaller units. The grid systems used by print designers have more flexibility and variation, but for Web designers, only a few types of grids are in common use (see Figure 10.4).

Grids

narrow-wide-narrow   narrow-wide   wide-narrow

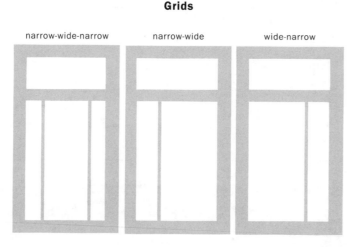

10.4
The most common grid types used in Web design.

One of the most popular—the narrow-wide-narrow grid—places a narrow column on each side of the page with a wide column in the center. This grid is used by a variety of portal applications, such as myYahoo!, MSN, and Fidelity Investments. The advantage of the grid is its adaptability to information of varying lengths presented in varying page widths. The grid also provides a clean and simple format for smaller amounts of content. Figures 10.5 and 10.6 illustrate this grid's adaptability to different situations.

10.5

Fidelity Investments uses a narrow-wide-narrow layout, separating its page into areas for content, tools, and advertisements.

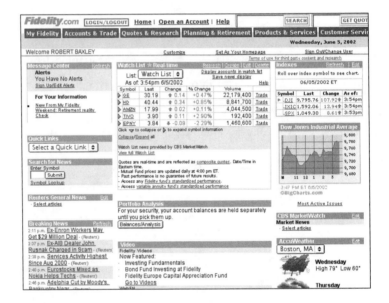

10.6

British Airways also uses a narrow-wide-narrow layout. Note how the grid handles a page with little content in the narrow columns.

Although there are other layout styles in common use, they are generally variations on the narrow-wide-narrow theme: narrow-wide, wide-narrow, and simply wide. Figures 10.7 and 10.8 illustrate two of these variations.

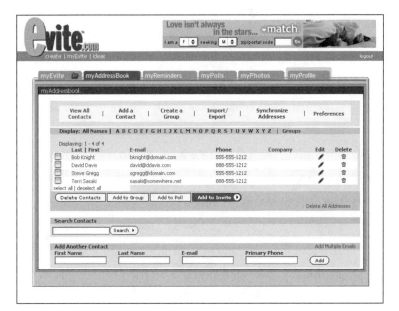

10.7

Evite's layout uses a single wide column of fixed width. Note the consistent inclusion of essential page elements, such as the company logo and the primary navigation links at the top.

10.8

Shutterfly uses a wide-narrow layout to great effect. By moving the corporate logo and page-level navigation to the right side, the layout breaks from the standard left-side orientation.

There are graphic design books filled with information about the value of grids and templates as well as techniques for creating them. Although the subject can hardly be done justice here, the following caveats are particularly relevant to Web applications:

- □ **Limit layouts to less than three columns.** Because of limited screen real estate, avoid layouts requiring more than three columns.

- □ **Avoid symmetrical layouts.** A two-column symmetrical layout sets an expectation of balance that is difficult to fulfill unless there is precise control over the content. Unfortunately, that level of control is rarely available with data-driven applications and templates.

- □ **Use a different layout for views and forms.** The difference between views and forms should be accented by the use of distinct templates for each. Although the different templates should be consistent in their placement of essential page elements, such as corporate identifications and page titles, other aspects of the layout can and should vary.

The best method for ensuring consistency throughout the interface is to visualize the entire application as a single functioning unit rather than a collection of individual, isolated pages. This can be readily accomplished by printing a number of pages and placing them so that they can be viewed simultaneously. By experiencing the application in one eye span, it is possible to identify inconsistencies and problems that are often lost when the application is viewed one page at a time. By approaching the problem in an integrated, cross-page manner, you are more likely to create an application that offers users a satisfying level of predictability, consistency, and control.

CONSISTENCY IN VISUAL DETAIL: STANDARDS AND GUIDELINES

Another level of consistency requires the development and use of a standardized set of visual details, such as the appearance of buttons and links, the placement of labels and page titles, and the use of color and typography. Designing, communicating, and enforcing a consistent visual language is a challenge for the designer of any Web application or site. However, the advantage of such a language can be felt in both the consistency of the interface and the ease with which new features and pages can be created.

A unique aspect of guideline development is that the design is only half the problem; the other half involves adopting and implementing the guideline. For small projects, it may be possible to enforce guidelines by limiting the number of people responsible for the interface's visual presentation. For larger projects, however, the design team is likely to be one component of a far-flung enterprise, and individual designers are unlikely to be involved in every decision. In these situations, making the guidelines as clear, accessible, and implementable as possible is important. The chances of a guideline being adopted is greatly increased if sample HTML and intelligent art production templates are readily available.

DESIGN VALUE: ORDER

If cleanliness is indeed next to godliness, order can't be far behind. As a design value, order is present when all elements are arranged so that their relative importance and relationships to one another are apparent. The importance of order in supporting the interface's more fundamental behavioral and structural aspects cannot be overstated. When a page is ordered, it has the overall appearance of neatness, precision, and thoughtfulness.

Although order is an easy quality to recognize, being able to consistently produce and create order requires an understanding and mastery of the principles of grouping, hierarchy, alignment, and balance. Independently, these principles can improve any layout. Working in concert, they can produce a truly superior design.

PLACING LIKE ELEMENTS TOGETHER: GROUPING

The first step toward ordering a layout is to arrange the individual page elements into groups. These groups form the basis of the layout, functioning as its primary elements.

The visual effect of a group can be created by using a variety of the visual variables that Gestalt psychologists described in the 1920s. They defined various perceptual biases and visual principles, including the following:

- **Proximity.** Objects appearing near one another are perceived as a group.
- **Similarity.** Objects that share visual qualities are perceived as a group.

☐ **Continuity.** The preference to see lines, figures, and areas as continuous, uninterrupted forms.

The use of these principles is evident on MSN's home page (as shown in Figure 10.9).

Links for editing content look similar to the left column but are placed in the center column— a conflict between proximity and similarity

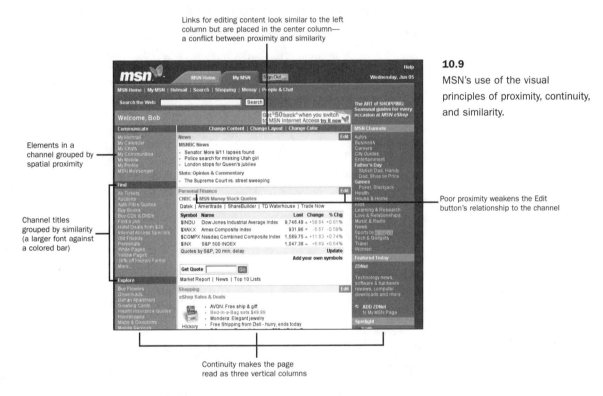

Elements in a channel grouped by spatial proximity

Channel titles grouped by similarity (a larger font against a colored bar)

10.9
MSN's use of the visual principles of proximity, continuity, and similarity.

Poor proximity weakens the Edit button's relationship to the channel

Continuity makes the page read as three vertical columns

Although it requires experience and skill to master the subtleties of these principles, even with these simple definitions, it is possible to increase your understanding and control of the perceptual workings of visual design.

VISUALLY RANKING ELEMENTS BY IMPORTANCE: HIERARCHY

In addition to grouping, visual *hierarchy* is another useful technique for creating order. By manipulating the visual variables of size, color, and position, you can generate contrast and direct the viewer's attention.

By definition, hierarchy requires that some elements become more prominent at the expense of others. Many designs fail to take advantage of the value of hierarchy because they are unwilling to elevate one set of elements over another. This often results in a page absent of visual hierarchy, contrast, or order. Unfortunately, such designs leave users to find their own way, without the benefit of visual landmarks or direction.

You can use hierarchy to great effect by manipulating only one visual variable at a time. For example, because the upper-left corner of the page is the most visually prominent, placing an element in that location elevates it in the visual hierarchy. In other words, if you place your logo in the upper-left corner, you don't have to also make it the largest or brightest element on the page. As a general rule, *multiple coding*—using two or more visual variables in combination—is unnecessary. The most subtle, simple, and refined visual designs use variables one at a time.

Figure 10.10 from RedEnvelope is a good illustration of visual hierarchy. This design uses variation in type size to establish a hierarchy between the page title, the area titles for returning versus new customers, and the form labels. For comparison, look back at Figure 10.9 from MSN. What stands out on the page? What does the designer want you to look at? Although MSN uses color to distinguish one area from another, because there are three colors and three areas, each area appears equal to the others and no contrast or hierarchy is established.

10.10
The login page from RedEnvelope
communicates a visual hierarchy
by varying type size.

Establishing visual hierarchy and contrast is critical to creating order. Every page should have some elements that are more prominent and some that are less so. If everything is talking at the same volume, be it a shout or a whisper, it's impossible for the user to pick up the conversation.

SUPPORTING VISUAL FLOW: ALIGNMENT

Alignment, another design principle that contributes to order, refers to how the elements are spatially related to one another. Do they align to a left-hand border? Or do they align to a single right-hand edge? Do they align vertically along the top, or are they centered through an axis?

In keeping with the Gestalt principle of continuity and the general theme of grids, alignment should occur in both vertical and horizontal axes. In addition, the number of alignment points should be kept to a minimum, ideally less than four. Figure 10.11 from JetBlue illustrates how poor alignment can make even simple forms look unnecessarily complex and disordered.

10.11

Shown top, JetBlue's flight search form suffers from poor alignment. The version at bottom improves the layout by establishing clear alignment points and grouping related elements.

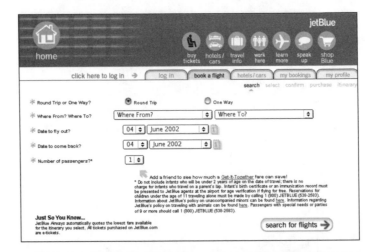

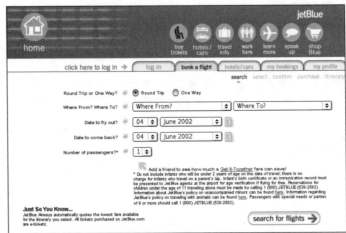

In forms, a common alignment problem involves the relationship between form elements and their labels. Because of the importance of proximity in associating the label with the input control, keeping the two close together is critical. The length of a label can vary, so left-aligning the labels often creates too much space between the label and the control. A better solution is to right-align the labels, ensuring that they appear within a few pixels of their controls. Although this can destroy other vertical alignment axes in the layout, the usability benefit outweighs the aesthetic disadvantage. Figure 10.12 illustrates the advantage of right-alignment.

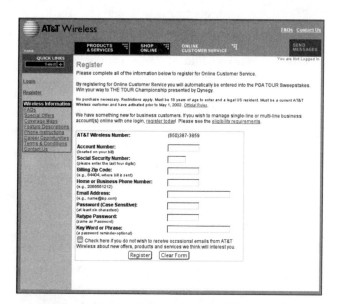

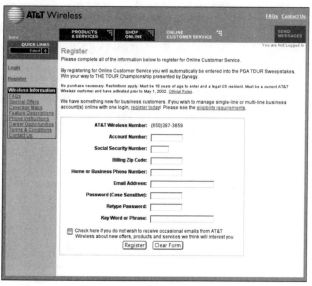

10.12

These AT&T forms show the difference between left- and right-alignment of input control labels. In addition, visual clutter is reduced by removing the unnecessary input examples.

A second option places the labels above the controls, preferably out-dented a little. However, there must be enough space between elements to make the association between the label and the control clear.

The design value of order is central to any visually pleasing, intelligent layout. Although it requires judgment and careful choices, creating a sense of order is not overly difficult. Taking the time and effort to instill order in the layout helps users focus on their work, relieves them of the visual noise and distraction prevalent in many Web applications, and improves their overall impression of the experience. Most important, order contributes to users' level of control by helping them understand the interface.

Precise Approximation

Much to the consternation of countless Web designers, the Web is not a medium that readily lends itself to precise control. If you approach the Web expecting the fine-tuned control associated with print design, you're destined for frustration—for yourself, for the engineering staff, and most importantly, for the users who have to suffer the pains of using an design inappropriate to the medium.

"The negative is comparable to the composer's score and the print to its performance. Each performance differs in subtle ways."

—Ansel Adams, *The Portfolios of Ansel Adams*

A more realistic option is to think of the Web as a design medium offering *precise approximation*—"precise" because the placement of elements is expressed with specific numeric values, and "approximation" because the countless permutations resulting from variations in browsers, operating systems, monitor settings, and viewer preferences make it impossible to create a uniform experience. Compounding the variation in browser and monitor settings, the dynamic, data-driven nature of Web applications introduces another dimension of variation. In most cases, for example, the challenge is not only to design a page that will render gracefully in different environments, but also to ensure that the design can function as a template, presenting a variety of content in the same layout.

As a visual designer on the Web, the challenge is to fully appreciate that although the Web does not offer the precise control of other mediums, it does offer a rich and fluid vocabulary for describing a page's visual presentation. In addition, the ethics of the Web dictates a level of shared control between the designer and the user. That means the design has to gracefully allow users to adapt parts of the visual presentation to fit their unique computing environments and needs. If you find yourself attempting to wrestle control from the user to achieve some aesthetic ideal, you need to stop and ask whether you're acting in the user's best interest or your own.

PUTTING IT ALL TOGETHER

Up to this point, the discussion has focused on design values and principles working in isolation of one another. Extraordinary solutions, however, go beyond the independent application of these techniques to find unique and sophisticated ways of harmonizing and balancing their effects.

Designs that succeed at this level do not result from an algorithmic or solely analytical approach; rather, they combine the values of simplicity, consistency, and order with the aesthetic ideals of restraint, balance, harmony, and integration.

Of the sites pictured in this chapter, RedEnvelope and Shutterfly (see Figures 10.13 and 10.14) come the closest to embodying all the values and techniques mentioned. Most noticeably, both designs exhibit restraint in their extensive and tasteful use of white space. By not attempting to fill every last pixel with meaning, they give both the page and the user some much-needed breathing room and foster an impression of professionalism, consideration, and control.

10.13
RedEnvelope's combination of restraint, balance, harmony, and integration make it one of the most beautiful and pleasing sites on the Web.

10.14
Shutterfly's use of white space, nonstandard logo placement, and vibrant color palette combine to create a balanced, well-ordered, and visually appealing design.

SUMMARY

As the initial layer of the Presentation tier, the Layout layer is the visual component most tightly integrated with the interface's behavioral and structural components. To ensure the integrity of this relationship, the design solutions in the Layout layer should reflect an awareness and understanding of the decisions and solutions made in the preceding layers.

Ideally present throughout the interface, these three core design values should be clearly evident in the layout of every page:

☐ **Simplicity.** Communication that is direct, clear, and concise

☐ **Consistency.** Communication that is uniform and harmonious

☐ **Order.** Communication that expresses priority and relationship

For the uninitiated, the task of creating a layout that reflects these values and principles might seem like a daunting task. With a bit of practice and observation, however, the basic use of these tools is easily mastered. Although the layout forms the structural frame that supports the other visual elements of the interface, because Web applications are largely template driven, changing this layer of the interface without greatly affecting the underlying technology is relatively easy. In other words, even if you don't start out with the ideal layout, it's not a horrible burden to fix it later.

With the discussion of the Layout layer at a close, the focus now shifts to the more emotional, more subtle, and more artistic world of the Style layer.

"There is nothing worse than a brilliant
image of a fuzzy concept."

Ansel Adams

11

STYLE

Defining Visual Appearance

The penultimate layer of the interface, Layer 8: Style, contains the application's visual details and graphic expression. The elements most people expect to see at the beginning—fonts, colors, imagery, icons, and logos—finally make their appearance here near the end. In most Web applications, the primary role of the Style layer is to support the more fundamental components of the design, described in the previous layers. Thanks to the power and persuasion of visual communication, however, the Style layer has the potential to exert significant influence on the user's overall experience. In the context of a Web application in particular, the challenge of the Style layer is to find a solution that works in concert with the other layers of the interface, rather than one that overwhelms the other members of the orchestra.

Because an exhaustive discussion of the Style layer would encompass nearly the whole of graphic design, the goal of this chapter is a bit different from previous ones. Instead of focusing on the techniques and skills useful in creating the design, this chapter focuses on a handful of guiding principles useful in evaluating solutions created by others. To aid in that evaluation, the chapter concludes with a discussion of how to prevent the Style layer from overshadowing and disrupting the other layers.

The techniques and artistry associated with the Style layer could easily fill a book in and of themselves. In fact, they already have—at least a few hundred, if Amazon is to be believed. For a list of recommended books on graphic design and other related topics, please visit www.bobbaxley.com.

EVALUATING STYLE

The Style layer contributes to the fundamental design goals of control and satisfaction to the degree that it embodies the values of elegance, novelty, beauty, and enjoyment. A well-designed Style layer not only reflects these values, but it does so in support of the interface's other components. To further the challenge, it also supports the established brand values of the company, while remaining sensitive to the underlying technology's abilities and limitations.

In contrast to other components of the interface, the Style layer is uniquely concerned with emotion and feeling. Through the use of color, typography, and imagery, the Style layer can contribute a sense of fun, excitement, variety, comfort, safety, trust, integrity, novelty, simplicity, or enjoyment to the user's experience.

Similar to a corporate brand, the way emotions are balanced and prioritized gives the application a unique and identifiable personality. Whether a particular design solution communicates the desired personality traits in a clear and memorable way should be the primary criteria for judging the solution's success. Obviously, this requires the personality traits to be explicitly defined before creating the design.

In addition to consistency with defined product personality traits, a solution should also be evaluated in light of its individuality, its consistency with established corporate brand values, and its appropriateness to the Web as a design medium.

For a look back at establishing a product personality and emotional goals, see Chapter 2, "Putting the User First: Describing Target Users and Product Goals."

INDIVIDUALITY

A primary goal of the Style layer is to give an application individuality: a distinctive, memorable, and unique look and feel. Because all Web applications are presented in the same browser environment, visual appearance is one of the most effective variables for quickly differentiating one application from another. Visual differentiation can often be more compelling than even functional differences, as users easily recall that a certain site was "cool" or "clean" more than they recall what it could actually do.

Unfortunately, the desire for a completely individual experience must always be balanced with a respect for the established visual and interactive design conventions that form the basis of Web usability. In addition, HTML's equalizing force as a presentation technology prevents the design from relying on the subtlety or precision of more established mediums, such as print or industrial design.

Compared to designers working on print projects, graphic designers working on the Web have to contend with a variety of technology-induced limitations. Some of the more notable obstacles include the following:

The Layout layer is discussed in Chapter 10, "Layout: Positioning Elements to Maximize Under-standing and Readability."

☐ **Variability of presentation.** As described in the chapter on visual design, visual design for the Web is a game of precise approximation. Differences in browsers, operating systems, monitor settings, and user preferences make it impossible to finely control how a design is going to appear. Because they are crafting a physical object, print designers do not have to contend with these factors.

☐ **No control over page size.** Web applications are displayed in a browser window, the size of which is controlled by the user. Compared to print designers who can precisely determine the physical dimensions of their work, the Web designer must contend with an unknown page size.

☐ **Limited typographic choices.** Because of the dynamic, data-driven nature of Web applications, a large portion of any page contains text displayed with HTML. Unfortunately, the range of typefaces typically available on user's systems is limited to fewer than 10. Compounding the problem, the low resolution of computer monitors renders many of those typefaces unusable. By contrast, print designers have at their disposal literally thousands of different typefaces to choose from.

☐ **Complex set of standards and conventions.** The increased degree of complexity and user knowledge required to use Web applications means that they are more reliant on visual and interactive conventions. Although consistency is a fundamental principle of interactive design, it clearly runs counter to the goal of individuality.

☐ **Bandwidth concerns.** Print designers don't have to concern themselves with how long an image takes to download. Web designers do. Throughout an application's visual design, there are countless tradeoffs between aesthetic values and bandwidth concerns.

Creating a visual design that successfully navigates these technical considerations and still succeeds in producing a unique and engaging experience is no simple task. When comparing and evaluating design solutions, a primary criteria should be how well the solution balances the conflicting requirements of consistency, technical practicality, and individuality.

BRAND CONSISTENCY

Another key factor in the success of a design is whether it is appropriate and consistent with established corporate brand values. Clearly, the issue here goes beyond simplistic concerns over the correct use of logos and colors. True brand consistency has to address core brand values, including the overall customer experience. For example, Target's online store (see Figure 11.1) reflects a brand personality consistent with its "physical" stores: The brand traits of price, value, variety, and order are all clearly visible. Similarly, Pottery Barn's online store elicits the same feelings of calm and comfort reflected in its catalogs and stores (see Figure 11.2).

By contrast, the online offerings for Fidelity and Schwab both fail to communicate the values of reliability, trust, and personal service that are critical to their brands. As seen in Figure 11.3, the portal approach and visual design of these online services are overwhelming, impersonal, and lonely.

11.1

The visual style of Target's online store is an appropriate and successful solution because it is consistent with its core customer experience and brand identifiers of price, value, variety, and order.

11.2

The Pottery Barn's online store conveys a sense of calm, comfort, and home, which is consistent with the company's catalogs, stores, and brand values.

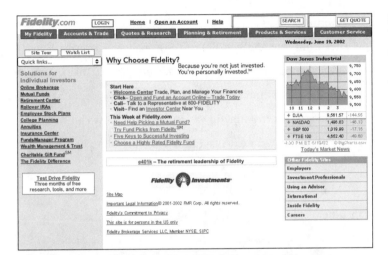

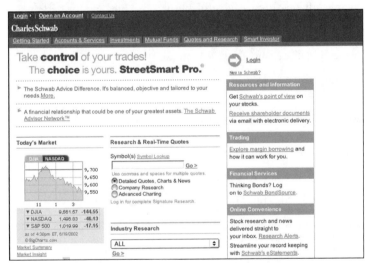

11.3
The visual style for both Fidelity and Schwab is neither distinctive nor consistent with their brand values.

There is nothing in these sites to guide or comfort the user or to suggest any degree of personal service. Rather, both sites offer a cacophony of choices, hoping that users will somehow be able to find what they need. Considering that both companies pride themselves on trusted advice and service, these pages feel about as personal as a warehouse office supply store when the staff has left for lunch.

In terms of individuality, there is little more than color to differentiate the sites from one another. Both sites heavily rely on simple rectangular shapes, repeating the theme throughout the primary navigation area, the command buttons, and the channel layout. Finally, neither site makes use of any imagery or meaningful variation of color. As shown here in black and white, you could exchange one site for the other by simply switching the logos.

Although brand consistency is a relatively obvious concern for consumer sites such as Target and Pottery Barn, it is also a concern for licensed Web applications. Companies such as Siebel, Oracle, and PeopleSoft have precise, identifiable brand values and the designers of these companies' applications have to be cognizant of those values. Reliability, professionalism, and flexibility are all values that can be communicated through visual style.

APPROPRIATENESS FOR THE AUDIENCE AND FUNCTION

Another critical concern when evaluating style options is their appropriateness to the application's function and target users. Vivid colors and highly stylized graphics can be appropriate for entertainment sites, although they rarely are for financial applications. A design that might seem boring or conservative could be the best solution for some applications, depending on their context and purpose.

Yahoo! is a prime example of this concept (see Figure 11.4). Although you'd be hard pressed to find anyone who would defend Yahoo's! style based on principles of aesthetics, beauty, or elegance, the solution is clearly appropriate to the application's purpose and functionality. The style could be made more attractive, but it clearly communicates Yahoo!'s core brand values of speed, economy, breadth, and depth.

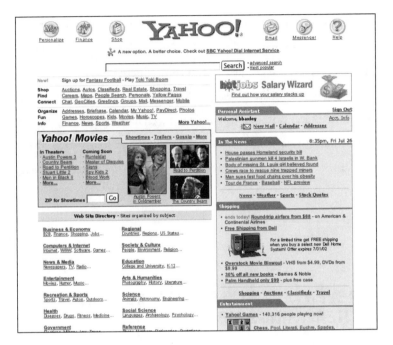

11.4
Yahoo's visual style can hardly be envied for its artistic merits. However, the solution is appropriate, given the context.

Determining whether a solution is appropriate also involves understanding cultural issues. The notion of culture doesn't merely refer to national or geographic cultures; it also includes the culture of specific professional groups, age groups, and others. For example, if a design features the color red, it's important to consider whether it has an unintentional meaning to a certain culture. Members of the financial services community, for example, are not particularly fond of the color red because it universally signifies declining prices.

Other considerations of appropriateness include type size or images versus words. If the application is targeting an audience older than 40, for example, 9-point type is guaranteed to send everyone running for their glasses. Similarly, a site targeting young children is going to be more successful if it relies on icons and pictures in place of words. Finally, a corporate accounting application that uses bright colors, decorative fonts, or gratuitous animations is hardly going to elicit the feelings of stability or security typically associated with such products.

Although evaluating design solutions is certainly easier than creating them, it is not without its own set of challenges. To play a useful and constructive role in the process, you should establish clear goals before the work begins and then use those goals as the criteria for evaluating alternatives.

PREVENTING STYLE FROM MESSING OTHER THINGS UP

What's dangerous about style is that it can—and often does—get out of control. In an effort to bring the aesthetics and precision of print to the medium of the Web, designers can unwittingly sacrifice the fundamental usability concerns of legibility and Web-wide consistency. In addition, the desire for novel or precise design solutions often leads to technical implementations that require excessive bandwidth, exhibit cross-browser incompatibility, or are generally unstable.

Any successful design solution must accommodate the basic limitations and constraints of the Web as a medium while being sensitive to users' physical and cognitive needs, as they work to understand and use the application.

WORKING WITHIN THE MEDIUM

If an application's visual designers are not reasonably well versed in the basic functioning of HTML, there is a significant risk that their solutions will unwittingly become a major source of additional engineering efforts. An unrealistic desire for precise control of typography, color, and placement can quickly lead to code contortions that tax engineers' sanity and users' patience.

Echoing an important theme of Layer 7: Layout (discussed in Chapter 10), visual design on the Web, particularly for Web applications, is an exercise in approximation. HTML does not, will not, and cannot provide a level of control on par with print design.

In the same way that print designers have to accommodate a printing press' constraints and abilities, Web designers have to accommodate HTML. This constraint is neither bad nor good; it simply means that the visual design must be sensitive to the medium through which it communicates.

LEGIBILITY

In contrast to readability, which is the property of a user being able to understand the meaning of the text based on vocabulary, grammar, and tone, *legibility* refers to the visual presentation of the text. Can the user visually parse and perceive individual letters, words, and sentences?

Unfortunately, legibility is one of the qualities most often sacrificed in the name of style. Without legibility, however, the interface is largely rendered useless. After all, it doesn't much matter what you write if no one can read it.

Legibility is influenced by a variety of visual variables, including contrast, line length, typeface, type size, font styling, and density/leading, discussed in the following sections.

Contrast

The quality of *contrast* refers to the difference in brightness between the text and background. A quick look around the library reveals that maximum contrast is not only the most common in print but presumably the ideal. It's no random chance that paper is generally white and ink is generally black. Excepting *Wired* magazine, the majority of print designers have recognized that maximum legibility results from maximum contrast: ideally, black text on a white background.

Although there's obviously some wiggle room here, it's best not to wiggle too much. Light gray is close to white, dark gray is close to black, and the brightness of any hue can be adjusted to produce a suitable foreground or background. The point remains, however, that for text to be legible, it has to be easily distinguished from the background.

Line Length

Line length refers to the horizontal width of a text block. It's hard enough to keep your eye focused on a single line of text as it moves across a printed page, much less a computer screen. Keeping line length to a reasonable distance improves legibility because the reader's eye doesn't have as far to travel.

Owing to this fact, most newspaper and magazine sites limit line length by using fixed-width layouts. Although that approach works for the long blocks of text typical of such sites, it's not necessarily the best solution for most Web applications. Financial applications in particular often need to present wide tables of data, and fixing their width unnecessarily limits the user's control. In these types of applications, users should be able to open the windows as wide as they want to see as much data as possible.

Legibility can be improved in these situations by adding background shading or borders to table rows. Something as subtle as a light gray background alternating between rows is typically enough. If the table's primary orientation is vertical, shading can also be applied to alternating columns instead of rows.

Typeface

Despite the mumblings and grumblings of countless Web designers, the state of the Web leaves only a handful of font choices—Arial, Verdana, and Times being the most popular options. At a more general level, the choice comes down to serif versus sans serif.

Serif fonts, such as Times, have decorative lines on the strokes used to compose letters, and sans serif fonts, such as Arial and Verdana, don't. Serif fonts are typically used in books, magazines, and other print publications because the serifs can help readers more quickly recognize letter and word shapes. In other words, the serifs increase legibility. Unfortunately, the same is not necessarily true for text on a computer monitor.

Because of their low resolution, computer screens lack the fidelity to accurately display serifs, especially at smaller type sizes. As a result, the serifs actually diminish legibility. Therefore, the best choice for Web applications tends to be a sans serif typeface, particularly if the text is smaller than 12 point. For text larger than 12 point—page titles, for example—either option is acceptable.

Type Size

Again, owing to the low resolution of computer screens, larger type sizes are more legible than smaller ones. The larger the type, however, the less information can appear on a page. Given the limited screen real estate, the challenge is to identify the minimum type size that is still legible. Depending on the quality of your user's eyesight, that's probably somewhere between 10 and 12 points. The best option, however, is to put the user in control of this variable by using a fluid layout that gracefully accommodates the font size preference of the user's browser.

Font Styling

In addition to the "normal" version of any font, there are styling options—bold, italic, and underlined being the most common. Unfortunately, thanks again to the resolution factor, there simply aren't enough pixels to render italics legibly. Similarly, although underlining is an option, because it serves as *the* universal Web convention for a hyperlink, you should never use it as simple text styling. Any text that's underlined appears as a link, regardless of color, typeface, or other formatting. Unless the text you're emphasizing truly is a link, you should not use underlining. With italics and underlining generally out, the only remaining option is bold. Unfortunately, even bold has its limitations because there is not enough screen resolution to distinguish bold text from non-bold text at smaller font sizes.

Despite all that bad news about font styles, there are methods for emphasizing and differentiating small blocks of text that don't involve font styling. Placing the text in different areas of the page or altering its color can render the text more or less prominent. Finally, used in small doses, all caps or small caps can also be an appropriate way of distinguishing text.

Finally, applying multiple styles to a block of text should generally be avoided. You can usually achieve enough visual coding by altering a single variable, such as size, color, style, or case. Double coding—bold italic, for example—is typically heavy-handed and unnecessary.

Density/Leading

A final variable affecting legibility is *density*, the space between lines of text or between the cells of a table. Legibility is almost always improved by decreasing density and increasing white space.

As a general rule, the text *leading*, or line spacing, should be 120% of the font size. For example, 10-point text should use 12-point leading. For tables, a good starting point is 4 units of cell padding and spacing combined—cell padding of 2 and cell spacing of 2 *or* cell padding of 4 and cell spacing of 0, for instance.

Although there is always pressure to add more information to a page, leaving an appropriate amount of "air" and white space is a welcome relief to users. By reducing the visual density of text and tables, the impression made by the page is less cluttered, less overwhelming, and more inviting.

Balancing the Variables Affecting Legibility

Legibility is critical for every site, application, and design. Unfortunately, it is often overrun by the desire for aesthetic coolness, individuality, or beauty. Figure 11.5 shows a table of data breaking with too little contrast in the sort key's (Date, in this example) column header and too little white space between the cells. Figure 11.6 corrects those errors, resulting in a much more legible table.

11.5

The legibility of this table suffers from too much density and too little contrast in the column header for the sort key.

LEGIBILITY

Title	Type	Gain/Loss	Date	Size	Actions
Lorem ipsum dolor sit amet	Euismod tincidunt	x.xxx.xx	03.31.2001	150Kb	delete
Consectetuer	Laoreet euism	x.xxx.xx	03.31.2001	230Kb	delete
Euismod tincidunt ut laoreet euismod tincidunt	Tincidunt	x.xxx.xx	02.28.2001	113Kb	delete
Quis nostrud exerci tation	Euismod	x.xxx.xx	02.28.2001	90Kb	delete
Lorem ipsum dolor sit amet	Tincidunt ut	x.xxx.xx	10.31.2000	150Kb	delete
Consectetuer	Euismod tincidunt	x.xxx.xx	10.31.2000	230Kb	delete
Euismod tincidunt ut laoreet euismod tincidunt	Euismod tincidunt	x.xxx.xx	09.30.2000	113Kb	delete

11.6

This figure corrects the problems in Figure 11.5, resulting in a more legible page.

LEGIBILITY

Title	Type	Gain/Loss	Date	Size	Actions
Lorem ipsum dolor sit amet	Euismod tincidunt	x.xxx.xx	03.31.2001	150Kb	delete
Consectetuer	Laoreet euism	x.xxx.xx	03.31.2001	230Kb	delete
Euismod tincidunt ut laoreet euismod tincidunt	Tincidunt	x.xxx.xx	02.28.2001	113Kb	delete
Quis nostrud exerci tation	Euismod	x.xxx.xx	02.28.2001	90Kb	delete
Lorem ipsum dolor sit amet	Tincidunt ut	x.xxx.xx	10.31.2000	150Kb	delete
Consectetuer	Euismod tincidunt	x.xxx.xx	10.31.2000	230Kb	delete
Euismod tincidunt ut laoreet euismod tincidunt	Euismod tincidunt	x.xxx.xx	09.30.2000	113Kb	delete

Ultimately, the purpose of every application is to serve the user's needs. Clearly, one of those needs is being able to read what's on the screen. Although the quest for legibility imposes a variety of limitations on the design, a successful solution carefully balances legibility and aesthetics.

PROVIDING VISUAL CUES TO BEHAVIOR

In the same way that a visual design should present text legibly, it should also present an application's functional controls in a manner that indicates their behavior. This requires the design to accommodate a variety of visual cues to communicate to the user, "Hey. You can click this thing here, but you can't click that thing over there." Because onscreen interfaces are disassociated from the physical world and the affordances it provides, there is nothing you can place on a screen that inherently makes it look clickable to a viewer totally unfamiliar with the medium. Instead of true affordances, the Web as a medium has developed a vocabulary of visual cues to indicate whether an element is clickable. For example, blue underlined text is a visual cue indicating that the underlined text is linked to other content and can be clicked. Nothing about the color blue or underlined text inherently means that the text is a hyperlink. Rather, the Web has associated blue underlined text with a hyperlink as a visual convention—one that continues to evolve to this very day.

The Term "Affordance"

The perceptual psychologist J.J. Gibson coined the term *affordance* to refer to actions that could take place between the physical world and the sentient beings operating within it. Gibson's goal was to explain the properties of physical objects that "afforded" how they could be used and manipulated. How, for example, can we tell that a rubber ball will bounce, but a steel one won't?

Later, Donald Norman introduced the concept of affordance into the lexicon of product designers in his book *The Psychology of Everyday Things*. Norman's discussion expanded the concept of affordance to the design of physical, real-world objects, such as doors and door handles. For example, how do we know how to open a door?

The concept of affordance eventually entered the vocabulary of interface designers, although its original meaning has suffered in the process. As Norman has observed, although industrial designers can rely on a wide variety of affordances resulting from the physical laws affected by shape, weight, material, texture, and so forth, software interfaces are not governed by these physical laws. Interface designers, therefore, are not concerned with affordance per se, but with the "perceived affordances" that result from what users perceive about what they are seeing on their screens. How, for example, do we know where to click in an interface?

It's important not to confuse visual feedback with visual cues that communicate whether an object is clickable before the user explores it. Rollover behavior—highlighting a screen element when the cursor hovers over it—does not communicate anything until the user explores the object. Rollover behavior does nothing to inform users of an object's behavior *before* they place their cursors over it. Therefore, rollovers rarely add to a user's understanding of an interface, although they can contribute a measure of fun and interactivity.

Compared to other interactive medium, in the world of Web applications, only one behavior really needs to be communicated. Onscreen elements can't be lifted or thrown; in general, they can't even be dragged from point A to point B. In typical HTML implementations, the only interaction that onscreen elements support is clicking. In addition, there are only two types of onscreen elements: text and graphics. Some text is for reading and some text is for clicking, in the same way that some graphics are for viewing and others are for clicking.

From the perspective of visual design, the fundamental question is "What are the visual conventions that indicate whether an onscreen element can be clicked?" Based more on personal experience than true research, there appear to be two important visual cues affecting text and one affecting graphics, explained in the following sections.

Visual Cues for Text-Based Hyperlinks

There was a time when voices in the design community preached that all hyperlinks should be forever and always blue and underlined. Those voices have now been replaced by an evolving visual convention that allows hyperlinks to be indicated with a variety of color and font style options.

When it comes to text, underlining is perhaps the strongest visual cue, although color runs a strong second. Users perceive any underlined text on the page as a clickable hyperlink, regardless of the text color. Unfortunately, if there are a *lot* of links on the page, the amount of underlining can become visually overwhelming. To accommodate for this problem, many designers now use color as the primary visual cue, sometimes coupled with the feedback of underlining the text when the user rolls over it. On the Web today, almost any combination of underlining and/or color is now interpreted as a hyperlink, with or without visual feedback. The unfortunate result is that color has almost been eliminated from the visual vocabulary as a way to distinguish bits of text.

When creating a visual style for an application's hyperlinks, be aware of the various conventions already familiar to users. In particular, avoid designs that mislead users into thinking some screen elements are links when they are not.

Visual Cues for Clickable Images

The visual cues indicating whether an image or button is clickable are more complicated than those affecting text links. For example, before the availability of color, the Macintosh operating system relied exclusively on shape. With a relatively simple but effective visual language, the Mac used rounded rectangles to represent buttons and simple circles and squares for radio buttons and check boxes. The Mac UI also featured drop shadows to communicate depth for document windows and pull-down menus. Microsoft later upped the ante with the Windows 95 use of color to create three-dimensional shading and beveling effects intended to make interface elements look clickable. Mac OS X has now gone one step further by introducing a visual effect that relies on sophisticated highlighting and reflection to create the illusion of depth.

Because desktop computing environments make use of multiple stacked windows, however, they are inherently three-dimensional environments. Therefore, it makes sense to use three-dimensional effects, such as shading and beveling, as visual cues. By contrast, the Web is a page-based environment, so it does not include the concept of depth. As a result, the three-dimensional effects characteristic of desktop computing environments are not particularly appropriate for Web applications.

In the absence of three-dimensional effects, the Web has adopted shape as the primary visual cue indicating whether an image can be clicked. Following the precedent established by the original version of the Mac OS, many Web applications include buttons shaped like rounded or squared rectangles. Figure 11.7 illustrates this button style from a variety of sites.

11.7
These buttons from various applications rely on shape to communicate to the user that they are buttons.

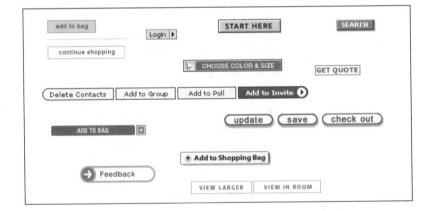

Text and location are additional cues used to indicate that an image is a button. An element containing text looks more like a button than ornamentation, as do elements placed in conventional areas of the page. Elements near the top of the page are expected to be navigation, whereas elements in the page's content area are expected to be command buttons or other input controls.

Tab-style navigation areas also rely on a combination of shape and text labeling to communicate their function. Figure 11.8 illustrates how navigational elements can be affected by removing the vertical lines between them. With the lines, the sub-navigation elements are perceived as individual navigation choices, but if the lines are removed, these elements run together into a single line without a clear indication of their function. Convention dictates separating each element into its own "box," and breaking the convention makes it more difficult to see the element as navigation.

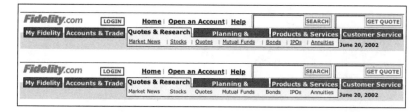

11.8

At the top, vertical lines "box" the sub-navigation elements. At the bottom, the "clickability" of the sub-navigation elements is affected by removing the vertical lines and the text underlining.

The delicate balance involved in working with these visual conventions requires a conscious understanding of the conventions themselves. For example, with buttons, a reasonable amount of variation is possible in both color and shape, certainly enough to achieve a measure of individuality. However, if the convention is violated by placing the button's label outside the button, the function of the button is left unclear.

Designs that alter and stretch convention are a necessary and vital part of ensuring the Web's continued evolution and development. However, these efforts always run the risk of taking things too far and destroying the user's ability to use the application. As a result, designs that run counter to established convention should be always be tested with users.

SUMMARY

Working in the realm of the Style layer is one of the most exciting and enjoyable aspects of interface design. The visual components of an interface tend to steal the spotlight from some of the more thorny and analytical aspects of the overall design. Ultimately, however, like all forms of design, visual design is about problem solving, not about personal preference or unsupported opinion.

Whether a particular visual design is appropriate for the interface of a Web application lies in how it balances a variety of competing demands, including:

- Consistency with corporate brand values and desired product personality traits
- Desire for individuality and unique identity
- Accommodation for the Web as a medium and for the technical realities of HTML
- Legibility of text and tables
- Consistency with the Web's established visual conventions

The final layer of the interface is Layer 9: Text. Looking forward to the next chapter, the focus will turn from the subject of pictures and images to the world of words and language.

"All writing is a process of elimination."

Martha Albrand

12 TEXT AND LABELS

Writing for the Web and Calling Things by Their Right Names

The final layer of the interface is Layer 9: Text, which includes the textual elements, such as menu titles, button names, form labels, page titles, and instructional text. Thousands of years of history have shown the written word to be an effective and useful form of communication, but in the practice of interface design, it can also be a seductive crutch. Although it invariably fails to improve the situation, adding text as a way to "explain" an otherwise poor design is an omnipresent temptation.

The design challenge in this layer centers on two concerns: when to speak and what to say. When to speak means identifying the situations where a text element is both necessary and vital, and what to say means choosing the words for those situations with the utmost care. Keep in mind that the Text layer is not concerned with a site's text-based content. Content itself is outside the scope of the interface, falling in the realm of editorial goals and standards. The issue here is the use of text as a supporting element of an application interface, not "how to write for the Web."

ELIMINATE SUPERFLUOUS TEXT

Before the advent of the Web, superfluous words rarely appeared in application interfaces. As a rule, desktop applications, ATMs, cell phones, dashboards, and other interactive media have minimized labels and eliminated instructions wherever possible. In these mediums, there is the clear expectation that the user is trying to accomplish a task, so the most polite and prudent thing to do is keep the chatter down to a minimum.

Compared to other interactive mediums, the Web is considerably more text-based. However, the Web is also an interactive medium, and Web applications in particular are an interactive task-based medium. If the interface's ultimate goal is to put the user in control, it must deliver a focused environment where users have everything they need and nothing they don't. Providing this type of environment means putting the user's needs first, and that means, among other things, eliminating extraneous text.

You might ask, "What's wrong with a few extra sentences here and there? If users aren't interested, they can just ignore them." The problem is that users don't know what they can and can't ignore until they look at it, and the simple act of looking at it distracts them from all the other things they *do* need to look at.

There is no zero in design. Each individual element plays a part, adding to or subtracting from the effectiveness of the whole. Therefore, words, sentences, and paragraphs that aren't contributing to the experience are subtracting from the things that are contributing.

Figure 12.1 from eBay exemplifies this problem. The page contains so much superfluous text that the important elements are simply swallowed by the clouds. Simply eliminating these distractions goes a long way toward lifting the fog and brightening the view.

In Figure 12.2, the unnecessary text has been eliminated and the alignment and spacing of the layout has been adjusted. The result is a simplified page with less distraction, more focus, and less clutter. If there's a rule here, it goes like this: Eliminate every word you possibly can and then eliminate some more. Be brutal and you'll at least get in the ballpark.

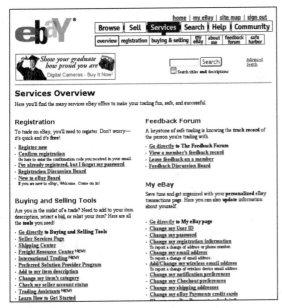

12.1

An example of the detractive nature of superfluous text taken from eBay.

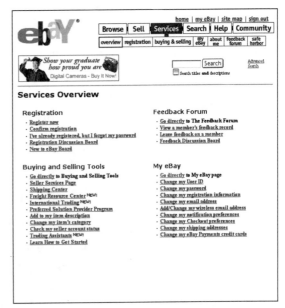

12.2

Eliminating unnecessary text reduces visual noise without reducing functionality.

TEXT: WHAT'S IT GOOD FOR?

Although text is one of the most direct ways to communicate with users, it also requires them to read, recognize, and understand the words. By contrast, visual forms of communication, such as icons, color, or proximity, can communicate more efficiently and effectively without requiring the same level of cognitive processing. The downside of visual communication, however, is that it often lacks the precision and specificity of written language. After all, if icons always communicated effectively, they would never need labels.

Clearly, some types of messages and information can be communicated only through text. The trick, then, is to identify and recognize which aspects of the interface truly require text and which ones don't.

NAVIGATION

Navigation and text are largely synonymous on the Web, thanks to its origins as a hypertext system. Text plays a critical role in supporting site navigation by serving as basic text links and labels for other navigational elements, such as tabs. When using text as navigation, choose language that clearly communicates the destination of the link and is familiar to the user. Unfortunately, the specialist vocabulary of the site developers' organization can often creep into the interface's text. The designers of WebMD (see Figure 12.3) know what they mean by "WebMD Health," "Medscape from WebMD," and "WebMD Office," but do you?

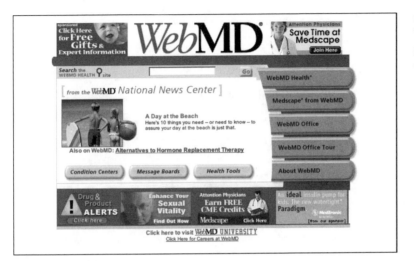

12.3
The vocabulary of WebMD's main navigation does little to tell users which area they should visit.

TITLES

Text is also the primary method for identifying individual pages as well as sections within a page. Well-written titles should serve as micro-messages giving the user as much context as possible with a bare minimum of words. Page titles in particular should be able to communicate the page's purpose even when they appear on a whiteboard by themselves. For example, specific titles, such as "Buy Stock," "Edit Contact," and "Purchase Tickets," communicate on their own in a way that nondescript titles, such as "Transactions," "Edit," and "Purchase," don't.

LABELS

Text is also used to label input controls on forms. In the interest of efficiency, labels for input controls, such as text boxes, radio buttons, and check boxes, should generally be nouns. A text box for a user's name, for example, should be labeled "Name," not "Type your name here."

By contrast, command buttons are best labeled with active, precise verbs. Save, Cancel, Delete, Edit, Purchase, Search are all good examples. Depending on the context, you could also reduce the button's label by eliminating the noun associated with the button's action. For example, if the page contains a list of email messages, the purpose of a Delete button will be just as clear as a Delete Messages button.

INSTRUCTIONS AND HELP

As a general rule, you should avoid instructions in the interface. Instructions are almost universally ignored and only serve to distract users and take up space—with form input examples being one of the few exceptions. If the design fails to adequately communicate how to operate the page, instructions are hardly going to make up for the design's shortcomings. Figure 12.4 from American Airlines includes a full paragraph of unnecessary instructional text.

12.4

If the page can't carry the day on its own, this instructional text is hardly going to help.

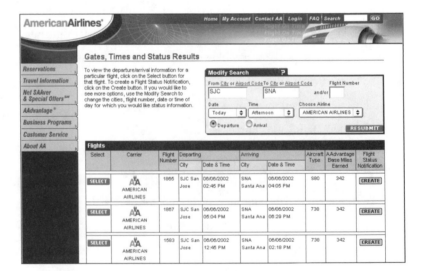

MARKETING MESSAGES

Banner ads and other marketing messages are the Web's equivalent of dinnertime phone calls from loan consolidators. Consumers hate them because they are a constant interruption. Businesses and marketers love them because they get users' attention. Although marketing messages can be accommodated in some Web applications, they are few and far between. Obviously, in applications sold and licensed as standalone software, such messages should be completely eliminated. After all, users have already bought the software. Leave them alone already.

However, if the application's business model requires the design to include marketing messages, the goal should be to keep the noise to a minimum. Ideally, the messages can be reduced to small graphic elements or short text links that lead users to pages with more information about the offer. If the offer isn't interesting to users, no amount of shouting will get them to accept it.

The free portfolio tracker at SmartMoney has five different marketing messages all vying for the user's attention, distracting from one another, and distracting from the user's information (see Figure 12.5). Although economic support for the application requires some level of advertising and marketing messages, the messages diminish the application's utility.

12.5
SmartMoney's portfolio tracker
has five different marketing
messages distracting users
from what they're trying to do.

Although there are legitimate uses for text in the interface, the general
rule is to keep it to a minimum. Because the design will need to rely on text
in some places, however, understanding what it means to write for the Web
is also important.

WRITING FOR THE WEB

It's a cold, hard fact, but people don't read on the Web. Certainly they don't read the Web in the same way they read books, newspapers, or other printed material. Instead, they "scan," moving about the page looking for isolated nuggets of meaning with a speed and ferocity that borders on manic. If you expect to add value in the midst of this activity, you'll need to keep a few things in mind.

BE COURTEOUS, NOT PATRONIZING

Using a Web application is not like a face-to-face conversation. Although being courteous is still important, simply being relevant and succinct is often the most polite thing you can do. Phrases such as "Please provide us with your email address" are just so much noise when a simple text box labeled "Email" would suffice.

LEVERAGE THE CONTEXT

Often you can eliminate words by leveraging the context in which they appear. For example, a reservation form doesn't need a Departure Date label right next to the controls for selecting a date. "Departure" alone serves the need and reduces the word count by half.

DON'T REPEAT YOURSELF

Don't fill up the page repeating the same words over, and over, and over again. Figure 12.6 illustrates repetition in a couple of different ways—how fitting. First, the instructional text does little more than repeat the page title and should be eliminated. Second, the word "recommended" appears multiple times next to each picture, when an icon alone would clearly suffice.

Other simple improvements include eliminating the explanatory text about printing on the back of photos, and changing the name of the Next button to reflect the next step's actual content. The "enhanced" version is shown in Figure 12.7.

AVOID MULTISYLLABIC WORDS THAT OBFUSCATE

Strive for clarity. Because users scan rather than read, any words that can't be instantly recognized and understood are almost guaranteed to be ignored.

Don't, however, pull your hair out trying to choose between two synonyms. Debates about the merits of "Submit versus Save" or "Edit versus Change" are unlikely to produce any meaningful improvements in your application.

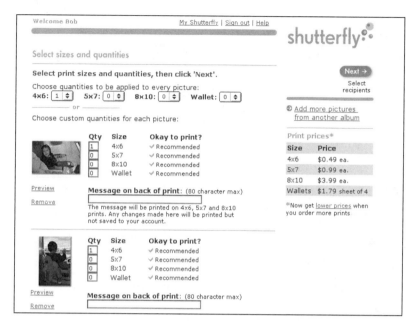

12.6
The Order Prints page from Shutterfly repeats the words *select*, *quantities*, and *recommended* unnecessarily.

12.7
An "enhanced" version eliminates repetitive instructions.

SUMMARY

Because it's easy to add words to an interface, there is always the temptation to try to talk your way out of a difficult problem. Like a discussion with a traffic cop, however, explanations and pleadings rarely alter the situation. Text can't repair problems in more fundamental areas of the interface, although it can play an important role in supporting them. The critical issue is knowing when and where text can help and then knowing exactly which words will be most effective. You will get further along that path by keeping the following in mind:

- ☐ Eliminate as much text as possible. Eliminate some more.
- ☐ Be relevant and concise.
- ☐ Select a vocabulary familiar to users.

Lest you find all the dos and don'ts a bit overwhelming, take comfort in realizing that text is the most easily modified aspect of the interface. In other words, you don't have to get it right the first time around. More so than with any other aspect of the interface, correcting problems in the Text layer is fairly easy, after you've vetted the design with actual users. Text is certainly important, but compared to everything else, it's more fixable.

With the discussion of the Text layer complete, the Presentation tier and the overall interface are also at an end. The remaining chapters have the enviable task of taking the theories and ideas discussed in the past nine chapters and applying them to two specific Web applications, beginning with the Web's most influential online store, Amazon.com.

Case Studies

PART V

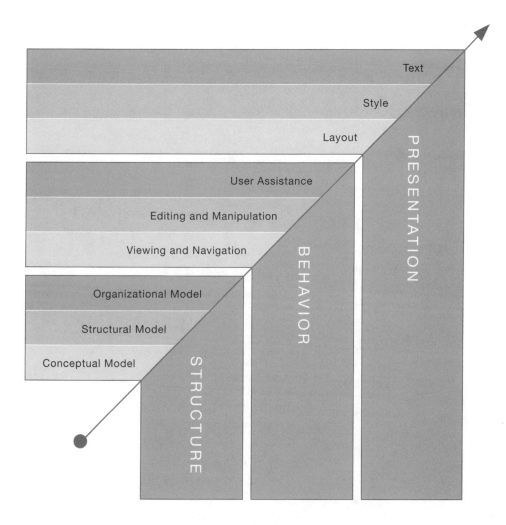

Text

Style

Layout

User Assistance

Editing and Manipulation

Viewing and Navigation

Organizational Model

Structural Model

Conceptual Model

PRESENTATION

BEHAVIOR

STRUCTURE

"You can't have everything.
 Where would you put it?"

Steven Wright

13

AMAZON.COM

Browsing the Aisles
of the Web's Supreme Retailer

Opening for business in July 1995, Amazon.com started with the mission "to use the Internet to transform book buying into the fastest, easiest, and most enjoyable shopping experience possible." Today, Amazon stands not only as a pioneer of the Web, but also as the undisputed leader of online shopping.

Since its beginnings, Amazon's customer base has steadily grown along with its product selection. The site now serves over 220 countries, under the slogan of "Earth's Biggest Selection." In addition to books, music, and video, the site boasts a diverse set of offerings—toys, electronics, computers, kitchenware, cameras, cell phones, and gardening supplies, to name a few (see Figure 13.1).

13.1

The home page of Amazon.com, the Web's largest and most influential retailer.

As a Web application, Amazon makes for an instructive case study for these primary reasons:

☐ **Market supremacy.** As the leader in online shopping, Amazon sets the standards that others follow. Right or wrong, there's simply no ignoring what happens on Amazon.

☐ **Quantity of content.** Thanks to the quantity and complexity of content, Amazon includes a variety of unique design problems and solutions. As a result, Amazon's interface, is weighted toward Layer 3: Organizational Model and Layer 4: Viewing and Navigation (see Figure 13.2).

☐ **Sophisticated checkout process.** As one of the most complex, sophisticated, and well-designed guides on the Web, Amazon's checkout process is an example clearly worth studying.

Unfortunately, the variety of content and functionality on Amazon makes it impractical to write an exhaustive case study. Therefore, the focus here will be on Amazon's bookstore and checkout process. In the context of those two areas, notice how Amazon's breadth of content and sophisticated navigation features support the commitment to an "educational and inspiring shopping experience."

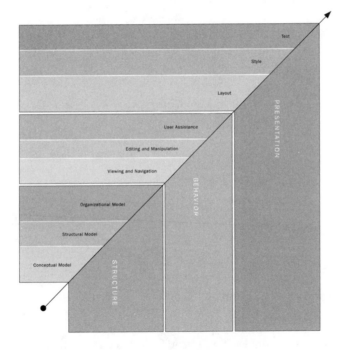

13.2
The variety of content on Amazon requires an interface biased toward organization and navigation.

TIER I: STRUCTURE

As with all Web applications, the success of Amazon's interface relies on the integrity of its structural components. In addition to the normal difficulty of creating a strong conceptual and structural model, the variety of Amazon's product offerings presents a unique challenge for the design of the organizational model. Whether users have a satisfying experience of "Earth's Biggest Selection" ultimately relies on their ability to simply find their way around.

LAYER 1: CONCEPTUAL MODEL

At the base of Amazon's interface is the conceptual model of a reference catalog. As opposed to magazine style-catalogs designed for browsing and exploration, reference catalogs, such as office supply or auto part catalogs, are optimized for directed, product-specific searches. The model is particularly appropriate and useful for fairly uniform product categories, such as books, music, and video, because users refer to those products by a unique title.

Like physical reference catalogs, the conceptual model of a reference catalog implies that each product is presented in a relatively uniform manner. In addition, the model implies the presence of several methods for finding specific products, such as a table of contents and multiple indexes. One example of Amazon's consistent implementation of this conceptual model is the book details page. Regardless of title or subject, Amazon relies on a single template for presenting each book, even though the information available for each title varies.

Of course, the real value of Amazon is not strict adherence to its conceptual model. Rather, the magic of Amazon is its ability to expand that model into a dynamic, personalized experience. Unlike a printed catalog, Amazon's technology enables the site to display different products based on users' past purchases and recently viewed items. Although Amazon's "clairvoyance" can be a nuisance, more often it feels like a personal shopper helping you make your way through the bewildering assortment of choices and products.

In addition, Amazon has expanded the conceptual model in a manner that would be impossible if it was a physical store. Amazon's product offerings are so varied and voluminous that housing them all in one location would require a warehouse of epic proportions. Even with an army of sales clerks, a physical store couldn't come close to the selection, advice, or personalized recommendations available on Amazon.

Amazon is able to provide this unique value and experience by exploiting one of the Web's exclusive resources: a community of users. Unlike most other online stores, Amazon allows users to review and rate products, in effect democratizing the book-buying experience in a way unimaginable before the advent of the Web. In addition, Amazon makes use of users' purchase and navigation patterns by using them as the basis for its personalization.

As the basis of Amazon's interface, the conceptual model of a reference catalog model not only gives users a clear understanding of what the site offers and how it is organized, but also provides a solid foundation on which the interface can grow and innovate.

LAYER 2: STRUCTURAL MODEL

Because of its huge volume of content, Amazon's primary structural model is a hub, as shown in Figure 13.3. The center of the hub contains the product detail and category index pages, and the spokes link to functional areas, such as checkout and account management. Amazon also uses the structural model of a guide for its checkout process and another hub for its account management area.

13.3

Amazon's structural model is a hub, with the product pages at the center and functional areas at the spokes.

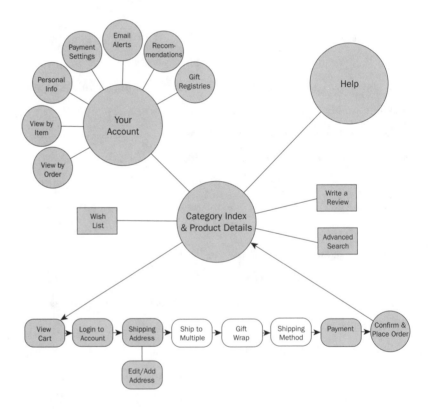

The most instructive aspect of Amazon's structural model involves its checkout process. Originally designed as a wizard, the process is now implemented as a guide. A notable improvement, this change enables users to edit discrete elements of a purchase without having to revisit the unaffected elements. For example, with the guide structure, a user can navigate directly from the order summary page to the shipping page and back again. In its previous implementation as a wizard, the user had to pass back through the payment page, even though he or she had not made any payment changes.

In addition to this improvement in task flow, Amazon's checkout process benefits from an obvious respect for the differences between view and form pages. Throughout the checkout process, the standard tab-based navigation is replaced by a prominent step counter, signaling to users that they are now in a different mode. In addition to communicating current and remaining tasks, replacing the standard navigation with the step counter eliminates distraction, focuses users' attention, and helps them understand the process.

Even more efficient than a guide, however, is Amazon's 1-Click ordering (see Figure 13.4). With this feature, users can buy an item without having to go through the checkout process at all—the ultimate in simplicity and efficiency.

13.4
Amazon's 1-Click feature allows users to bypass the checkout process guide altogether.

As with the conceptual model, Amazon has done an excellent job of choosing and implementing appropriate structures for the site's functional areas.

LAYER 3: ORGANIZATIONAL MODEL

One of Amazon's most notable strengths is the sophistication and richness of its organizational model—or, more accurately, *models*. As evidenced in Figure 13.5, Amazon's bookstore makes use of no less than five different organizational models, offering users a variety of methods for locating an item, whether they're searching for something in particular or just browsing.

☐ **Topical hierarchy.** Represented in the tab-based navigation structure, Amazon uses a topical classification scheme combined with a hierarchical model of association. This organizational model divides the site into different stores and organizes the products within those stores. In addition, the Browse channel on the left side of the page contains the top level of a topical hierarchy used to categorize books based on subject.

☐ **Alphabetic index.** Amazon's most used and most efficient organizational model uses an alphabetic classification scheme with an index as the model of association. Even though users don't experience the scheme directly, it is present in the search functionality, which allows users to search the collection by a text-based field, independent of any categorization.

☐ **Topical web.** One of Amazon's greatest strengths and unique features is its extensive use of a topical classification scheme with a web model of association. As seen on the home page and the product details pages, Amazon makes liberal use of topical hyper-links to guide the user to a wide variety of product groupings and related products. For example, the page in Figure 13.5 contains topical links to the Harry Potter Store, the Summer Reading Store, Editor's Choice books, and the Celebrate America store.

☐ **Chronologic index.** Another of Amazon's organizational models is seen in the New & Future Releases area, which is organized as a chronologic index based on release date.

☐ **Numeric index.** Yet another of Amazon's organizational models is a numeric index, represented by the Amazon.com 100 channel. This organizational model allows users to navigate and locate books based on popularity and sales figures.

13.5

The home page of Amazon's bookstore contains at least five different organizational models, providing a rich variety of navigation options.

Topical hierarchy —

Alphabetic index —

Chronologic index —

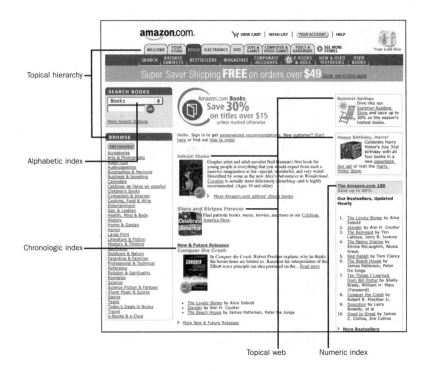

Topical web   Numeric index

Even more impressive than the range of organizational models used on the home page, however, is the sophistication and utility of the organizational options on the product detail pages (see Figure 13.6). In addition to the persistent navigation and search functions, the page contains topical links based on at least eight different associations.

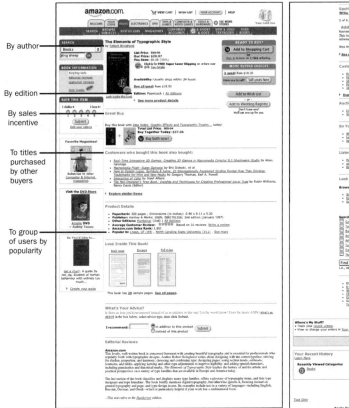

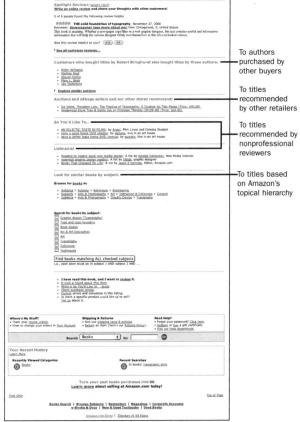

By author

By edition

By sales incentive

To titles purchased by other buyers

To group of users by popularity

To authors purchased by other buyers

To titles recommended by other retailers

To titles recommended by nonprofessional reviewers

To titles based on Amazon's topical hierarchy

13.6

Amazon's book details pages contain an extraordinary range of product associations and navigation options.

Amazon's rich organizational model spans the entire site, providing a compelling and educational browsing experience. The site's ability to expose the user to other books and products is unparalleled and surely lies at the heart of Amazon's success. Although Amazon lacks the physical experience and immediate gratification of a brick-and-mortar bookstore, it succeeds by exploiting its unique advantages over physical stores—the most obvious being selection, but selection alone is not enough.

More than selection alone, however, the magic of Amazon is its ability to expose buyers to other books and products based on past buying and browsing behavior. In other words, it's not that Amazon as a store carries the world's biggest collection of books; it's that Amazon as a Web application allows users to navigate through that collection in meaningful, useful, and serendipitous ways.

TIER II: BEHAVIOR

In addition to the navigation features required to support Amazon's complex organizational model, the dominating element of Amazon's Behavior tier is the checkout process. The following sections analyze those two elements as well as Amazon's help and customer service center.

LAYER 4: VIEWING AND NAVIGATION

Because of the lack of user-created data, the Amazon interface does not require any of the view manipulation features typically associated with tables of text-based data. There are no columns to sort, no objects to edit, no datasets to filter. Although Amazon's interface lacks viewing function-ality, it is full to overflowing with navigation options, thanks to its rich organizational model. Even here, however, Amazon's designers do a great job of not letting the sheer quantity of options lead to a corresponding increase in complexity. In fact, Amazon's Viewing and Navigation layer is extremely simple from an interaction perspective, even though it is a critical element of the interface as a whole.

As shown previously in Figure 13.6, except for the high-level navigational elements represented in the tab bar, Amazon's navigation scheme relies almost exclusively on the humble hyperlink. If you know how to use a Web page, you know how to use Amazon. There are no hidden options—nothing tucked inside a menu or two levels down inside a hierarchical tree. Everything is immediately visible directly on the page in a clear, concise manner.

Another notable aspect of Amazon's navigation mechanism involves the use of highlighting to indicate location. The only level of navigation that's highlighted is the top-level tab, which indicates the current "store." However, despite this fact, the design is one of the most effective navigation systems on the Web. The implication here is that it's not necessary to communicate users' current locations if they are navigating through a deep and complex information space, especially if multiple organizational models and navigation schemes are available.

Another result of the variety of organizational models is that no single navigation mechanism dominates the interface. Despite the tab bar being one of the most prominent visual elements of the application, from a usage perspective, the Search form is undoubtedly more popular. In addition, the few pages that are represented in the tab bar serve less as hubs than they do as starting points. For example, although users can navigate to the New & Upcoming Releases page through the secondary navigation area of the tab bar, once there, they are as likely to navigate directly from one item to the next as they are to return to the index page. With all the different navigation options, users are likely to follow different paths derived from different organizational models at nearly every turn.

One problem with Amazon's navigation is the way the tab bar's contents change as the user navigates from one tab to another. Because some of the tabs take the user to "stores" operated by one of Amazon's partners, navigating to toys, for example, completely changes the tab bar and destroys the experience of Amazon as a single, cohesive site. Regardless of this flaw, however, Amazon has clearly succeeded in creating a true hypertext experience by providing such a rich and varied number of navigation options.

LAYER 5: EDITING AND MANIPULATION

Amazon's Editing and Manipulation layer is dominated by s sophisticated guide that serves as the checkout process. The following pages are required steps (four of these pages are shown in Figure 13.7):

> Shopping cart
>
> Shipping address
>
> Shipping method
>
> Payment method
>
> Payment address
>
> Order confirmation

1

2

3

4

13.7

The shopping cart, shipping address, payment method, and order confirmation pages from Amazon's checkout process.

The checkout guide also includes optional pages for gift wrapping and multi-address shipping.

There are a number of instructive aspects to this design:

- ☐ **Elimination of navigation.** As mentioned in the context of the structural model, once the user enters the checkout sequence, the persistent navigational elements are removed. In addition to helping users focus on their tasks, this helps prevent them from inadvertently exiting the sequence by clicking one of the navigation options.

- ☐ **Informative step counter.** The step counter at the top of each page provides meaningful information about the checkout process as well as a quick way for users to see where they are and how many steps they have left.

- ☐ **Simultaneous access to existing and new data.** As seen on the shipping address and payment method pages, users can easily use information they've already supplied to Amazon or enter new information without having to go to a different page.

- ☐ **Obvious access to the next step.** The large Continue and Place Order buttons provide distinct mechanisms for moving to the next step or completing the sequence.

- ☐ **Robust navigation in the order confirmation page.** This page is the strongest element of the checkout process, thanks to its clear layout and robust navigation. The page summarizes the order details and provides an obvious way to alter any order details with the clearly labeled array of "Change" buttons.

- ☐ **All options made visible.** Throughout each of the guide's pages, virtually every available option is visible on the page. For example, on the shipping address page, every saved address is visible on the page instead of being hidden inside a menu.

Although there are some minor problems with Amazon's checkout process—too much instructional text, for example—those criticisms pale in comparison to how many things Amazon got right.

LAYER 6: USER ASSISTANCE

Amazon's User Assistance layer is composed primarily of online help and customer service, both of which are available from the utility navigation icons in the upper-right corner.

Online Help

Amazon features an unusually rich amount of online help, as shown in Figure 13.8. The help system is procedural in nature and follows a FAQ style. In addition to the topical hierarchy seen on the help index page, users can also use the "Search Our Help Department" feature as a quick way to search across all help pages. Another helpful feature of Amazon's design is the topic summary on the category index page. As shown in the Ordering via 1-Click page (top-right page in Figure 13.8), the summary can be useful in answering users' question without requiring them to go down to the next level. As an improvement, using that same layout for the third-level pages would also be helpful so that users could quickly go to another topic without having to navigate back to the category index.

1

2

3

13.8

Amazon's rich online help is presented in an FAQ style using a three-level hierarchy.

Customer Service

In addition to one of the best e-commerce sites on the Web, Amazon also boasts one of the best order fulfillment and shipping operations of any online vendor. Among other places, this is highly evident in the depth and sophistication of the Your Account page, shown in Figure 13.9. Because Amazon conducts business completely through the Internet, all ordering operations have to be available in a self-service manner. Clearly, the variety of actions in the customer service area is a critical factor in Amazon being able to run a multi-billion-dollar business without an 800 number.

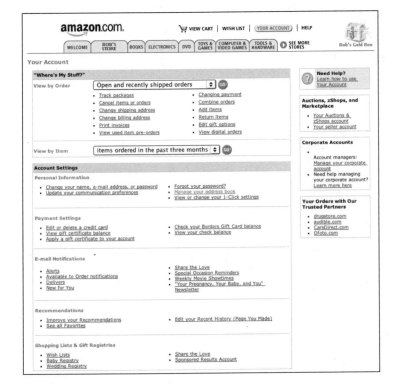

13.9
Amazon's Your Account page uses a procedural-style FAQ page to communicate the available self-service operations.

Alerts

Similar to other online stores, Amazon's interface does not include many alerts or confirmations. The primary source of input errors is either a failed user ID or password on the login page or an incorrect credit card number on the payment page. Although input errors can occur in other pages, they are in less-traveled areas.

Figure 13.10 shows Amazon's alert for a failed login. Notice the visual strength of the alert message and how the page clearly communicates that an error has occurred. Although the message text runs longer than necessary, there is no mistaking what has taken place.

As with the Structure tier, the strength of Amazon's design is apparent throughout the Behavior tier. The site consistently uses the most direct and obvious interaction mechanisms, requiring little or no additional learning on the part of users.

13.10
Amazon's login page clearly communicates when an error has occurred.

TIER III: PRESENTATION

The Presentation tier is the one aspect of Amazon's interface most in need of attention. Although it generally supports the previous layers, it fails to add as much to the experience as it could.

LAYER 7: LAYOUT

Amazon primarily uses two layouts: one for view pages and one for forms. The book details page shown in Figure 13.6 is representative of the layout for view pages, as are the checkout process pages shown in Figure 13.7 for forms.

The layout on the book details page uses a two-column grid, dedicating the left-side column to navigation options and the other column to product information. In some situations, such as the bookstore's home page, Amazon extends the grid, adding a third column to the right side for more navigation options. In either case, the main content column expands and contracts to accommodate the width of the page. This allows users to adjust the length of text elements in the main column, giving them a level of control consistent with the Web.

For forms, Amazon uses a single-column layout. The form layout also dynamically adjusts to the width of the browser window, offering more control over the presentation. Although the form elements do not resize to the window, the spacing between elements varies as the window expands and contracts.

Amazon consistently places different classes of elements—navigation versus content, for example—in clearly delineated areas. For example, the tab bar, search box, and utilities such as View Cart and Help appear in the same location across every page. Even though the content varies from product to product, the placement remains consistent so that users can quickly orient themselves. This is true not only in Amazon's bookstore, but also across the site as a whole.

In addition, the layout of Amazon's various pages presents a clear visual hierarchy by placing critical elements at the top of the page and using horizontal rules and color to identify different sections and groups. Perhaps the biggest problem with the Layout layer is simply the overabundance of information on each page. Although Amazon's current design strikes an acceptable balance between functionality and clutter, each new element it adds pushes things toward the messy end of the scale.

LAYER 8: STYLE

The bulk of Amazon's brand identity and visual style occurs in the top 110 pixels of the page. No single element more clearly says "This is Amazon.com" than the tab bar. Even without the logo, the site is instantly recognizable by the tab bar. Although the channel borders and title areas certainly support the visual identity set up by the tabs, they play a supporting role to the tabs themselves.

In addition to the strength of its visual identity, Amazon's Style layer supports the elements of the Behavior tier by using a conventional shape and consistent color for command buttons, such as Add to Cart and Place Your Order. The design also supports the large volume of text by using effective color, contrast, legible font sizes, and appropriate font styling. For example, almost all text is black on a white background and underlining is exclusively used to indicate a hyperlink.

Although the design succeeds in establishing a clear and consistent visual identity, it fails to come across as harmonious or elegant. Compared to more visually appealing designs, such as RedEnvelope or Banana Republic, Amazon looks like an advertising insert in the Sunday paper. Although that look is consistent with the conceptual model of a reference catalog and may even represent the exact feeling the designers were intending, the visual experience certainly lacks beauty.

As the penultimate layer of the interface, Amazon's visual style may or may not have much effect on its success. After all, two of the Web's strongest brands, Yahoo! and eBay, also lack a compelling visual presentation. Even so, considering the number of visitors and the time spent looking at these pages, it's unfortunate that the experience isn't more elegant.

LAYER 9: TEXT

The final layer of the Amazon interface is the Text layer. In keeping with the criticism of the other Presentation layers, the biggest problem with the Text layer is that there's just too much of it. Almost every page is filled with text related to the current item or other related items. Unfortunately, the Amazon interface tends to make matters worse by adding superfluous instructional text and marketing messages, filling the page with even more words.

This is particularly true of the checkout process, where page after page is filled with unnecessary instructions and endless footers and disclaimers. Figure 13.11 shows what the order confirmation page would look like with the extraneous text removed. In the spirit of giving them the benefit of the doubt, it may be that Amazon's usability studies have shown that the extra text has value. The reduced version is certainly an easier page to digest, however.

However, there is one aspect of the Text layer where Amazon excels: labeling buttons, hyperlinks, and input fields. Throughout the site, command buttons and hyperlinks are clearly labeled with simple, obvious language, using both a noun and a verb to ensure clarity. Place Your Order, Add to Shopping Cart, and Buy Now with 1-Click are all examples.

Although the different layers of Amazon's Presentation tier fulfill their requirements, they lack the sophistication and elegance of the solutions in the layers of the Structure and Behavioral tiers.

13.11

Although the design shown on the right is more visually manageable, only a usability study could show if less actually turned out to be more in this case.

SUMMARY

As the leader of online retailing, Amazon is not only a model worth emulating, but also a standard that's impossible to avoid. Fortunately for the designers and users of the Web, Amazon generally gets things right, particularly in the areas where it's most important. As a Web application interface, Amazon's example is most useful for the following problems:

☐ **Structural model.** Over time, Amazon has been willing and able to modify the structural model of one of its most important components: the checkout process. Here and elsewhere, Amazon demonstrates the differences between guides and wizards and shows the value of clearly differentiating between view and form pages.

☐ **Organizational model and navigation scheme.** Amazon's organizational models and navigation schemes work in concert to provide a flowing, seamless browsing experience virtually unparalleled in online shopping. The manner of moving through the available inventory at Amazon is fundamentally different from that of a physical store in terms of its sheer volume and the multiple ways in which items are related.

☐ **Editing and manipulation.** The simplicity of Amazon's interface is evident in both the checkout guide and the forms associated with the customer service center. The interactive design of these forms tends to be as obvious and natural as possible with a minimum of hidden options or complex dependencies between input controls.

With the analysis and critique of Amazon's bookstore completed, the next subject for examination is the Web's leading photo processor, Ofoto. In contrast to Amazon's relative lack of user-created data and volumes of content, Ofoto contains virtually no content and nothing but user-created data.

14 OFOTO

Looking at the Leading Online
Photo Processor

Founded in July 1999 and subsequently acquired by Kodak in June 2001, Ofoto is the premier online photography service available today. As stated in its company mission, Ofoto's goal is "to provide top-quality silver halide prints for digital and film camera users."

As a photo-processing business, Ofoto and its competitors are a natural outgrowth of the trend toward digital photography. Because digital cameras capture photographic images as computer files rather than physical film negatives, Ofoto's customers upload their images to the Ofoto Web site (see Figure 14.1), either through the site or with the desktop utility, OfotoNow. After the images have been transferred, the Web site can be used to order prints in a variety of sizes and formats. The site also provides tools for users to store and manage their photos, to share their photos with family and friends, and to edit and crop their photos.

14.1

The home page of Ofoto.

As shown in Figure 14.2, Ofoto's interface features a variety of complex and unique design challenges in the structural model and the Behavior tier that make Ofoto an example worth studying. Those challenges include the following:

☐ **Creating and managing user data.** In addition to storage and management of photos, Ofoto enables users to create and manage photo albums, shipping addresses, slide shows, and print orders. In addition to the forms that support creating these data objects, the view pages have mechanisms for selecting and managing users' stored data.

☐ **Editing and enhancing images.** Because images cannot be directly edited through HTML input controls, Ofoto's image-editing features present unique technical and design challenges for Layer 5: Editing and Manipulation.

☐ **Designing for the consumer market.** Compounding the inherent difficulty of providing sophisticated functionality through a Web application, Ofoto targets the mass consumer market. As a result, Ofoto's interface must be particularly easy to use, as shown in the significant support from Layer 6: User Assistance.

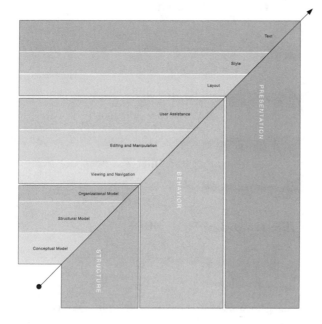

14.2
Ofoto's emphasis on functionality rather than content results in an interface that emphasizes the structural model and the Editing and Manipulation layer.

In addition to examining these three challenges, the goal here is to analyze Ofoto's interface, looking at it as a single, unified design. As a consumer-based online service, Ofoto's site boasts one of the most thoughtfully designed interfaces on the Web. Unfortunately, however, the type of functionality it offers does not easily lend itself to the Web as an interactive medium. As a result, many of the weaknesses discussed here should be considered commentary on the capabilities and limitations of Web applications as a medium rather than criticisms of the Ofoto design in particular.

TIER I: STRUCTURE

The dominant design challenge of Ofoto's Structure tier, if not the interface as a whole, is the conceptual model. Almost as challenging, however, is Ofoto's structural model, with its relatively complex collection of interdependent hubs and wizards. Fortunately for the designers at Ofoto, the minor volume of content—compared to an online store like Amazon—means that the interface does not require a sophisticated organizational model.

LAYER 1: CONCEPTUAL MODEL

Like other online photo-processing services, Ofoto's core functionality includes the following:

- **Photo upload.** Electronically transferring photo files to Ofoto through the Ofoto Web application or the desktop utility OfotoNow.
- **Photo storage and management.** Organizing photos into different groups so that they can be easily accessed later.

- ☐ **Print ordering.** Indicating images to be printed on photographic paper, including each print's size and quantity as well as shipping location and payment method.

- ☐ **Photo sharing.** Selecting images to publish in a "slideshow" and inviting guests to view the slideshow via email.

- ☐ **Photo enhancement.** Rotating, cropping, editing, and enhancing photos. including red-eye removal, brightness and contrast adjustment, and other effects, such as sepia tone, black-and-white, and so forth.

Unfortunately, this functionality does not easily lend itself to a single, unified conceptual model. Although the obvious conceptual model might be that of a photo-processing store, that model fails to accommodate any features unique to digital images, such as sharing, editing, or enhancing. Similarly, even though some areas of functionality suggest the model of a photo album, a mail system, an address book, or a photo-editing tool, none of those options adequately encompasses the full set of features.

Although it isn't labeled as such, the first page users encounter after logging in, the View and Edit Albums page, serves as the application's home page and effectively establishes the conceptual model (see Figure 14.3). Because of this page and others, the model or photo album most clearly comes through in Ofoto's design.

14.3

Right from the start, Ofoto establishes the conceptual model of a photo album. Shown here is the View Albums page, the first page displayed after the user is logged in.

Unfortunately, the model of a photo album captures only the storing and sharing features, virtually ignoring the print ordering and image-editing functions. A different model the designers of Ofoto could have considered is a storage system for negatives. In that model, "digital negatives" are stored in a single, non-hierarchical library, augmented with keyword and text-based searching. Some desktop applications, such as Apple Computer's iPhoto, use this model.

As a conceptual model, a storage system for negatives has a variety of advantages, including the following:

☐ **Positions photos as the primary object.** By focusing the interface on individual photos, the model would emphasize Ofoto's print-ordering and image-editing features.

☐ **Positions albums as temporary containers.** In this model, albums serve as temporary containers that can be modified or deleted independently of the images in them. This would allow users to create a variety of highly customized albums without affecting the organization or storage of their digital negatives.

☐ **Allows images to be modified without affecting the original "negative."** Because the model creates "digital prints" for placement inside albums, it implies that those prints can be manipulated and edited without affecting the stored original. This would encourage users to explore the editing and enhancement tools because it gives them a safe environment to work in.

☐ **Enables searching across the universe of stored images.** Because images are stored in a single library, the model would allow users to search across all their images instead of requiring them to view one album at a time.

☐ **Consistent with the model of film-based photography.** Because the model retains the notion of negatives and prints, it would reflect the established model users have derived from film-based photography.

Despite these advantages, however, the model of a storage system for negatives has some serious drawbacks in the context of a Web application. The most obvious problem is the amount of time it would take to download a user's photo library. The inescapable constraint of network bandwidth would require users to browse their photo libraries one page at a time or rely on the search and keyword functionality used by stock photo libraries, such as PhotoDisc or Getty Images. These navigation methods work for stock photography, but they would require users to assign keywords to every image, which is simply incompatible with how users are accustomed to browsing their personal photos. With these limitations in mind, it's easier to understand why Ofoto adopted the photo album model. Despite its noted drawbacks, Ofoto's approach is more practical in the context of a Web application because it limits the number of images available in any single context.

In a larger sense, the issues surrounding Ofoto's conceptual model call into question whether the Web is the right medium for this type of application. It's worth asking whether the conceptual model of the Web— a page-based hypertext system—is ultimately appropriate for the storage, organization, and manipulation of file-based media, such as digital photos or digital music. As the discussion moves to other areas of the interface, note how weaknesses in the other layers can be traced back to these fundamental concerns with the conceptual model.

LAYER 2: STRUCTURAL MODEL

As shown in Figure 14.4, Ofoto's structural model is composed of a series of hubs and wizards. The hubs are used to manipulate albums, photos, and user accounts, and the wizards are used to add photos, share photos, and buy prints.

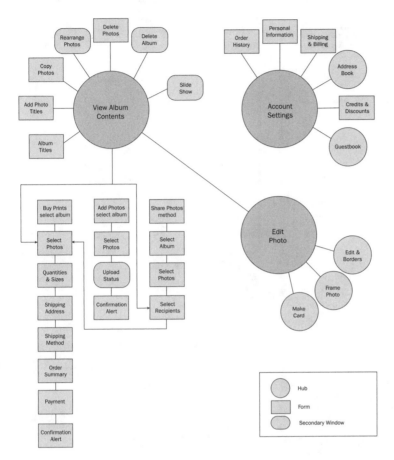

Figure 14.4

This figure illustrates Ofoto's main structural elements.

Ofoto generally makes appropriate use of the hub and wizard structures. In particular, the task flow for selecting a photo from an album is well suited to the hub structure. However, there are notable problems resulting from Ofoto's noncompliance with the view/form construct and the selection of a wizard for the print-ordering task (see Figure 14.5).

1

2

3

4

14.5

Ofoto's Buy Prints wizard.

Four of the pages from Ofoto's print-ordering wizard are shown in Figure 14.5. Unfortunately, the wizard suffers from a variety of problems, including the following:

☐ **Navigation**. Except for the first page of the sequence, none of the pages contain navigation to preceding steps in the sequence. This problem is particularly evident on the Order Summary page, which displays the ship-to address of all recipients but does not provide a way back the shipping page so that the recipient list can be modified. Similarly, the detailed view of the order summary dedicates significant space to each photo but does not have any mechanism for removing or modifying the images.

☐ **Choice of structural model**. Although the task of buying prints does require the user to supply a collection of information, the process is better suited to a guide than a wizard. The guide structure would offer a simple mechanism for users to complete the process and also provide a more efficient method of modifying individual aspects of the order. From the Order Summary page, for example, it should be possible to navigate back to the order contents or recipient pages without having to pass back through all the subsequent steps. Because there is no dependence between the order's contents, payment method, or recipients, there is no reason to force users into a wizard.

☐ **Inappropriate conceptual model**. Another factor affecting the efficiency of the print-ordering process results from the choice of a photo album as the conceptual model. In particular, the album model requires users to constantly navigate among albums if they want to order a group of photos that aren't stored together. This cumbersome interaction ultimately affects which photos get printed or shared because users tend to follow the path of least resistance. By contrast, if the conceptual model included a universal photo library, users could browse the entire collection, select any group of images, order prints, and optionally save the group for later reordering or sharing.

A more universal issue affecting the entire Structural Model layer of Ofoto is the inconsistent and noncompliant use of the view/form construct. For example, Ofoto includes forms that appear in the main window, such as the Copy Photos form, as well as forms that appear in a secondary browser window, such as Update Album Details (see Figure 14.6). To make matters worse, forms opening in a secondary window have a Cancel button, but those appearing in the main window do not. In the current implementation, a Cancel action is implied when the user navigates out of the form.

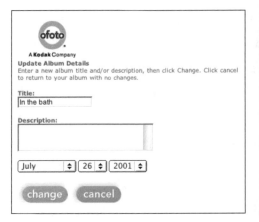

14.6

These forms demonstrate Ofoto's inconsistent use of the view/form construct. Not only do some forms open in the main window and others in secondary windows, but forms in the main window do not contain a Cancel button.

Despite the problems described here, Ofoto's structural model is generally well designed and implemented. The navigation concerns with the print-ordering process could easily be improved, even if the deeper issue of photo selection could not be. Unfortunately, the problems created by not respecting the view/form construct are not as easily addressed. At this layer of the interface, those features are probably quite rigid from a technical perspective. As a result, there aren't any easy fixes from an engineering or a design perspective.

LAYER 3: ORGANIZATIONAL MODEL

As evidenced by the main tab bar, Ofoto's organization model pairs a functional classification scheme—View & Edit Albums, Share Photos, Buy Prints, Add Photos, and Ofoto Store—with a hierarchical model of association. In most cases, the organization is limited to two levels of hierarchy, but it does extend to three in some places. For example, the Copy Photos form shown in Figure 14.6 lives at View & Edit Albums → Edit Album → Copy Photos.

Although Ofoto's functional classification scheme helps push the user to action, the specific categories again point to weaknesses in the conceptual model. The lack of a top-level category for editing or viewing photos is the most obvious example. This problem could be easily fixed, however, by simply renaming the tab "View & Edit Photos." Although the first page in the tab would involve selecting an album, relabeling the tab to focus on photos would be consistent with the Add Photos and Share Photos tabs, which also require the user to select an album before going further. By renaming the View & Edit Albums tab, albums would be reduced to simple navigational and organizational aids instead of a major interface object.

A more radical alternative to Ofoto's organizational model is to eliminate the tabs and rely solely on the low-level navigation area. Looking again at Figure 14.6, with the exception of Ofoto Store, all the tabs are also represented in the low-level navigation area on the right side of the page. Because the user has to select both an image and a command to complete any operation, the two mechanisms simply serve as different ways of answering the same question. Where the tabs ask the user to specify the command first and then the image, the low-level navigation simply flips the order and asks the user to first select one or more images. Although eliminating the tab bar would be a substantial change, it would simplify the interface by reducing redundancy and offering users a single, consistent way to operate.

Looking at Ofoto's structural components, it is easy to see how a difficult decision at the level of the conceptual model gets amplified throughout the rest of the interface. Although there are some specific problems in the Structural and Organizational Model layers, those problems are largely solvable. The ultimate strength of those and other supporting layers, however, is limited by the conceptual model's integrity.

TIER II: BEHAVIOR

Building on the strengths and weakness of the three structural layers, the layers of Ofoto's Behavior tier bring a new set of challenges. The problem of object selection is a conspicuous aspect of the Viewing and Navigation layer, as are the technical and design concerns related to photo editing in the Editing and Manipulation layer. In addition, the User Assistance layer carries the burden of educating a mass consumer audience about the capabilities and limitations of digital photography in general and a photo-based Web application in particular.

LAYER 4: VIEWING AND NAVIGATION

Except for the Address Book, the viewable data stored in Ofoto consists of albums and photos, both image-based objects. As a result, Ofoto's Viewing and Navigation layer is thin, especially compared to Web applications that deal exclusively with text-based data.

Viewing Table-Based Data

Together with the Address Book, the Guestbook shown in Figure 14.7 is one of the few pages to display text-based information in a conventional table format. As the figure shows, this view follows a shared control motif to delete entries by using a check box to select each row. Although this same function could have been accomplished by placing a Delete link in each row, the shared control approach is more efficient for deleting multiple items—the most likely usage, considering the data.

Table sorting is accomplished with the conventional use of column headers. Unfortunately, this design fails to indicate the column associated with the current sort order or the sort key. Although not having a sort order indicator is of little consequence, not indicating the sort key is a confusing omission that leaves the user to wonder whether the data is sorted or not. In addition, the lack of a stronger visual distinction between the column headers and the first row of data blurs the boundaries between the two and confuses the interaction.

14.7
The Guestbook page includes a table that can be sorted by clicking the column headers.

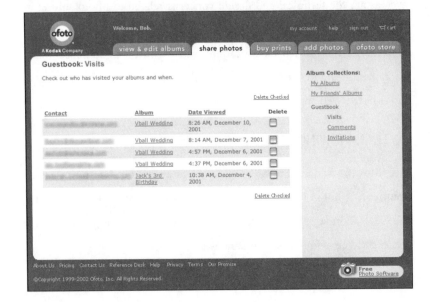

Navigating to Imply Selection

One of the most interesting aspects of Ofoto is the intersection of navigation and selection. Because the user is required to select a photo before editing, the navigational path to the edit photo form starts with View & Edit Albums → Select Album → Select Photo → Edit & Borders. By eliminating any direct navigational paths to the edit photo form and including the photo as part of the navigation path, the interface is able to infer a selection in a seamless but subtle manner.

A less fortunate result of the interdependence between navigation and selection is that the availability of commands is based on whether an album or a photo is currently selected. This effectively places the application in a different mode, depending on the selection, and unnecessarily limits when certain commands can be used. For example, if a photo is selected, it is impossible to edit the album properties, even though selecting a photo also implies selecting a specific album because photos exist only in the context of an album. Even worse, frequently used photo-specific operations, such as delete, duplicate, and share, can be performed only in the context of the album, even though they are useful and relevant in the context of a photo.

Another confusing aspect of the intersection between navigation and selection occurs when the user tries to navigate from an individual photo back to the relevant album. This problem also occurs in online email applications as the user moves back and forth between messages and the inbox. In desktop applications, this is easily accommodated by opening the photo or message in a separate window, leaving the context of the album or inbox intact. With Ofoto, the user can click the Return to Albums link from the low-level navigation area or the View & Edit Albums tab. This navigation, however, does not adequately convey movement between a container and its contents, leaving users confused about where they are at any single point. In addition, the interaction requires an unnatural back and forth movement between albums and photos that quickly becomes tedious.

Another confusing behavior is the inconsistent relationship between the currently selected album or photo and the high-level navigation (see Figure 14.8). For example, if the user is working with an album and the View & Edit Albums tab is active, the current selection is not carried over to the Share Photos tab. Instead, the selection is discarded and the operation starts from the point of selecting an album. By contrast, the low-level navigation links bearing almost identical labels to the Buy Prints and Share This Album tabs *do* retain the selection of the current album. For example, if the user is viewing an album and clicks the Share This Album link from the low-level navigation, the application logically assumes that he or she wants to share the current album.

Although there are clearly some critical problems resulting from the design of the Viewing and Navigation layer, at least some of the instability has to be traced back to the conceptual model and the difficulty of providing this type of functionality in a Web environment. Despite the desire to be truly photo-centric, the interface is constantly saddled with the intervening object of an album, flipping back and forth between the two objects in sometimes explicit, sometimes implicit, and often confusing ways.

14.8
Although they share identical labels, the Buy Prints tabs and Buy Prints link have different behaviors.

LAYER 5: EDITING AND MANIPULATION

In addition to the unique interactions related to manipulating and enhancing photos, Ofoto's Editing and Manipulation layer contains interactions related to editing conventional text-based data. As discussed in the context of the structural model, however, many of these interactions are hampered by the inconsistent use of secondary browser windows and a failure to utilize the view/form construct. For example, if the user is on the Copy Photos page and clicks the Update Album Details link, the Album Details form appears in a secondary window. Besides the confusion resulting from opening a form in a secondary window, after changes are made in the secondary window and the form is submitted, the contents of the main window are inexplicably switched back to the View & Edit Albums page.

Another behavior of Ofoto's Editing and Manipulation layer worth examining is the Shopping Cart page. As with all photo-processing services, Ofoto's shopping cart form is complex (see Figure 14.9). The page displays thumbnails of every photo, size recommendations based on image resolution, and size and quantity options for each photo. In an attempt to streamline and simplify the operation, the page also contains shortcuts for ordering identical quantities and sizes of every photo in the order.

14.9

Ofoto's shopping cart contains a myriad of options for each print in the order.

Because each photo is typically associated with three indicators, three optional links, and three quantity controls, the amount of information in the shopping cart is substantial. Fortunately, the page's layout manages this challenge by arranging the controls and indicators in an uncluttered, digestible manner that helps the user focus on the specifics of each photo.

With the repetition in the controls, a tempting approach would be to eliminate some controls by using them to affect multiple photos or expressing them in more compact ways. This approach, however, would likely require using menus and other less obvious interaction mechanisms. Although such a design might be less overwhelming on first glance, it is unlikely that it would be more usable. Despite the visual complexity, Ofoto's Shopping Cart form exemplifies the benefits of placing all options and information directly in the user's view.

LAYER 6: USER ASSISTANCE

The focus of Ofoto's User Assistance layer is on application-related help, customer service, and the typical error and status alerts.

The application contains a persistent Help link in the utility navigation in the upper-right corner of the page. As shown in Figure 14.10, the help system follows the style of a conventional FAQ. The list of topics is extensive and searchable. Unfortunately, the benefits of the help content are undermined by displaying the information in the main browser window rather than its own secondary window, making it impossible to retain the context of the user's current operation.

For example, if users are viewing the shopping cart and click the small + icon next to a recommended print size, they are teleported out of the shopping cart and over to a help page with information about the relationship between image resolution and print size. This action is consistent with standard hyperlinking behavior, but help is the one place that almost always deserves its own window. By not retaining users' context when they access help, this approach adds to the frustration by requiring them to find their way back to the page where they were first having trouble.

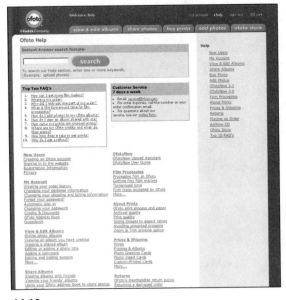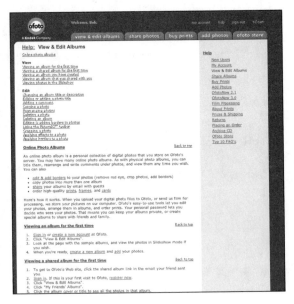

14.10

Ofoto includes substantial amounts of procedural help presented in the common FAQ format.

Ofoto's User Assistance layer also contains a variety of input error alerts. Figure 14.11 highlights one of them, illustrating how clearly Ofoto reports input errors. Error messages are highlighted in red text *and* positioned next to the fields containing the errors. The application also detects and communicates all errors at once, so the user can correct all of them in one operation.

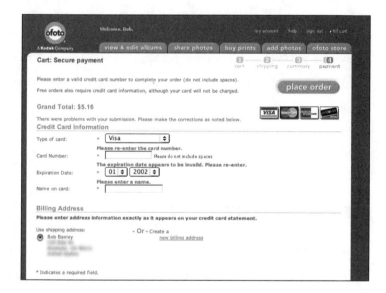

14.11
Ofoto's error alerts clearly communicate the nature and location of input errors.

The Uploading Photos status alert is another component of Ofoto's User Assistance layer. As shown in Figure 14.12, this alert appears in a secondary window, featuring an animated GIF to create the impression that the operation is continuing. Unfortunately, the alert does not provide any estimate of how long the operation might take, so users are left to wonder how long they have to wait.

14.12

Ofoto's Uploading Images status alert does not answer the critical question "How long will this take?"

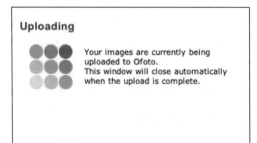

Building on the foundation of the Structure tier, Ofoto's Behavior tier exhibits a variety of interesting problems, solutions, and tradeoffs. The most instructive is how the Viewing and Navigation layer interweaves navigation and selection.

TIER III: PRESENTATION

As the most visible means of distinguishing itself from competitors, the Presentation tier is a critical element of the interface for a company like Ofoto. With companies such as Shutterfly and Snapfish offering similar functionality and pricing, it is far more economical for Ofoto to emphasize the Presentation tier than to engage in a hard-fought feature or price war.

LAYER 7: LAYOUT

Ofoto's layout is grounded with a consistent and simple two-column grid. The layout has a fixed width, with the user's content in a wide column on the left and the low-level navigation in a narrow column on the right. Because Ofoto is an image-centric application, a fixed-width layout is clearly appropriate.

The layout follows a slightly unconventional but perfectly acceptable right-hand orientation. In addition, the layout uses conventional placement for standard navigation elements, including the tab bar, the company logo, and the persistent utilities, such as the Account, Cart, and Help links.

Content and navigation areas are clearly delineated by the two-column grid and background colors. The white background behind the main content area is particularly effective at focusing the viewer on the current photo or album. Most pages contain enough white space, although the small advertising-like images that occasionally appear on the site can be distracting.

One problem worth noting is derived from the confusion between form and view pages. For example, the Delete Photos form (see Figure 14.13), can't be easily distinguished from the View Album page. Other than the primary command button to perform the action—in this case, the big orange Delete button—there is little to clearly identify a form from a view. This further contributes to the problems already mentioned in the Structural Model and Viewing and Navigation layers.

14.13

The Delete Photos form can barely be distinguished from the View Photos page.

Another issue in the Layout layer is evident in the forms that open in a secondary window. The Rearrange Photos form, for example (see Figure 14.14), lacks a clear header area, a distinct page title, correct button placement, an obvious grid, or anything else to anchor it to the window.

With the exception of forms that appear in a secondary window, however, Ofoto's Layout layer sets an example of simplicity and restraint worth following.

14.14
The secondary window for rearranging photos in an album lacks the well-considered layout and visual style of Ofoto's other elements.

LAYER 8: STYLE

Ofoto's graphic style is the single interface element that could most clearly distinguish the application from its competitors. However, as shown in Figure 14.15, both Shutterfly and Snapfish have visual styles strikingly close to Ofoto's. All three sites use similar layouts, grid systems, and typography. Even with the slight variation in color scheme, they all communicate the same general feel, leaving little to distinguish these sites or brands from one another. To the benefit of everyone involved, however, the style is clean and direct and does not distract from the underlying utility or purpose of the applications.

14.15

Two of Ofoto's primary competitors, Shutterfly and Snapfish, have very similar visual styles.

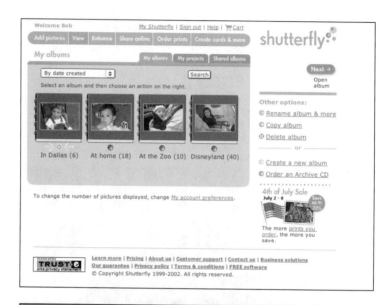

As a rule, text is presented legibly. This is particularly evident in the text-heavy pages of the help system. A notable faux pas, however, is the use of underlined text to distinguish headings on the answer pages of the FAQs (see Figure 14.16). Although the headings are already identified with bold text, the underline has been inappropriately added because the headers do not function as hyper-links.

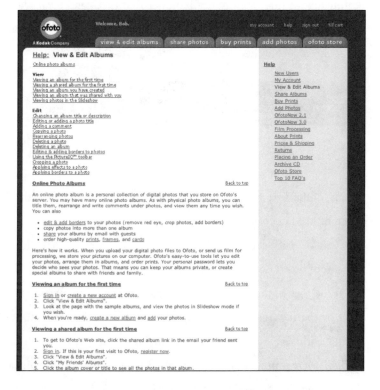

14.16
Ofoto's help pages make inappropriate use of underlined text to highlight headings that are not hyperlinks.

Finally, the visual style follows the convention for communicating which elements can and can't be clicked by using rounded rectangles for command buttons. Although the buttons are perhaps too large, they are obviously controls and, therefore, serve their primary duty well. The weakest link is the navigational links in each page's upper-right corner and footer. The position of these elements supports their function as links, but nothing about their appearance indicates that they can be clicked. In the top header, for example, there is no visual cue that the "Welcome, Bob" text is not clickable and the "My Account" text is (see Figure 14.17).

14.17
The utility navigation area at the top of the page lacks any clear visual cue as to what is and isn't clickable.

TEXT

Typical of the Text layer, the biggest problem here is simply that there's too much of it. Many pages contain instructional text when a descriptive page title would easily carry the day. In other cases, even though the overall amount of text is not onerous, the text is extremely repetitive. For example, the home page of the Share Photos tab contains eight instances of the word *share* or *sharing* (see Figure 14.18). The words *photos* or *prints* are not far behind with seven appearances. Looking at the area titled "Share Photos Online," there is practically no difference in the meaning communicated by the section title, the text under the title, or the link. Most of this text could be eliminated with absolutely no loss in what's being communicated.

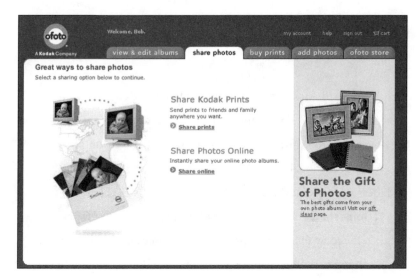

14.18
Enough already. I get that this page is for sharing photos.

To its credit, however, Ofoto minimizes the visual presentation of the instructional text, tucking it under the page title and away from the page's main content area. As a result, the text does not overly distract from the page, even though it is superfluous.

SUMMARY

Despite the criticisms in this case study, Ofoto stands as one of the Web's most thoughtfully designed and well-implemented online services. There are obviously problems, but many are the natural outgrowth of providing this type of functionality in a Web application. In terms of lessons learned and ideas worth borrowing, the following represents the highlights:

☐ **Importance of the conceptual model.** The type of functionality offered by Ofoto presents an almost unsolvable problem for the conceptual model. Although the photo album model is practical for a Web application, it results in a number of unfortunate consequences in other layers of the interface. From a pure interface perspective, the conceptual model of a storage system for negatives would give users a superior experience, although it would probably require a dedicated desktop application.

☐ **Interrelationship of navigation and selection.** The method of combining navigation and selection in Ofoto's Viewing and Navigation layer is an unavoidable aspect of the conceptual model and its container/object orientation. Because the Web does not provide any direct selection methods, inferring selection from navigation is a reasonable alternative. However, any implementation built on this mechanism should ensure that the relationship between selection and navigation is consistent no matter what navigational path the user follows.

☐ **Visual simplicity, clarity, and order.** With few exceptions, Ofoto's Presentation tier reflects the core design values of simplicity, clarity, and order. Despite the temptation to crowd and complicate the interface, Ofoto has taken the road less traveled and produced an experience that places users' needs at the top of the priority list.

September 23, 2002
Menlo Park, California

AFTERWORD

The writing of *Making the Web Work* took me from July 2001 to August 2002. A lot happened during the intervening months—to me, to my family, to the world. In the face of such times, it was sometimes hard to believe that the design of something as transitory as a Web page really mattered.

I eventually concluded, however, that it does matter. It matters in the same way that all forms of design matter. It matters because design is about making something for somebody else—about creating objects, interactions, and experiences that others will find rational, enjoyable, and beautiful. It matters because being a designer requires you to consider the needs and perspective of all those other people who are ultimately going to use what you've created. Building something that makes their day a little more sensible, a little more ordered, a little more enjoyable, and a little less frustrating—that's a job worth doing and worth doing well.

Thanks for reading. I hope to hear from you soon.

All the best... Bob

bob@baxleydesign.com

INDEX

A

Acrobat Reader, Adobe, 285

ActiveX, 28

Adobe Systems

Acrobat Reader, 285

online store

instructional help, use of, 293-294

progress alerts, use of, 301-302

Photoshop, 28

Save dialog box, as example of modality, 124

Portable Document Format (PDF), as used to deliver conceptual help, 285-286

Aetna.com, use of audience-based classification scheme, 171

"affordance," concept of, 357

AIGA (American Institute of Graphic Artists), use of dynamic menu navigation, 212-213

airline reservation Web sites, as examples of wizard structure, 134-136

alerts, 296-297, 305. *See also individual entries*

confirmation alerts, 304-305

error alerts, 297-300

on Amazon.com, 400

on Ofoto, 431-432

status alerts, 301-304, 431-432

completion alerts, 303-304

progress alerts, 301-303

alphabetic (objective) classification schemes, 151-152

Amazon.com

"1-Click" ordering, 387-388

alerts, use of, 400

bookstore

book details pages, 384, 390-391, 401

home page, 388-390

organizational models of, 388-392

placement of elements, as consistent, 402

tab bar navigation, 388-389, 393-394

brand identity of, as provided by tab bar navigation, 402

B

G

H

U

X-Z

HOW TO CONTACT US

VISIT OUR WEB SITE

WWW.NEWRIDERS.COM

On our Web site you'll find information about our other books, authors, tables of contents, indexes, and book errata. You will also find information about book registration and how to purchase our books.

EMAIL US

Contact us at this address: **nrfeedback@newriders.com**

- If you have comments or questions about this book
- To report errors that you have found in this book
- If you have a book proposal to submit or are interested in writing for New Riders
- If you would like to have an author kit sent to you
- If you are an expert in a computer topic or technology and are interested in being a technical editor who reviews manuscripts for technical accuracy
- To find a distributor in your area, please contact our international department at this address. **nrmedia@newriders.com**
- For instructors from educational institutions who want to preview New Riders books for classroom use. Email should include your name, title, school, department, address, phone number, office days/hours, text in use, and enrollment, along with your request for desk/examination copies and/or additional information.
- For members of the media who are interested in reviewing copies of New Riders books. Send your name, mailing address, and email address, along with the name of the publication or Web site you work for.

BULK PURCHASES/CORPORATE SALES

The publisher offers discounts on this book when ordered in quantity for bulk purchases and special sales. For sales within the U.S., please contact: Corporate and Government Sales (800) 382-3419 or **corpsales@pearsontechgroup.com**. Outside of the U.S., please contact: International Sales (317) 581-3793 or **international@pearsontechgroup.com**.

WRITE TO US

New Riders Publishing
201 W. 103rd St.
Indianapolis, IN 46290-1097

CALL US

Toll-free (800) 571-5840 + 9 + 7477
If outside U.S. (317) 581-3500. Ask for New Riders.

FAX US

(317) 581-4663

VOICES THAT MATTER

New Riders

WWW.NEWRIDERS.COM